Sweet Encore

A Road Trip from Paris to Portugal (via northern Spain)

D0557178

Karen Wheeler

SWEET ENCORE

Copyright © Karen Wheeler 2015

First published as an e-book, by Sweet Pea Publishing, 2015

Sweet Pea Publishing
www.sweetpeapublishing.com

ISBN: 978-0-9571066-2-8

Typeset by Mach 3 Solutions Ltd (www.mach3solutions.co.uk)

Printed and bound in Great Britain by CPI Group Ltd,
Croydon, CR0 4YY

To my readers and Gabriella Mellen, with love

About the Author

Karen Wheeler is a former fashion editor of the *Mail on Sunday*. She wrote for the *Financial Times How to Spend It* magazine for over fifteen years, and her work has appeared in the *Daily Mail*, *Sunday Times Style*, *You*, *ES* magazine, *Living France* and numerous international publications. More information can be found on her blog www.toutsweet.net and Twitter.com/mimipompom1.

Also by Karen Wheeler:

Tout Sweet: Hanging up my High Heels for a New Life in France

Toute Allure: Falling in Love in Rural France

Tout Soul: The Pursuit of Happiness in Rural France

The Marie Antoinette Diet: Eat Cake and Lose Weight

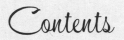

Contents

'I may not have gone where I intended to go, but I think I have ended up where I needed to be'.

Douglas Adams

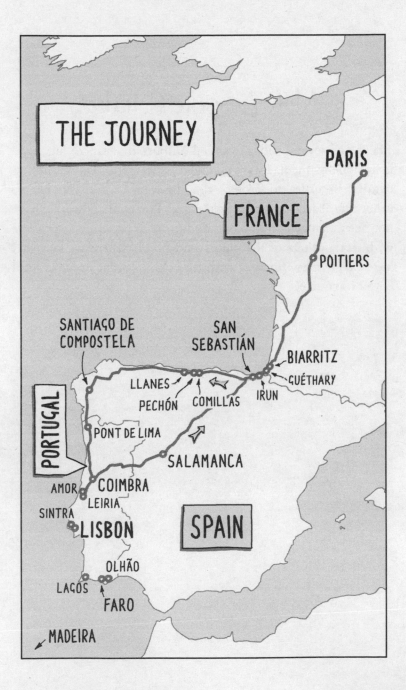

Note from the Author

There are several villages called Villiers in France, but mine is not one of them. I have changed its name, along with other details, in order to protect the innocent – and the not so innocent. Place names in Spain and Portugal, however, have not been changed and I have tried to be as accurate as possible with descriptions of the places and hotels where we stayed. I have taken a few liberties with timings, in order to make for a better narrative.

Chapter 1

What's New, Kangaroo?

THE CALL FROM my brother comes at the end of June, as I'm rushing around trying to find two matching shoes. I haven't heard from him in several years. There is no particular reason for this; it's just that he lives in the Caribbean, I live in France, and neither of us is very good at keeping in touch. After some basic niceties, he gets to the point: 'Can Arianna come and spend the summer with you in France?' he asks.

The request takes me by surprise. The last time I saw my niece, she was sitting under my desk in London, playing with a Buzz Lightyear doll as I typed out a feature entitled 'Rubies are a Girl's Best Friend'. Every now and then, I threw her a Chocolate Button, in much the same way as I throw dog biscuits to my little black terrier, Biff. It wasn't difficult to entertain her as a toddler, but how would I keep a sixteen-year-old amused in a small French village, where it's lights-out-and-everyone-under-the-duvet-by-10-pm, even in the summer?

Villiers, where I live, has many charms – chief among them, for a writer, being the peace and the plentiful supply of Sauvignon – but not much to appeal to a teenager, and especially not a teenager who has grown up on a lively Caribbean island with the ocean on her doorstep and, by all accounts, a dynamic social life.

I point this out to my brother, but he is curiously persistent. 'It will be good for her. She'll have a great time,' he says. 'And she can learn French.'

'In a few weeks?'

'Well, she can learn the basics – *bonjour* and all that.'

'And what does Arianna think about this?'

'She's already packed her bag.'

'Listen, I'm running late to visit a friend,' I say. 'Can we talk about this tomorrow?'

I figure that my sibling will forget the plan. He often has crazy ideas – most recently to buy a holiday home in Papua New Guinea – that usually disappear when hosed down with the cold-water jet of reality.

'OK,' says my brother. 'I'll be in touch.'

I glance at the kitchen clock. I'm supposed to be at Gabriella's at 8 pm and I don't want to keep her waiting. 'Come on, Biff,' I plead, holding up a silver-hooped sandal. 'Where's my other shoe?'

Stealing my shoes and hiding them in strange places, like the woodpile, is his favourite thing. I spend a lot of time begging for them back. I know he understands because he looks at me intently, as if considering the request.

As I search behind the sofa, he trots out of the room and returns, his little tail bobbing, with my shoe between his teeth. 'Thank you,' I say, extracting it from his jaw. He looks thoroughly pleased with himself, but, realising that I am about to go out without him, rushes to park his enormous paws in front of the door, where he tilts his head to one side and assumes his most beguiling pose. For a second, my resolve wavers. But the last time I took him to Gabriella's he barked his head off for most of the evening, probably because he felt left out of the conversation. Gabriella is ninety-five years old, deaf and almost blind, so it wasn't helpful.

After some fancy footwork to get past him, I head down the cobblestone slope that leads to Gabriella's, catching the scent of honeysuckle on the warm evening air. It's on nights like this that I really love France. Gabriella's house, a former coaching inn, is one of the oldest in the village, flanked by lavender bushes and a mass of snowball-like hydrangeas. The door is open and she is sitting at the farmhouse table in her kitchen, waiting for me. She is always nicely dressed – Dolores, her housekeeper, visits every morning to help with the cleaning and ironing – but tonight she looks particularly crisp in a mustard cotton dress.

'*Coucou*, it's me,' I shout.

'Is that you, Keren?' (No one in France calls me by my correct name.)

'Yes it is.'

I kiss her on the cheek, inhaling the essences of lemon and tuberose in the expensive Italian cologne that she wears.

'Come on in. Have you got your little dog with you?'

'No. He is at home.'

'The dog is in Rome? How did he get to Rome?'

'No, he's at home,' I say, a little more loudly.

'Wait! I need to adjust my hearing aids,' she says. Then, after fiddling around with them for a few minutes, 'Say *merde*,' she commands.

'*Merde*!' I shout.

'Good. Now I can hear you.' She motions for me to sit down next to her at the wooden table. 'So what's new, kangaroo?'

'Nothing much,' I reply, deciding to spare her the details of how I spent today leaving countless messages for Victoria Beckham, for a newspaper article that I am writing.

'How was your day?' I ask.

'I've just been listening to a French political show,' she says. 'Our stupid governments say they are fighting for peace, but fighting for peace is like f*****g for virginity.'

When I've stopped laughing, she takes my hand and squeezes it. 'Now, I've made us some soup. Be so kind as to get spoons from that drawer over there. And in the icebox you will find a bowl of vegetables. On the second shelf down.'

Her kitchen is chaotic – copper pans simmering on the stove, fruit and vegetables strewn across the table, a string of garlic swinging from the ceiling – but Gabriella knows exactly where everything is. The jars and tins in her kitchen all bear big white labels, their contents marked in giant capital letters.

'There is a metal stand next to the gas ring. Can you see it? Good, now bring it here to the table.' I follow her instructions like a robot. 'And put the vegetables in the computer (she means the microwave) and turn the dial to the right. That's it. Now come and sit down and tell me your news.'

'Actually, I'm feeling a little… restless,' I say, hoping for one of the nuggets of wisdom that she often pitches my way. The former wife of an American diplomat, Gabriella was born in Italy, grew up in a decaying former convent in Mexico, and lived all over the world, including a stint in Washington, before landing, at random, in rural France. Much like me, in fact, except that I came here via west London and a career in fashion journalism, rather than the diplomatic service. Along the way, Gabriella has learned to speak five languages fluently – 'including swear words!' – and collected friends in the manner that others collect shoes or wine.

'You're feeling reckless?' she says, getting up and moving slowly to the stove to stir the pan of soup.

'Restless,' I repeat, loudly. 'I want something exciting to happen. To be surprised by life, but in a good way.'

'My dear, life is full of surprises, even when you are as old as me. But you can't just sit back and wait for them to happen,' she says. 'You have to make a move. Do something.'

I'm not sure why, but magical and unexpected things seem to happen after visiting Gabriella. I nearly always leave her house feeling happier and more inspired than when I arrived. She makes you feel as if you are the most important person in the world. 'If I were your mother-in-law...' she will say, before delivering some pithy piece of advice.

But I must admit that she is my friend in spite of myself. I did my very best to dodge her acquaintance, when she knocked on my door unannounced one day. I stuck my head out of the upstairs window and saw a thin woman with white hair and a walking stick below.

'Are you the writer?' she asked.

'Who wants to know?' I said, annoyed by the interruption.

'I'm Gabriella. Gabriella Mellen,' she replied. 'Someone at the *mairie* told me that we have a writer living in the village and I thought I would investigate.'

'I am a writer, yes. But I'm very busy right now.'

'Well, is there a time when it would be convenient to call back?' Gabriella was determined to be friends with me and I think I was swept along by the sheer force of her personality. I did not know at that point that Gabriella was nearly blind and deaf. For her even to have found my house was testament to her character and tenacity or, as she calls it, 'grabbing life by the balls'. We laugh about it now, but the truth is that I was not as polite as I could have been that day. 'Don't even mention it,' she says, whenever I do. 'The most important thing is that we are friends now.'

Over dinner of minestrone soup followed by Italian-style vegetables – Gabriella's favourite diplomatic posting was Rome during the Kennedy era – I tell her about the call from my brother. 'MORON!' cries Gabriella. (I like to think this is a term of endearment, as she calls me this often.) 'You should have bitten his arm off. Of course you should let your niece come. What have you got to lose?'

By the end of dinner, Gabriella has convinced me that a visit from Arianna is the best possible thing that could happen this summer. 'Do you need me to read any letters before I go?' I ask.

'Not tonight,' she says, and I'm almost disappointed. She usually has a basketful of letters from friends around the world, waiting to be read. They're always handwritten and sometimes up to twenty pages long; and before I start to read, Gabriella gives me a potted history of the writer, such as: 'Her parents survived the Titanic' or, 'She left her husband for another woman, who then ran off with the family tiara.' People have written novels with less happening.

'Remember,' she says, as I get up to leave. 'One of the secrets of life is to recognise the opportunities when they come along. You've got to grab life by the balls.'

'Got it,' I say.

She sends me back into the summer evening with her usual sign-off: 'See you later, alligator.'

'In a while, crocodile,' I reply.

I'm still smiling as I walk back up the cobblestone slope, past a stone wall topped with a froth of wisteria. I stop to admire the sky, turning milkshake pink above the church spire, and breathe in the sweet, warm air. Tonight is the summer solstice.

Biff is lying along the back of the sofa, his hairy face pressed up against the window waiting for my return. He races to the door, dangling his lead in his mouth. I get the hint. Heading up rue St Benoit for our usual evening walk, I can hear live music and laughter coming from the square. After 10 pm. What's going on? And then I see that the Café du Commerce on the corner is lit up, and there is a crowd outside.

The café appears to have finally reopened. A couple of months ago, a sign in the window announced that it was under new ownership and would reopen soon. (Cafés in rural France change ownership frequently. If someone lasts eighteen months they are doing well; but most have closed the doors by year three, thanks to the punitive French tax system.)

Opaque white screens subsequently appeared in the windows, hiding the mysterious makeover that was taking place within. But often when I took Biff for his bedtime walk, I would notice that the lights were on, sometimes as late as 2 am, and I could hear the sound of hammering and drilling inside. Occasionally, I would see two men – one chubby and short, the other thin and with long hair – enjoying a cigarette break in the moonlight.

As I walk down one of the side roads leading off the square, I hear someone say *'Bonjour!'* When I turn around, I see a man, barefoot, in khaki shorts and a dark T-shirt, smoking a cigarette in his garden. He's in his late forties, with floppy hair and a five o'clock shadow. He reaches over the stone wall to pat Biff, before striking up a conversation in French.

'Nice evening,' he says.

'Yes, it is.'

'You live in the village?'

'Yes. And you?'

'I've just arrived.'

'Nice house,' I say nodding at his cottage.

'Oh, it's not mine,' he says. 'I'm renting it for six months, while I renovate a barn nearby.'

I start to laugh. 'You're English?'

'I am.' He grins, switching to our native tongue. 'You too?'

'Yup.'

His French is excellent, and although I detected the faintest hint of *anglais* in his accent, it was the mention of the renovation that did it: if someone is mad enough to take on an old barn in my region, the Poitou-Charentes, they are almost certainly British. 'Well, welcome to Villiers,' I say. 'Don't get the wrong impression. It's not normally as lively as this.'

He laughs. 'You mean the *pot d'acceuil* in the café?' he says, revealing that his French is a cut above average by using the phrase for 'welcome drinks'. 'I was just about to wander over. Do you want to come along?'

I hesitate. I have to be up at 7 am tomorrow to work on 'Who Wore It Best?', a newspaper feature I recently agreed to write, about a Victoria Beckham dress that countless celebrities have worn.

'It looks like a private party,' I say.

'Nah, it's an opening party. And anyway, I *am* invited.'

In my head, I can hear Gabriella shouting, 'What are you waiting for, you MORON? GO!' This is, after all, an opportunity to get to know a neighbour and meet the new owners of the café.

'Well, I suppose... maybe for half an hour. But I might just take my dog home as it looks a bit crowded in there.'

'Great,' he says. 'I'll get my shoes and meet you on the square. By the way, I'm Matt.'

'Nice to meet you,' I say. 'I'll see you shortly.'

Biff looks outraged that I'm leaving him at home for the second time this evening. Cocktail parties, with their stray crisps and canapés and distracted humans, rate second only to barbecues as his favourite social event. I feel rather guilty as he fixes me with an intense, black-eyed stare.

'I know. Life can be cruel sometimes,' I say, waggling his ears, 'but I won't be long.'

My fellow *Anglais* is waiting for me at the top of rue St Benoit. 'My wife Zoe is arriving in a few days,' he says, as we walk over to the café. 'Hopefully, you'll meet her soon. I'm hoping that you'll give us the lowdown on the village, as we're probably going to be here for a while.'

'So how far have you got with your barn?'

'Put it this way: you can still see stars through the roof.'

The Commerce is rocking as we arrive – literally, thanks to the live band playing in the corner. And what a transformation. Under the previous owner, Clément, the interior decor was like something you'd find in Soviet Russia, circa 1970. (Think beige vinyl seating, Formica tables and fluorescent strip lighting.) But all the late-night activity has paid off. The grim, vinyl furniture and flooring has been stripped out and replaced with rustic wooden tables and chairs; and the ugly suspended ceiling has been hacked back to reveal the original plaster cornicing and centre rose.

It is easy to spot one of the new proprietors. Short and solid, with a cheeky grin, he looks quite pleased with himself.

'That's Basile,' says Matt, 'the owner. Apparently, he's worked for restaurants in Paris, Bordeaux and La Rochelle.'

This of course, begs the question: what is he doing in Villiers? 'His wife is from the region,' says Matt, as if reading my mind. 'And wanted to move back.'

'Is she going to help out in the restaurant?'

'I think his friend Guy is going to run it with him.' He nods towards a thin, rather wan-looking man, with long dark hair. He's not from the village, but I recognise him as the man who helped Basile with his midnight renovations.

Our fellow guests are a mixture of local business owners and people that I haven't seen before, many of them young and unusually well dressed for a Thursday night, in rural France.

Where have they all been hiding, I wonder? This is clearly the start of a whole new era for the Café du Commerce.

We take our complimentary drinks – chilled lychee juice with sparkling wine, which is quite exotic for these parts – and move outside. 'Beautiful evening,' says Matt. And it is. The sky is a stunning royal blue and there is a silvery new moon above the *mairie*.

'You've arrived in France at a good time,' I say. 'Just in time for summer.'

'I know,' he says, sitting back in his chair, with a smile. 'So what do you do?' he asks, squinting his eyes, so that I have the impression that I am being analysed.

'I'm a freelance writer. You?'

'An architect.'

'Sounds fun.'

'Not really. I spend a lot of time on my own, surfing Twitter – oops, I mean drawing up plans – as I imagine you do. What kind of stuff do you write?'

'All sorts, but if I were to appear on *Mastermind* right now, my specialist subject would be the life and designs of Victoria Beckham.'

'Oh,' he says, looking puzzled.

'I write lightweight stuff,' I say. 'Otherwise known as fashion and lifestyle features, for national newspapers.'

'And it's possible to do that from rural France?'

'It's not always easy,' I say, with some understatement. 'How do you know Basile?'

'I don't. I met him in the *boulangerie* this morning.'

It's a little surreal, I think, that a couple of hours ago I was eating soup with my ninety-five-year-old friend. Now, here I am enjoying cocktails and a musical quartet with a stranger. This is not at all a typical summer's night in Villiers.

'Let me show you a picture of the barn,' says Matt, getting out his smartphone and showing me a photo of a cluster of stone buildings with the roof falling in, of the kind I see everyday when walking Biff in the nearby countryside.

'Well, good luck with that,' I say. 'Where exactly is it?'

'On the outskirts of Villiers, surrounded by green fields, but only a ten-minute walk from here.'

He swipes through the pictures to a three-dimensional plan of the finished house. At the front, you see only the traditional stone facade; but at the rear, there is a glass box with floor-to-ceiling windows opening on to a terrace and swimming pool. It is certainly going to break new ground in Villiers.

'It looks like it's going to be quite a party house,' I say.

'That's the idea. Another drink?'

'Um, I have to start work early tomorrow.'

'One glass won't do you any harm. It's not like you have to go far to get home.'

'OK,' I say, showing the self-discipline that got me where I am today.

Inside the café my new neighbour stops to chat to Basile, before reappearing with a bottle of white Burgundy and two glasses. 'They've got a cracking wine list,' he declares as he pours the wine. He clicks my glass. '*Santé*! To the good life in France.'

'So have you actually started work on your barn?' I ask.

'Not yet. We only bought it a few months ago. We haven't got planning permission yet. It's difficult because I have to keep flying back to the UK to deal with work projects.'

'Would I recognise any of your work?' I ask.

He laughs. 'Sadly, no. We can't all be Norman Foster,' he says, referring to the famous architect. 'Some of us have to design boring office blocks and public buildings.'

This seems unusually modest for a new arrival in France. Most expats tend to embellish their achievements and, in his shoes, many would claim to have designed half of London.

When I glance at the clock on the *mairie*, it has gone 1 am. In the three hours that we've been chatting, we've covered all the usual ground – septic tanks, solar panels and French bureaucracy. I learn that he has two daughters from a previous marriage, both of them at university; and that Zoe, his second wife, is a textile designer and twelve years younger than him. She is currently in India on a work trip.

'Or at least that's what she tells me,' he says, with a wink. 'You and Zoe are going to get on like a house on fire.'

I'm not sure what makes him so certain of this, but in France it is quite usual to strike up instant friendships with fellow expats, the common bond being that, for whatever reason, you both felt motivated to cross the Channel and acquire a pile of old stones. At the very least, he and his wife will be interesting additions to the village.

Inside the café, the saxophonist is hitting his stride and the party is still going strong. 'Time for me to go,' I say.

'Yeah. Me too.'

We say good-bye to Basile, who appears to have been partaking liberally of his own largesse, and walk back across the square, tailed by the soaring saxophone.

'Thanks for the drinks,' I say, when we reach rue St Benoit.

'Pleasure,' he says with a grin. 'Thanks for the company and the conversation. See you around.'

Back home, I find an email from my brother. 'Please let me know ASAP if there are any dates that you can't do,' he has written. I type back a reply, though I'm still not convinced that the visit will happen.

But Gabriella was right: life does keep delivering surprises. And, like buses, there are none for ages and then they come along in threes: the call from my brother; a new expat in the village; and, most surprising of all, the fact that the local café has reopened with, by all accounts, a halfway decent chef. As for my niece, I cannot wait to see how the sweet, chubby-cheeked toddler has turned out. All I have to do is follow Gabriella's advice, and grab any opportunities by the balls.

Chapter 2

The Dangerous Aunt

I'M AT MY desk at 7.30 am, the following morning, dressed as if I were going to a drinks party in my lucky, cherry-red 'desk shoes' – so-called because the heels are as high as the Shard and I can't actually walk in them. Many people assume that if you work from home, 'career dressing' means pyjamas or similar 'leisure' attire, but if you're psyching yourself up for eight hours of liaising with fashion publicists and agents – I use the word 'liaising' optimistically as most don't bother to return calls – it helps to be sharply dressed.

I am braced for a day of humiliation and the phrase, '*Yeah, who exactly are you again?*' repeated with varying degrees of indifference. Saner folk would give up. But I am determined to 'land the plane', as Gabriella would say. I can almost hear her shouting, 'Get it finished. Don't take any crap from these morons. Land the plane. *Basta!*'

The piece in question is on the advent of the 'It' dress and follows a rash of photographs of famous women wearing an identical Victoria Beckham design – a demure grey dress with a peplum. I had some qualms when the newspaper sent me the brief: *1200 words on the VB dress plus at least three other 'iconic' dresses, each to have been worn by a minimum of four celebrities, with no overlapping of celebrities or labels.* It sounded like a problem in a maths exam, requiring an algorithm or, at the very least, a Venn diagram, before I could even start.

My commissioning editor also wants comments from the relevant designers and the celebrities who have worn the various dresses. And what a commissioning editor wants, I strive to deliver. Unfortunately, after a week's worth of phone calls and emails, it is clear that not a single celebrity or designer wants to speak to me.

Undeterred, I draft another round of emails. Then, because it is too early to start the bombardment by phone, I walk Biff over to see my friend Pierre-Antoine, who owns a fashion boutique on the square. He is busy unpacking a consignment of biker jackets in pastel-coloured leatherette.

'Oof,' he says. 'They're jumping off the rack; I can't keep them in stock.'

'Listen,' I say. 'The Commerce has reopened. Would you like to have lunch today?'

'Why not?' he replies.

'I'll meet you over there at noon.'

And so, after another unproductive morning, I walk over to the Commerce to meet Pierre-Antoine. I spot him by his paisley shirt – patterned shirts are very much his thing – waiting at a corner table. The restaurant is packed with many faces that I recognise, including Biff's beautiful vet and her husband; Jérome the local estate agent; and several town hall clerks. An air of expectation fills the room, fanned by the delicious aromas wafting from the kitchen. I can't believe how different it all is. Under Clément, the previous owner, the Commerce had all the ambience of an operating theatre.

'Oh, la, la,' says Pierre-Antoine, shaking his head as I slide into the chair opposite him. 'I think they might be overwhelmed.'

I see immediately what he means. Basile's sidekick, Guy, is the only waiter for the expectant throng. Sweating profusely in a thick, plaid shirt, he lacks the brisk competence of your typical French waiter. For a start, he is not moving anywhere near quickly enough, but lingering at the tables with a startled look in his eyes.

'Do you know where Clément has gone?' I ask Pierre-Antoine.

'No idea,' he shrugs. 'But I think we all knew that he wasn't the ideal candidate for the job.' This is an understatement. In the three years that he ran the café, Clément never once looked pleased to see me. And I was his most regular customer. As I hurried in through snow, rain or fierce sunshine, for my morning caffeine hit, he invariably greeted me with a frown.

Often I would be the only customer, sipping my coffee in silence, in the bleak surroundings. It didn't bother me, as I'm not excessively sociable myself in the mornings. Plus Clément made a halfway decent *café crème*. Sometimes, as I arrived, he would be outside with his chef, enjoying a leisurely cigarette and an espresso. In such situations, he never rushed or troubled himself – even if there were several customers waiting inside to be served. We were under no illusions: we knew that we were an inconvenience.

The menu of the day looks good,' I say, nodding towards the blackboard propped up on the bar.

'We'll see,' says Pierre-Antoine, sounding unusually sceptical.

Guy doesn't seem to be serving people in the order that they arrived, so our food arrives surprisingly quickly: gazpacho soup to start, followed by roast chicken with thyme, and then a pear charlotte for dessert – all of it, Guy confirms, homemade.

It is one of the best lunches I've had in rural France – and all for €12. Admittedly, the bar is low, because, despite France's reputation as a place of gastronomic excellence, most of the restaurants that I've encountered fall into two categories: establishments serving frozen food and stuff from industrial catering cans; or places of tortured perfectionism, where the chef wields tweezers or a pipette as he dribbles a coulis of *quelquechose* onto a beetroot brioche or something equally ridiculous.

So I can't believe my luck that a restaurant serving edible, unpretentious food has opened in my village, two minutes from my house. No need to drive forty kilometres for a decent dinner with friends, anymore. Pierre-Antoine, however, seems hesitant. 'Let's see if it lasts,' he says, as a flustered-looking Basile emerges from the kitchen to help Guy with the service. Some diners who arrived before me, are only just being served their main course. Fortunately, the people of the Poitou are known for their patience and slow approach to life (except that is, when they are behind the wheel of a car).

Back at my desk, there has been no response to this morning's emails. In despair, as the piece is due in tomorrow, I google again the celebrities who've worn the Beckham dress. There is one that I've missed, who actually looks better in the pale grey number than most of the models or actresses who've worn it: Carol Vorderman.

The TV presenter looks amazing in the dress, which clings and pulls in in all the right places. She also seems to have an uncanny eye for a high-profile frock, as she owns several of the designs I'm featuring. Why on earth did I not think of her before?

I fire off an email to her agent, begging for even a second-hand comment. To my amazement, he replies almost immediately, saying that he's been in touch with Carol and she is happy to speak to me directly. I can't quite believe it, but, ten minutes later, she has practically written my feature. A celebrity with an eye for a good design and a degree from Cambridge, I discover, is a fashion journalist's dream.

Carol is warm, funny and down-to-earth. She explains the appeal of several of the frocks that I'm writing about and gives a fascinating glimpse into dressing for the red carpet. The 'secret' behind the success of one of the dresses, she explains, is the in-built power-mesh 'that acts like an enormous girdle'.

I am practically weeping with gratitude by the end of the call. I've 'interviewed' many celebrities during my career – by which I mean that I've spent five minutes with them in a room or, if I've been really lucky, fifteen minutes on the phone – but Carol Vorderman shoots straight to the top of my list of favourites, second only to Aerin Lauder of the Estée Lauder dynasty (charming, professional, punctual and waiting to greet me in the corridor of her Manhattan skyscraper).

Inspired by the lovely quotes from Carol, I start to write the feature and by the end of the afternoon I've landed the plane. Gabriella would be proud of me. And just as I zap the piece over to the commissioning editor, an email pings into my inbox with news of another plane. My brother has sent Arianna's flight number. She will be arriving at Heathrow airport in the first week of July.

This is followed by an email from my niece herself, politely enquiring about the possibility of attending a 'rave'. How to explain that the only disco is fifty kilometres away and that the liveliest it gets in my village is when the wood-fired pizza van rolls into the square on a Thursday evening?

I spend a couple of hours stalking my half-Venezuelan niece on Facebook, clicking through photos of her at beach parties, lying under palm fronds, scuba diving and riding in speedboats – never, I note, wearing a life jacket – and always surrounded by a lively-looking entourage. Her life looks like a Bounty bar advert, but with oxygen tanks. How can my poor little village compete with all of that?

I lie awake for several nights, worrying about the impending visit. I compile a mental list of friends who have a stable of teenagers of a similar age, and make subtle enquiries as to how they keep them occupied during the summer months.

Inspiration strikes during a 3 am bout of insomnia. I am reading an eighteenth-century travel memoir by William Beckford, the richest man in England of the time, and best described as the Bill Bryson of his era, by which I mean that he was a witty and wonderful writer. (I should point out that Bryson, unlike Beckford, was not forced to go travelling as a result of a liaison with a sixteen-year-old boy.) As I devour his lovely descriptions of Spain and Portugal, I decide that I will take my niece on a road trip around the Iberian Peninsula.

In truth, her visit is well timed. I've been planning a pilgrimage to Portugal for a while, on account of my former Portuguese boyfriend, Luis. When we were together – he was, for several years, my neighbour in Villiers – he spoke often and with great affection of Leiria, the city closest to where he grew up. 'You would love it, *chérie*. Lots of Portuguese writers lived there,' he would say, before reminding me again of the fabulous seafood, magnificent forest and wildly beautiful beaches of Portugal's Silver Coast (so called, because on some days, the sun's rays turn the ocean a shimmering metallic). And then he provided another, sadder, reason to visit Leiria: it is close to Amor, the village where he was born, and is now buried.

The only reason that I haven't already made the journey is that my twenty-year-old car – or the Biffmobile as I fondly refer to it – can no longer be relied upon to make it home from dinner in the next village, let alone Portugal. This has certainly added a frisson to life in the French countryside over the last six months, but if you're about to embark on a 3000-kilometre trip, you need to know that your vehicle will actually start.

Transport issues aside, in all other respects, it is the perfect summer plan. We will drive through southwest France, across the top of Spain and then drop down into Portugal at its northern-most point, hugging the coastline and stopping over-night in little fishing villages, where we will eat simple but freshly cooked food with the locals.

If not exactly a Grand Tour of Europe, I will at least be taking my niece on a Grand Tour of the Iberian Peninsula and giving her an introduction to European art and culture. We will be following in the footsteps of Beckford, Napoleon and er... thousands of Ryanair passengers since. The planned route will take us past the key pilgrimage sites of Santiago de Compostela in Spain, and Fátima in Portugal, so we might even find some spiritual enlightenment en route. Unable to delay the inevitable any longer – putting the Biffmobile into retirement – I arrange to collect a new car in London and drive it back with my niece, after picking her up at Heathrow.

And so it is that one morning a couple of weeks later, I am running up an airport escalator, when my phone rings. 'Where are you?' snaps my sibling, from the laboratory thousands of miles away where he thinks of new ways to stop mosquitos breeding. 'Arianna has been waiting for nearly ten minutes and is really freaking out.'

I look at my watch: 8.30 am. It's five minutes since the plane officially landed. Either it arrived early, or my niece moved at the speed of fibre broadband from aircraft to arrivals hall. Either way, it is disconcerting to hear that a ten-minute wait has sent her into a tailspin. It means that I am about to spend my summer with an impatient diva. And there is room for only one of those in my small French house.

My brother, it must be said, does not panic easily. Once, while collecting sandflies on a mountain in Venezuela for his

PhD, he and his driver were held up at gunpoint and robbed of their cigarettes, beers and cash. When he recounts this incident, he makes it sound positively jolly – almost a 'must have' travel experience. After declaring himself 'a little shaken', he managed to persuade the bandits to give him a cigarette, before sitting down to enjoy one of his confiscated beers, with them.

But he is not so laid-back when it comes to his daughters. 'She's wearing jeans and a football shirt,' he snaps. 'Call me back the minute that you've found her.' I wince. In Facebook photos, my niece was invariably on a beach and minimally dressed. But a football shirt? For the first time, it occurs to me that she might actually be a nerd. If not a nerd, almost certainly a tomboy, I think, remembering the small person who preferred a Buzz Lightyear doll to Barbie.

I don't have to wait long to find out. I spot her immediately, leaning against a pillar in the arrivals hall with the kind of bored, slightly sullen look that only the young and good-looking can carry off. She is tapping away at her phone and nothing about her demeanour suggests that she is 'freaking out'.

'Auntie Carrie?' she says, in a languid American accent. (In case you're wondering, I am called many things in France including Madame Willer, Madame Wheel-AIR, and *Kar-enne*, but among certain close friends and family, I answer to the name 'Carrie'.)

'Hey, Ari,' I reply, throwing my arms around her.

Dressed in a tight-fitting purple shirt – if it's a football shirt it's not the kind that you see on the terraces of Old Trafford – and a hoodie, the sleeves pushed up to reveal a band of woven bracelets around her slender wrists, everything about my niece suggests laid-back beach babe. She has big brown eyes, long dark hair and the kind of tan that comes from a childhood spent in and around the ocean.

'How was your flight?' I ask, taking her bag.

'Yeah, cool.'

'Are you jet-lagged?'

'No. I'm excited.'

First lesson in dealing with teenagers: they are concise with their words. But the moment is not as awkward as I feared. Arianna is as sweet and adorable as the toddler who played under my desk. As we walk towards the taxi rank, I catch sight of my reflection, pale and freckled beside this tanned and exotic creature. It's hard to believe that we share the same DNA (twenty-five per cent of it, apparently, between an aunt and a niece).

It was Arianna who made me think that having a child of my own could be enormous fun, rather than just hard work. Unlike a dog, a biped pet would be welcome in restaurants and on planes – at least once past the bawling stage. In truth, I cannot remember Arianna crying even once, as a child. She was always so placid and sweet. The last time I came to Heathrow to meet her, she was sitting on top of a pile of suitcases as my brother pushed her into the arrivals hall on a trolley. At just two years old she was already a seasoned traveller, shuttling between Venezuela, Grand Cayman, Miami and er... Liverpool.

She lived too far away for me to witness her growing up, so my memories of my niece are a series of happy and vibrant snapshots: bobbing around in the Caribbean surf in a yellow swimsuit embroidered with daisies – one of many cute pieces of clothing that I bought and mailed to her in Cayman – or jumping off the side of a boat at Sting Ray City, a series of shallow sand bars off Cayman, undeterred by the mattress of sinister brown creatures lurking below the water. My brother brought her up to be a gutsy and joyous child, and I melted many times at the sight of those chocolate-brown eyes.

On another occasion, I remember Ari in a raspberry-coloured dress with navy polka dots, clutching my hand as we boarded a train to Chester. I noticed many admiring glances from other passengers as she sat quietly in the seat opposite me. 'What a good little girl, you've got,' proclaimed an elderly lady across the aisle, obviously thinking that Arianna was mine. I did nothing to contradict her.

The impeccable behaviour was down to my brother, who took a zero-tolerance approach to anything that might disturb the equilibrium of others. Unlike some of today's middle-class parents who feel that the rest of us have to take second place to their offspring's right to express themselves – kicking seat backs on airplanes or running amok on trains – if my nieces so much as squeaked in a restaurant, my brother would immediately scoop them up and take them outside for a stern 'talking to'. (Though once when he did this in a posh restaurant on Cayman, I followed my sibling outside to find him puffing urgently on a cigarette, while Arianna and her sister pretended to perform heart surgery on a toy panda in the grass nearby.)

My phone rings. It's my brother again. 'Find ya chill,' I say, using a phrase I picked up while stalking my niece on Facebook.

'What?' he says, and I hear him draw on a cigarette.

'Relax yourself. Arianna is safely in my custody,' I say, although some might think the phrase 'safely in my custody', an oxymoron.

'She is? Thank God.'

'Are there any rules that I should know about?' I ask.

'It is up to you to set them,' he says. Then, as an afterthought, he adds, 'No staying out all night.'

'Me or Arianna?'

'Both of you. And make sure she helps around the house.'

'Um,' I say, thinking back to the photo that Arianna posted on Facebook, her rubber-gloved hand poking through a broken wine glass, with the caption, 'F*** you, dishes'.

For someone who has only ever been left in charge of a dog before, the safekeeping of a teenager seems an enormous responsibility. I picture myself pushing through a field of frenetic dancing to extract her from a rave. At least dog ownership has given me grounding in the art of search and recovery, climbing into neighbours' gardens and, on one occasion, a chicken pen, in irate pursuit of an errant terrier. I reassure myself that Arianna won't be able to run as quickly as Biff. Though looking at her long legs, I'm not so sure.

'So when are we going to France, Auntie Carrie?' she asks.

'I've booked a cabin on the overnight ferry from Portsmouth, this evening,' I reply, 'so we don't have to leave until about 6 pm. I've organised a late checkout of the hotel room in London, so that you can sleep if you want.' (The research I've done suggests that teenagers like to sleep a lot, which is good because my worst nightmare is the guest who is up and ready to go at 7 am.)

'Cool,' says my niece. When she smiles, I notice that her eyes widen and she has the kind of cheeks that you want to tweak.

But first we have to collect my new car. We shuffle to the front of the taxi queue where, apologetically, I ask the cab driver to take us to Twickenham.

'Do you know how long I've been sitting here, waiting for a fare back to London?' he replies.

The only answer to this is 'What am I, psychic?' But since my niece is with me, I defy my better instincts and apologise again for the fact that we are not going somewhere that he finds more convenient. I also point out that it will still be a significant fare – licensed cabs at Heathrow, incidentally, are supposed to accept any journey within twenty miles of the airport – and hint that I will make it worth his while, by way of a large tip. But still he grumbles for the entire journey, interrupting my efforts to catch up on over a decade of my niece's life, with variants of the same question. *Will I be able to give him directions when we get to Twickenham? Do I know exactly where the garage is? Can I remember anything nearby?*

'No, but I've given you the address and postcode,' I reply, marvelling at his magnificent display of passive aggression.

'Why doesn't he just turn on his sat-nav?' whispers Ari.

'Because he's a moron,' I reply. Passive-aggressive people, along with tailgaters, Tony Blair, injustice of any kind, and UHT milk, are among my least favourite things in life. By the end of the twenty-minute journey, I would actually like to lean through the partition and throttle this man for sabotaging the start of my niece's trip to Europe.

Instead, I give him a generous tip. He responds not with thanks, but by reminding me, once again, that he will now be driving back to central London without a fare. As he pulls away I silently scream 'Moron!' and hope very much that his next passenger is a violent psychopath. I also resolve to open an account with Uber.

In the garage, Arianna sits patiently in the waiting area while I sign the papers and get to grips with the important stuff, such as how to operate the CD player. Finally, the salesman hands me the keys and we drive back to London in the morning rush hour.

An hour later, having dropped Ari's bags at the hotel, we are sitting outside a café on Kensington High Street, in the morning sunshine. I scan through the newspaper that asked me to write the piece on Victoria Beckham's 'It' dress. My feature hasn't appeared, which is disappointing, as the commissioning editor assured me it would.

I send her an email asking what has happened and receive an immediate reply saying that although she loved the piece, it has been bounced out of the style section by a piece on dog hairdos. Now, I love pictures of dogs with good hairdos as much as the next person, but I'm gutted that all those emails and phone calls were for nothing. I'll still get paid for the piece but I feel bad for having wasted Carol Vorderman's time. Worse, she might assume that I was some weird stalker fan, looking for an excuse to talk to her.

But I'm not going to worry about work now. As Arianna tucks into a full English breakfast, I tell myself, *this is all going to be fine*. My niece is fun and easygoing and does not have an eating disorder, which was just one of several tricky scenarios I'd envisaged. I won't be spending two months watching a moody teenager poke at a piece of lettuce. Finally, I can relax. And then I realise that I've left the car key in the ignition.

We leave London in the early evening, grateful that we still have a vehicle in which to do so. Fortunately, no one had spotted the gift in the underground car park with a bunch of keys dangling temptingly from the ignition. (Or possibly, it being Kensington, where f**k-the-environment, four-wheel drives are the norm, it just wasn't tempting enough.)

Arianna, it has to be said, seemed fairly unfazed by the sight of her aunt jumping up from the table with a cry of '*Oh, my God*!' and then sprinting along Kensington High Street towards the car park. At least it gave me an unexpected aerobic workout.

As we head towards the South Coast in the fulsome evening light, listening to Lana Del Rey singing mournfully of lost love and Californian swimming pools, Arianna provides some revealing glimpses of her life in the Caribbean. I learn that she likes to dive off cliffs for a dare, that her BMW-driving ex-boyfriend was significantly older than her, and that her father doesn't approve of her hard-partying friends. I suddenly understand why my brother was so keen to expedite his daughter to France for the summer.

It's also clear that, for Arianna, academic achievement is not a priority. 'Yeah, Dad's always on my case about *that*,' she sighs, when I ask about school. 'He thinks I'm really stupid.'

'The thing is, your dad measures intelligence by how good you are at science. So by his standards, I'm a thicko too,' I say.

Arianna seems quite pleased by this. She turns to me with a grin and says, 'Can I ask you a question?'

'Of course,' I reply, thinking of how much I am going to enjoy sharing my hard-won life experience, with my niece.

'Why does dad always call you "the dangerous aunt"?'

'He still calls me that?' I say, recalling the epithet that I was given (for reasons I don't remember) when Ari was a toddler.

'Yeah. He does.'

'What else did he say about me?'

'Not much. Just to make sure that I'm wearing my seat belt at all times.'

'Very funny,' I say, a little hurt at the slur on my driving.

We arrive in Portsmouth with an hour or so to spare. As we circle a roundabout, Arianna suddenly becomes strangely animated, leaning forward as if she cannot believe her eyes. Her face lights up like Paris at dusk. 'Oh. My. God,' she cries.

'What?' I ask, wondering if it is the DFS furniture store that is having this effect? Or maybe B&Q?

'A McDonald's,' comes the breathless reply.

'Have you not seen one before?'

'No! I mean, yes. But we don't have McDonald's where I live. It's all Burger King. The nearest McD's is in Miami. Oh please, Auntie Carrie, can we stop?'

Everything within me cries *NO* in 36-point, bold capital letters. McDonald's and its plastic food goes against all of my principles. I am a fast-food-phobic – the kind of person who scrutinises supermarket labels for additives and hydrogenated fats. There is no way I am even setting foot in McDonald's.

Less than ten minutes later, I'm watching my niece tuck into a Big Mac and fries. I'm ashamed, and worried about free-radical damage. But Ari seems happy. As we pull out of the car park, blinded by the brilliance of the evening sun, I resolve to rise to the challenge. During the next six weeks, I am going to impress on my niece the importance of good manners, eating fresh vegetables and making an effort at school.

We roll off the ferry in Ouistreham the next morning, in semi-darkness, listening to Rihanna's 'Shut up and Drive' – my niece is in charge of the music, so I hope this is not some kind of message – and join the traffic on the Caen *périphérique*.

I am convinced that this was designed as France's first line of defence against the British. On seeing a number plate featuring the initials GB [that's 'Great Britain', for my US readers], the French drivers on this ring road will do their best to kill you – especially if you are stupid enough to obey the speed limit of 90 km/hr, thereby becoming a danger to everyone on the road, including yourself.

To teach you a lesson, the native drivers will recklessly undertake and then cut back in front of you, lightly brushing your front bumper to emphasise their displeasure. Your other option is to move to the (supposedly) slower lane. But thanks to the treacherous road design and absurdly short entry roads, this is even riskier. Traffic does not so much 'filter' on to the *périphérique*, as hurtle suicidally on to it at an angle of ninety degrees. This leaves you in a constant state of terror as a car, often with a driver chatting on a hand-held phone, accelerates out of nowhere directly towards your door. If you haven't slept well on the night ferry over, a couple of minutes on this curving road will soon wake you up. Or send you back to the port for the first boat home.

But this morning we circumnavigate the highway from hell, and take the 'Gate for Paris' without incident. We speed past the flat fields of Normandy as daylight dawns, the sky a swirling molten pink above us, so that it feels as if we're driving through a lava lamp.

As we fly south, I learn that Arianna's nickname at school is 'giraffe and a half' (say it in an American accent pronouncing 'half' as 'haff' and it works) because she is tall; that her father calls her 'Barry' (to rhyme with Ari); and that she occasionally earns extra pocket money by acting as a lifeguard at children's pool parties. She is also very keen to know if Pop-Tarts, a kind of breakfast pastry, are readily available in France.

'I'm not sure, but the croissants aren't bad,' I tell her. 'And by the way, I've found you a rave to go to.'

'No way? Where?'

'In my village. To celebrate Bastille Day.'

Yes, indeed. We will be arriving back in France in time for July 14th. Unlikely though it might seem, my village celebrates the event with a giant outdoor rave. Or, at least it has for the past four years. While other communes in the region have polite little discos and play Boney M in the village square, my local *mairie* sets up an enormous dance floor in the municipal park, along with giant video screens, a bar and the kind of DJ that doesn't talk between songs.

'What's Bastille Day?' asks my niece.

'It's a French national holiday, to celebrate the freeing of prisoners in a jail in Paris.'

'Wow,' says Ari. 'France sounds insane. People celebrate a jailbreak?'

'Er... kind of. It was a symbolic jailbreak, during the French Revolution.'

'Oh. Well, tell me more about the party.'

'Last year it was... wild,' I say. And it's true that the dancing was frenetic and continued until sunrise, and that some villagers were rather desiccated by the end of it.

'Can't wait,' says Ari. 'France sounds *so* exciting.' Before I can disabuse her of that idea, a road sign looms in front of us.

'Oh look,' says my niece. 'Paris. Yay!'

Chapter 3

Cocktails in Paris

HOW DO YOU distil Paris into a day? The answer is that you don't. Instead, I decide to go for the edited highlights, imagining the day ahead as a montage of fun, memorable moments of the kind that you would find in a Woody Allen film.

Less than five hours after disembarking the ferry in Ouistreham, we are walking along the Seine towards the Eiffel Tower. Discouraged by the long queue to go up it, we decide to skip the world's most visited monument. Guiltily, we also skip the Louvre, the Musée d'Orsay, Notre Dame and Sacré Coeur, having abandoned the schedule of 'key sights' in favour of a more relaxed, meandering approach to Paris. To be fair, you need a certain level of energy to tackle the Louvre, and after the dawn start, we don't have it. Better to give my niece a flavour of the city, I figure, than rush around ticking monuments off a list.

In the early evening, we take the metro to Boulevard Saint-Germain, an area that many Parisian insiders avoid at weekends because, as the shoe designer Christian Louboutin once explained to me, it's overrun with a 'frighteningly chic' kind of tourist. I cannot claim that we belong in this category, but Arianna attracts quite a lot of attention as we pass the terrace of Les Deux Magots, or 'The Maggots' as I fondly refer to the famous bistro.

My niece, bless her, is oblivious to her effect on French teenagers, waiters and a species of French male that I call 'Left Bank Man' who, identifiable by his 'character' glasses, sits alone in Left Bank cafés, pretending to read *Le Monde* while checking out attractive women.

Watching the black-clad waiters in Les Deux Magots is, in my opinion, one of the top five unmissable Paris experiences. Dressed in their black suits and long white aprons and balancing enormous trays on their shoulders, they are at the pinnacle of their profession – and in Paris waiting tables really *is* a profession – treating tourists with a mix of disdain and arrogant competence. You mess with a French waiter, complaining that your food is over- or undercooked, for example, at your peril. In France, restaurants, in common with roads, are best regarded as a theatre of war. And much as I'd like to give Arianna an invaluable lesson in surviving the battle of wills that is Gallic service, I have another restaurant in mind for her this evening.

The Relais de L'Entrecôte does only one dish, *steak-frites* which, as a close relative of burger and chips, I figure is likely to appeal to my niece. The restaurant does that dish so well that there is an almost permanent queue outside, which means that the staff don't have time to engage in psychological warfare, or toy cruelly with the customers.

Once through the door, not a minute is wasted, in stark contrast to restaurants in my nearest town, Poitiers, where it is possible to arrive for lunch and still be waiting for a menu at dinnertime. This is the French version of fast food. There are no menus, just one question: how would you like your steak cooked? In little over an hour we have eaten and are walking up rue Bonaparte, towards the Seine. (It seemed rude to linger when thirty or more people were lined up outside, eyes boring in hungrily through the window.)

I point out the École Des Beaux-Arts, or *Boze-Aagh* as it is inelegantly pronounced, and tell Ari that former students of the prestigious art school include Renoir, Monet and Seurat. 'When I was a fashion editor, I watched quite a few Chanel shows there,' I say, recalling the excitement as a flock of over-dressed fashion people clipped across its courtyard.

'Was it fun being a fashion editor?'

'Some of the time,' I say, recalling how I first came to Paris to cover the shows for a trade publication called *Draper's Record*. Although the magazine provided a great grounding in fashion journalism, 'trade' journalists were considered to be second division, as far as fashion publicists were concerned. Not for us the gift left on the seat, the silk scarf, bottle of scent, or fawning attention to which the consumer magazines were treated.

Instead, we were lucky to have a seat at all, and, more often than not, stood in a crush at the back of the room with the 'friends of the designer' – aka the students and hangers-on who'd climbed in through a bathroom window, slept with a security guard, or otherwise blagged their way in.

In New York one year, I managed a stunning turnaround of this situation. Tired of my N-for-Nobody status, and of American publicists saying 'You work for *Raper's what?*' I shortened the name of my publication to a snappier-sounding *DR*, and told them that it was the British equivalent of *Women's Wear Daily* (*WWD*). This was entirely truthful in the sense that both magazines were aimed at the industry rather than the general public. The difference was that *WWD*, aka the 'global fashion bible', was read by 50,000 of the world's most influential fashion people; and *DR*... well, not quite so many. I should point out however, that it was a fine publication, and I was privileged to have worked for it, not least because several colleagues there became life-long friends.

But at this particular show in New York, my declaration – and on-the-spot rebranding of the magazine – had an electric effect on the guardian of the gilt seats. 'Come this way. I'm sure we can find you somewhere better to sit,' she replied, leading me to the front row. And right there, in the Grand Ballroom of the Plaza Hotel, I learned an important lesson: in fashion, as in life, how you present something, is everything.

Shortly afterwards, I was promoted into fashion's equivalent of the Premier League, by landing a job on a national newspaper. But colleagues I left behind at '*Raper's*', gratefully acknowledged my legacy with regards to the improved seating. 'I don't know what you said to those New York publicists, but they certainly remember *you*,' one of them declared, long after my Manolos had clipped up the ladder to newspaper land.

But I digress. Paris has that effect on me. It's like returning to my old office. As luck would have it, Ari and I reach the banks of the Seine just as the Eiffel Tower begins to shimmer like a Cartier charm, its 20,000 light bulbs bouncing light along the river like a million brilliant-cut carats. Only recently did I realise that this happens for five minutes on the hour, every hour, starting at dusk, transforming a Meccano-like construction of rivets and metal into a mesmerising light installation. Amazingly, many tourists miss this nightly light show, because it receives little publicity.

There is no doubt about it: Paris on a warm July evening is a fine place to be. We walk on towards the Pyramid of the Louvre – in my opinion, the most beautiful monument in Paris – its glass and metal sides shimmering like gold mesh, against the violet-blue sky.

Arianna, meanwhile, has spotted lights of a different kind: the fairground in the Tuileries Garden. 'Come on, Auntie

Carrie,' she says, pointing to a ride that replicates the vigorous action of a KitchenAid blender. It looks as though it could turn your insides to soup or, at the very least, re-arrange your internal organs.

'I think I'll pass on that,' I say, as a gaggle of Japanese tourists stagger off, gasping and disorientated, like the victims of a sarin attack. I also decline the waltzers, and when Arianna points to a ride that looks like a demented octopus, with punters dangling in pods at the end of its fast-moving arms, I reply with a firm, 'No way, José'.

Ten minutes later, I am being unbuckled from my pod and staggering back onto firm ground with the feeling that my cerebellum might never recover. My head hasn't spun like this since the night that I drank three champagne cocktails in Claridge's. (My French boyfriend of the time, who witnessed the aftermath, subsequently informed me that no French person would ever touch a classic champagne cocktail.)

It all becomes a bit of a blur after that, but eventually Ari and I end up on the Ferris wheel. I fear that its sedate revolutions are not quite the buzz that my niece is looking for, but it does provide some stunning views of Paris at night. It also gives my pulse a chance to return to normal.

As we rotate above the rue de Rivoli, it occurs to me that I should take Arianna to my favourite Parisian playground – the place where I invariably ended up after countless fashion shoots and beauty launches in the City of Light. My brother probably won't approve, but having failed to introduce her to the cultural landmarks of the city, the least I can do is give my niece a glimpse of Paris nightlife at its most glamorous.

'I'm going to take you somewhere that you won't forget,' I say, which is also a ploy to distract my niece from yet another stomach-rearranging ride. We leave the fairground, with its scent of spun sugar and onions, and head for the rose-scented haven of the Hôtel Costes, near the Place Vendôme. We are neither of us dressed for cocktails in one of Paris's most fashionable hotels, but the dark-suited doormen wave us into the lush, dimly lit interior, *pas de problème*. Although it is close to midnight and the lobby and bar are buzzing, we are led immediately to a table with two red velvet armchairs and a ringside view of the *beau monde*. There are advantages to travelling with an attractive niece.

I order two non-alcoholic cocktails, which seems like sensible aunt-like behaviour, but then remember my reputation as 'the dangerous aunt' and order myself a glass of champagne instead. Sipping her blend of exotic fruit juices, Ari seems suitably impressed by the pulsing house music and louche nightclub ambience. Grand Cayman might have beachfront bars, barbecues and Mudslides (the island's popular, sugar-packed cocktail), but it has nothing to compare to the sophistication of the Costes.

'How do you know about this place?' asks Ari, as a well-known model sweeps in, wearing a shell-pink dress that reaches to her ankles but leaves little to the imagination.

'I used to come here for work.'

'What was the most exciting thing that you did when you were a fashion editor?' she asks.

Good question. My salary and status doubled overnight when I moved to the newspaper. On one memorable occasion, I was invited by the hot label of the day to a 'private dinner' with Madonna, in Milan. I listened with mounting excitement as Signora Rinaldi, the label's publicist, repeated the words 'private' and 'exclusive', and I had to clutch the edge of the desk in my Kensington office to refrain from shouting, 'I'm in!'

I imagined myself clinking champagne flutes with the pop star, in the cosy dining room of a sumptuous apartment. It seemed feasible, as I had given the designer label in question, fabulous coverage over the previous years.

The only potential problem, added Signora Rinaldi, was that the dinner clashed with the show of Mr Giorgio Armani.

'Well,' I said, hyperventilating at the thought of bonding with Madonna over buffalo mozzarella and a glass of Valpolicella, 'I'm sure no one will notice if I miss his show just this once.' This event, it was clear, was not just going to be another mass grouping of fashion scribes, coldly raking over a few rocket leaves, as was the norm for a fashion week dinner. Indeed, so small and privileged was the planned gathering, that I would be required to exercise 'the utmost discretion'.

In particular, Signora Rinaldi requested that I desist from mentioning the invitation to fellow hacks. I readily agreed. At that point, I had not only imagined becoming best friends with Madonna and swapping tips on Pilates instructors, but also ghostwriting her official biography.

As promised, the address of the top-secret dinner was couriered to my hotel on the appointed day. I was surprised to find that it was in one of the less salubrious parts of the city – I'd imagined it would be in the private palazzo of the label's owners – but was feeling far too pleased with myself to question it. Waiting for a taxi in the hotel lobby that evening, I was surprised to find Lydia Bingle, the fashion editor of a rival newspaper, there too.

I'm not sure which of us was the most aghast to discover that we were both en route to the same select gathering. We were even more aghast when the taxi we had reluctantly agreed to share, pulled up in front of a seedy nightclub. *Surely some mistake?* I thought, spotting a brace of familiar fashion editors in the crush to get in. We encountered several more doyennes of the front row in the queue for the cloakroom, and it quickly became apparent that we'd all been had.

At least half a dozen other British fashion editors, it transpired, had received the same furtive but thrilling invitation, and were now furious to find that the 'small intimate dinner' was actually a standing finger buffet for several hundred.

Madonna and the label's designers, meanwhile, were cordoned off from the riff-raff of 'close friends', by a velvet rope and several burly bouncers.

The talk at the following morning's shows was not just of the hot fashion label's 'coup', but of Mr Armani's' fury at finding his front row decimated. His press officers had been spotted gravely surveying the empty seats and ostentatiously compiling a list of the AWOL, while warning that there would be 'consequences'. (Lydia, it transpired, had been smart enough to phone ahead and excuse herself with a fictitious bout of food poisoning.)

On my return to London, there was a further surprise waiting for me. Summoned into the editor's office, I was confronted with a handwritten letter from Mr Armani himself. In it, the great Italian designer announced that he would not, in future, be allocating a ticket to my newspaper, as its fashion editor had shown 'a lack of professional judgement'. I had not bothered to attend his show, the result of months of hard work, he wrote, but had instead gone out to dinner with friends. A similar letter was sent to other newspaper editors.

Fortunately, my editor had a sense of humour and although he took Mr Armani's complaint seriously, he also saw the funny side when I explained how we had all been hoodwinked. As for me, I was so touched that the legendary designer cared so much about my bottom on one of his beige velvet banquettes, that I framed the missive.

He was also, as I later discovered, big enough not to hold a grudge. A few years after 'Madonna-gate', he invited me to the opening of the flagship Giorgio Armani boutique on Madison

Avenue. Together with an exceedingly grand magazine editor, I was flown to New York first class, and put up at The Mark, an elegant hotel nearby.

Over a decade of working in fashion could not have prepared me for the glamour of the black-tie evening that followed. Assembled on the top floor of the Giorgio Armani boutique was a full roster of Hollywood stars. Standing right behind me in the buffet queue – think lobster and caviar rather than sausage rolls and quiche – were John F Kennedy Jr and Carolyn Bessette-Kennedy. The exceedingly grand editor meanwhile, with whom I'd enjoyed a martini in the hotel bar beforehand, ditched me the moment we arrived, and was now working the room with aplomb, signing up several years' worth of super-prime Hollywood stars for her covers.

I'd like to report that, while waiting in the world's classiest buffet queue, I enjoyed a little light-hearted banter with the Kennedys who, at that point, had been married for less than a month. But I didn't. I was too awestruck, despite having met Carolyn a couple of years previously. At the time, she was working as the publicist for Calvin Klein and I had gone to the label's headquarters with a colleague, Adrian, to borrow an outfit for a preview shoot.

This was always a tricky assignment because designers in the US were notoriously reluctant to lend clothes before – and so close to – their catwalk show. If they released an outfit at all, it was for a maximum of half an hour and accompanied by an armed guard. (OK, I exaggerate, but we were invariably chaperoned by a press officer, who would snatch back the outfit after ten minutes with a terse 'Time's up'.)

Carolyn Bessette, however, was a class act. Slim as a flute and fashionably dressed, she arrived in reception to meet us, exuding an effortless charisma. She was stunning. No photograph ever managed to capture that beauty, or the incredible presence that she had in real life. She was also significantly more beautiful as a brunette than the pale, icy blonde that she later became.

I don't remember what she was wearing that winter afternoon, apart from a knitted beanie hat – it was the height of the 'grunge' fashion era – but even dressed as a down-at-heel hobo, she was mesmerising. Everything about her was fluid, easy, effortless. She couldn't have been more different from the hard-bitten US publicists to whom I was accustomed. In her presence, I felt about as graceful as a Normandy cupboard. We didn't know at the time that she was already seeing the world's most eligible bachelor, which made her guilelessness all the more incredible.

'How many outfits would you like?' she asked, fixing us with clear, feline eyes. Adrian and I looked at each other. She was prepared to lend more than one? This was unheard of, before a catwalk show.

'Three or four?' I said, speculatively, not for a second thinking it would be possible.

'Sure,' she replied, and went off to get them, while we stood in the hushed white reception, unable to believe our luck.

While the presence of other US publicists was to be dreaded, I fervently hoped that Carolyn would insist on coming on the shoot. But she had more interesting things to do than escort garment bags around Manhattan.

Clutching the precious clothes, we rode the elevator thirty floors back down to the lobby, silenced by the vision of beauty and poise that had appeared before us. 'She was f**king gorgeous,' said Adrian, once he'd recovered the power of speech.

'In every way,' I agreed. Working in fashion you become immune to physical beauty, but we both agreed that John F Kennedy Jr had excellent taste. As for Giorgio Armani, he proved to be charming and intelligent when I interviewed him in his boutique the following morning. Fortunately, there was no reference to my misdemeanour in Milan.

Our waiter reappears. 'Another drink?' he asks, addressing the question to Arianna. She smiles and gives a sweet little shrug because she doesn't understand, so I translate.

'I'm cool with whatever you want to do,' she says.

'You know, you really remind me of your dad,' I say, signalling to the waiter for the bill.

'No way?' she says, her face filled with horror. 'He's pale and freckled and turns pink in the sun. He looks like a strawberry ice cream with sprinkles.'

'I meant in terms of personality,' I say, laughing at the astonishingly accurate description of my brother's freckled, Celtic complexion. 'You're both very laid-back.'

'Laid-back? No way! You should hear him ranting about my schoolwork.'

'You know, you're an intelligent girl, and with a little bit of effort you could really turn things around,' I say. 'What subjects do you like?'

'Art and English. I like reading books,' says Ari, which is music to my ears. 'But all dad goes on about is maths,' she adds with a grimace.

'Don't listen to him. With a bit of effort, you can be good at anything,' I say. 'And anyway, maths isn't everything. But the point is that you have to make an effort at *something*. Life has dealt you a good hand. Don't waste it.'

Ari looks unconvinced, but I figure that's enough of a motivational lecture for one night. I don't want to push it.

'Thank you, that place was amazing,' says Ari, as we walk back to the hotel. And I'm not sure, but I think that cocktails at the Costes might just have aced an evening at a rave.

The following morning, I retrieve my car from the under-ground car park near our hotel and, after a few hours of going nowhere on Paris's infamous ring road, we fly down an almost empty motorway towards my village in the Poitou-Charentes. I am *so* looking forward to showing my niece the smiling sunflowers, the vast open spaces and the spectacular sunsets. I hope that she will appreciate, as much as I do, the beauty of potted geraniums lined up against pale grey shutters, the sweet scent of the honeysuckle and lime blossom, and the sight of a white butterfly dancing on a blade of green wheat at dusk.

I am not sure how interesting such simple pleasures will be to a sixteen-year-old, but if all else fails, I do have one ace up my sleeve: Poitiers has a McDonald's.

Chapter 4

Two Weeks in the Poitou

SOME PEOPLE WILL go to any lengths to find happiness. I went to France. It has been my home for the past eight years, ever since I went to the Poitou to visit a friend for the weekend and bought, on impulse, an old village house.

It is here that I met the great love of my life. He lived with my friends Sarah and Steve, but from the moment that I first clapped eyes on him, at a New Year's Day curry party, I was smitten. Everyone assumes that I was cunning and manipulative in my pursuit of him – and I admit that I did feed him fresh crab and turkey when he came to stay with me – but the truth is that he made the first move.

If he hadn't flirtatiously nudged my ankle as I lingered by the onion bhajis that day, I might never have found myself saying to Sarah, 'If ever you need someone to look after Biff...'

Foolishly, she took me up on the offer and the rest, as they say, is history. Sarah and Steve had another dog, so I didn't feel too guilty when Biff made it clear, by climbing into my car one Saturday afternoon and refusing to get out, that he wanted to live with me. I even convinced myself that I was doing them a favour, since, as Sarah often said, Biff was the kind of dog who needed a lot of attention. But one of the conditions of letting me have him, was that they would occasionally have custody. This means that whenever I go away, I can leave my little black soulmate with his second family.

So, our first port of call on arriving back in the Poitou is to Sarah and Steve's hamlet to pick up my darling boy. When we arrive, he comes hurtling through the potted herbs like a black furry bullet. 'Oh,' I say, 'you've got a new haircut.'

Steve recently acquired a pair of dog clippers and it seems he has taken the opportunity to experiment on Biff during my absence. As a result, my woofer is now the proud owner of asymmetric eyebrows, while his tail has been shaped into a jaunty pompom.

'Not bad, eh?' says Steve, picking up Biff, in order to admire his own handiwork.

'He certainly looks... different,' I say.

'So what are your plans?' asks Sarah.

'I think we're going to spend a week or so here, before heading down to Spain.'

'Biff's looking forward to it, aren't you?' says Sarah. 'Lots of sausages in Spain. He's packed his swimsuit already.'

'He's got a swimsuit?' says Ari, wide-eyed.

'And a surfboard,' says Steve, deadpan. 'He's a well-travelled dog, aren't you, Biffy?'

'Right,' I say, laughing. 'We'd better be off.'

After giving Sarah and Steve a polite lick on the cheek, Biff picks up his lead, which impresses Arianna – 'Oh my God, look! He's taking himself for a walk!' – and trots down the garden path towards the car. He jumps in the back with his travel bag and his doughnut bed, and assumes his usual brace position under my seat. Then we are off, following the narrow, sunflower-lined road to Villiers.

'Wow, this is amazing,' says Ari as we drive through small villages, which are not so much sleepy as fully sedated, in the glare of the midday sun. 'Everything looks so old.' I assume she means the stone churches and dilapidated barns, rather than the inhabitants who, in any case, are rarely to be seen in the dead heat of the afternoon.

Villiers has been given a makeover in the week that I've been away: big pink spots have appeared on the bins and bike racks in the village square, like a plague of municipal measles. It is the work of Felix, the local artist (and flouter of planning regulations), but one of the things that I love about France is the indulgence that it extends to its artistic community. While other shopkeepers in the square are restricted to an official palette of colours for their shutters and shop fronts, Felix has artistic immunity and does whatever he pleases. And everyone is fine with that, because his artwork really cheers up the village.

It's lunchtime when we arrive in the square. The Café du Commerce, I am happy to see, appears to be thriving. Looking through the window, I can tell that most tables are occupied and there is even a tractor parked outside, which suggests that word of its *menu du jour* and fabulous homemade cooking, has spread to the nearby farming community.

'Oh, it's cute,' says Arianna, as I pull up in front of Maison Coquelicot or 'Wild Poppy House'. I love returning to my little cottage, with its pale blue shutters and its familiar smell of floor polish, firewood, and rose-scented candles. I throw open the downstairs shutters and lead the way up the old wooden staircase to the guest room, which is textbook French style: chestnut floorboards, cream iron bed with floral eiderdown, and a painted chest of drawers. The casement windows open onto an enclosed courtyard with hollyhocks, climbing roses, jasmine and potted hydrangeas. How I would have loved, when

I was a teenager, to have had an aunt – especially a 'dangerous' one – with a house in the French countryside.

'Wow, I'm going to love staying here,' says Ari, as Biff positions himself on her bed, fascinated by our exotic guest and eager to study her every move. Downstairs the phone is ringing. It is my friend, Delphine, calling – somewhat unexpectedly – from a cannabis plantation.

Delphine is the mayor of a local village, Puysoleil, where her duties range from issuing hunt licenses and dealing with 'naughty' farmers – one recently put stones in another's field; another ploughed over a public path – to organising a Halloween party for the local children, and the annual dinner for 'the oldies', for which she even makes the dessert.

Many would like to see her run for president, such is the flair and good sense with which she runs her tiny commune. The role of rural mayor requires the skills of a diplomat, accountant, lawyer, psychologist, marriage counsellor – a surprising number of people confide in her the details of their marital problems – and dog controller. She also teaches English part-time in an agricultural college, where her students, the farmers of the future, are also difficult to control. All of this, she does with a beaming smile, beautifully dressed in the brightest of colours, and wearing her favourite Chanel lipstick.

Dealing with problem dogs is a growing part of her 'mayor business' as she calls it. Today, she does not sound her usual calm self. It seems that the owner of the cannabis farm, which is hidden in the middle of a forest between Puysoleil and the nearby town of Douhé, was arrested during the night by the gendarmes, who then called Delphine to tell her that the two angry Rottweilers left on the premises were now her responsibility.

Unfortunately, Bruno, Delphine's capable and trusty council worker, who would normally take care of such matters – he does everything from putting up the commune's Christmas lights to driving the school bus – is on holiday.

'*Mon dieu*,' says Delphine. 'I don't know what to do. These Rottweilers are huge and growling and snarling at me through the window.'

It seems that the Poitiers branch of the SPA, the French equivalent of the RSPCA, doesn't have space for the dogs; while the district council, which serves many communes in the region, does, and can house the Rottweilers for up to two weeks. The problem is that it refuses to collect the dogs because Delphine's commune hasn't signed the relevant contract for the transportation of animals. Even the mayors, it seems, can hit the famous cliff face of French bureaucracy.

'I have one last option, which is to call the captain of the fire brigade in Poitiers,' says Delphine. 'He is a friend, so if I tell him it is an emergency, maybe he will help me out just this once. Otherwise, I will have to take the Rottweilers myself, in the back of my car.'

An image of Delphine driving her beaten-up metallic green car, with two large dogs hanging out of the rear window, flashes into my head. 'What a nightmare,' I say, thinking that the French mayors really do earn their modest monthly allowances – what with the mad dogs, frequently madder humans, and the middle-of-the-night calls from the gendarmes. Delphine's commune consists of less than 300 people, but it is astonishing how much happens there, from a combine harvester crashing over Puysoleil's seventeenth-century stone bridge, in the middle of the night, as happened two years ago, to the proprietor of the village café owner being jailed for (allegedly) running a brothel.

I wish her '*Bon courage*,' as Arianna comes down the stairs, closely followed by Biff – or 'Biff-dude', as she calls him. 'Did you just mention a cannabis farm?' she asks, eyes wide.

'Yup. My mayor friend was just called out to one.'

'Near here?'

'About twenty kilometres away, in the middle of a forest.'

'Boy,' she says. 'It's all going down in France.'

The following day we drive to Poitiers to meet Delphine and her niece and nephew, who are both Arianna's age, for lunch. The waiter greets us with a radiant smile, which is disconcerting. This is not the sort of behaviour one expects in French restaurants.

Delphine, wearing emerald-coloured beads, which stand out against her long dark hair, waves from a corner table. With her are Elodie and Jérémie. Elodie is blonde, tall, and looks like a teenage Cameron Diaz. Jérémie, who stands up to greet us as we approach the table – French teenagers really do have impeccable manners – is dark-haired, intense and super-intelligent. He also speaks good English. As he politely inquires about life in the Cayman Islands, I ask Delphine about the Rottweilers.

'My goodness, I am so grateful to the chief of the fire brigade,' she says. 'As a personal favour, he sent three firemen to help me out. The most senior of them was only twenty-seven-years old, but what a hero! He went inside to have a look and when he came out, he said, 'Well, *Madame*, they are not poodles, that's for sure.'

I laugh. The French sense of humour can be as dry as Sauvignon Blanc.

'The Rottweilers were growling and baring their teeth,' continues Delphine. It was very perturbating [sic]. But somehow, the firemen managed to get them into a van and take them to the district council kennels.'

'Thank goodness.'

'Yes, but this story is not over yet, because the kennels are already phoning the *mairie* to say that the dogs cannot stay longer than two weeks, and that I have to find them a long-term home.'

'What about the owner, the cannabis grower?'

'He was out on probation, but now he is going back to prison.'

'What a hassle,' I say. Honestly, who would want to be a mayor, playing the role of house-hunter for two angry dogs?

While Delphine and I have been discussing cannabis farmers and homeless canines, Jérémie has been giving Arianna a history lesson. 'In 1202, the English laid siege to the city of Poitiers,' he is saying.

'Much as they are doing today,' I add.

Arianna seems genuinely interested in the history of the region. At the end of lunch, Jérémie offers to take her on a tour of Poitiers and show her the church of Notre-Dame-la-Grande. I'm tempted to tag along myself, so knowledgeable is he on the city's history.

As our waiter brings the bill, I notice something familiar about him. 'You don't remember me, do you?' he says. It takes me a second to realise that it is Clément, the former owner of the Café du Commerce in Villiers. He looks as if he's had a personality transplant, or at the very least a large burden lifted from his slim shoulders. I don't think I saw him smile even once, when he ran the café in Villiers. And now, here he is, beaming.

'Clément, how are you? Is this your new restaurant?' I ask, although I'm sure it can't be, as the food was quite good.

'No, I'm not the owner; just an employee,' he says. 'It's much less stress. *Oof.* You have no idea how much work running a café involves.' Best not to tell him, I think, that the Commerce is thriving since he left, and probably involves ten times as much work.

Delphine and I decamp to a nearby café to wait. When Arianna returns, she seems quite fired up by her tour of the city. Before saying good-bye, Jérémie presents her with a pink origami rose, which he folds with a flourish before amazed eyes. Frenchmen, it seems, learn to practise their charms from an early age. While their British counterparts are playing with their smartphones or taking 'legal highs' behind the bike sheds, French teenagers are reading Baudelaire and learning to fold coloured paper into potential love tokens. I think it is fair to say that, with the exception of Elodie, we are all impressed.

A couple of days later, Ari and I visit a popular local tourist attraction, La Vallée des Singes, an open-air monkey park. The star billing, apart from a grumpy-looking gorilla – 'He needs a Mrs Gorilla,' says my niece – is the bonobos. Delphine, who recently visited Monkey Valley in an official capacity, told me all about these promiscuous little monkeys.

'The interesting thing about the bonobos is that the females are in charge,' she explained, 'and they sort out any problems within their community with sex.' On average, bonobos engage in sexual activity at least once every two hours. And that's just the monkeys that are in captivity. In the wild they really go for it: any major event, such as the discovery of a new feeding ground, is celebrated with communal sex.

On the day that Ari and I visit, they seem to be sorting out a lot of problems, as everywhere we look there is a pair of bonobos powering through the Kama Sutra. Two of them are having face-to-face sex – the only animals to do this apparently – with the female astride a squatting male, one hairy leg straddling another.

'*What the hell?*' says Arianna, as we stand on a viewing platform, watching.

'OK, let's go and look at the gorilla again,' I say. I feel uncomfortable staring at animals in captivity at the best of times – they always look so sad – but this is a whole new level of voyeurism.

At least the bonobos appear to be enjoying themselves. Their happy lifestyle of free love has even inspired a book: *The Bonobo Way: The Evolution of Peace Through Pleasure*. As I watch one of them recline with a post-coital banana, it occurs to me that it can only be a matter of time before someone writes a self-help manual entitled, *Be More Bonobo*, based on the premise that you can shag your way to happiness.

July 14th, Bastille Day, approaches and with it the promised outdoor party, which I have rebranded as a 'rave' for the purpose of impressing my niece. There is a sense of excitement in the air, along with the smell of barbecue smoke, as French families get together for a lunch that can last until sundown.

After a couple of hours spent getting ready, we make our way down to the lake in the municipal park, ready to dance until dawn. But to my surprise, and Arianna's disappointment, there is no one there. For a second, I wonder if I've got the date wrong. But it is definitely July 14th, as evidenced by the sound of fireworks in a nearby village.

We walk back to the square, where a party is taking place at the Café du Commerce. A chalkboard reveals that they are offering live music and *moules frites* for the Bastille Day celebrations. A significant proportion of the village is squished together at the trestle tables that have been arranged outside. Sitting at one of them is Matt, who waves at us.

'Come and join us for a drink!' he shouts. Next to him, pressed tight against his shoulder, is an elfin-faced woman with a wispy blonde bob. Dressed in a tiny white skirt and a tangerine top, she looks more St Tropez than Poitou-Charentes. 'This is my wife, Zoe,' he says, pronouncing it 'Zo'.

'Hey, pleased to meet you,' she says, flashing a smile as wide and as white as a slice of coconut.

'And this is my niece Arianna. She is visiting for the summer.'

'Why don't you join us?' Zoe says. I look around, but apart from on Zoe or Matt's lap, there is nowhere to sit.

'We've just come from the lake,' I say. 'I thought there would be fireworks and a party.'

'Oh, didn't you hear?' says Matt. 'The mayor decided to cancel the celebrations at the last minute, under pressure from the gendarmes. Something to do with the number of alcohol-related incidents last year.'

'Really?' I say, thinking that for a newcomer to the village, Matt seems remarkably well informed.

'I was in the *mairie* yesterday,' he says. 'So I heard it from the mayor himself.'

Zoe rolls her eyes. 'Matthew went to the town hall to give the mayor a bottle of whisky and introduce himself,' she says. 'He thinks it is going to speed up planning permission for the barn, don't you darling?'

'Oh,' I say, feeling a little put out that it didn't occur to me to introduce myself to the mayor, or take him a bottle of whisky, when I arrived in the village. Not that I need planning permission, but you never know.

'I've done better than that,' says Matt. 'I've invited him to dinner next week.'

'Darling, you haven't?' she says, pretending to cuff him around the ear. As she moves, her metal bracelets jangle, making a sound like a glockenspiel.

'I have,' he says. 'We'll cook him dinner, ply him with fine wine and we'll have his official seal on the planning application forms before you can say *"merci bien"*.'

Somehow, I don't doubt it. Matt has the confidence of a man used to getting his own way. 'How were the *moules*?' I ask.

'We haven't had them yet,' says Zoe. She looks pointedly at the owner, who is casually enjoying a beer with a group of male friends. He looks as happy as a bonobo but, frankly, not that focused on feeding his customers.

'Shouldn't Basile be in the kitchen?' I say.

'Yes,' says Matt. 'He should.'

'Maybe his wife has it all under control,' says Zoe.

'I don't think she is even here,' says Matt.

'Perhaps we'll wander back over in an hour or so,' I say. 'And join you for a drink after dinner.'

'I think an hour might be optimistic,' says Zoe. 'But you will come back won't you? Matthew says that you've lived in the village for a while. And I want to know all the gossip.'

In the end, we don't go back. Ari is in her room texting and reading; I am working, and before I know it, it's 2 am. As I take Biff for a nocturnal walk around the square, I notice that the lights are on in the apartment above the Café du Commerce. The doors to the first-floor balcony are open and through them, I can hear raised voices. Basile and his long-haired waiter are inside and they appear to be having a heated argument. Oh dear.

Chapter 5

Bollywood Nights

THE FOLLOWING EVENING, my niece and I head to a rave of the middle-aged kind, namely a Bollywood evening at the house of my friend Charles, in the nearby village of Bonillet. I'm not a huge fan of themed gatherings as they usually involve quite a bit of effort and, with the exception of the Halloween party that I attended dressed as a cat – black leotard, black tights, white pompom pinned to my bottom – I do not look good in fancy dress. As for the cat, I was eight years old at the time, and that look would not work for me now.

But expats in France are exceedingly fond of a themed get-together, perhaps because a significant number of us suffer from a condition known as 'too-much-time-itis'. Since moving here, I have variously attended an airline-themed party ('boarding at 7.30 pm for take-off at 8 pm'), a Jubilee gathering, which required dressing as one of the Royal Family (by far the most tricky), and a summer solstice party (dress code: 'druids and hippies').

But it is worth getting dressed up for the Bollywood evening as Charles has a nice mix of friends – French and English – and there is curry on the menu. This is a rare treat in rural France, where anyone who can demonstrate flair with a jar of garam masala and a cardamom pod is likely to find themselves hugely popular.

A rummage around in the attic yields a red chiffon Prada skirt from my fashion editor days and a pink sarong, which I wrap and tie into a suitable outfit, while Arianna finds a tunic trimmed with gold coins, which she wears with denim shorts. We paint bindis on our foreheads and we're good to go.

As we follow the meandering road to Delphine's house, Arianna gasps – not at the beauty of the summer evening or the fields of glowing sunflowers and vibrant green corn stalks, but at something on her phone.

'What's up?' I ask.

'One of my friends is on the run from the police. She's hiding in some bushes with a bong,' she replies.

'A bong?'

'To smoke.'

'Yup, I get that, but smoke what exactly?'

'Chronic.'

'R-i-g-h-t.' I don't know what 'chronic' is, but I'm guessing it's not green tea. 'Why is she on the run from the police?' I ask.

'For possessing drugs.'

'What the hell?' I say, and I'm about to launch into a lecture about the dangers of friends who take drugs, when I think better of it. I have to choose my moment.

'Wow,' says Ari, as I pull up in the farmyard in front of Delphine's cottage, which has dove-grey shutters and banks of orange dahlias around the door. 'We don't have anything like this in Cayman. It's adorable.'

Delphine emerges looking furtive in a mélange of purple and orange fabric. 'I hope I don't bump into anyone I know,' she says. (Fancy dress parties, like baked beans and Marmite, are something that most French people don't understand.)

'Have you found the Rottweilers a forever home yet?' I ask.

'No,' she says. 'I think it is going to be difficult. They are not their own best advertisement. I'll show you some photos of them, and I think you will see what I mean.'

As we pull up in front of Charles's stone house, she produces her phone and shows us pictures of the snarling beasts.

'Boy,' says Ari. 'They look like they're raging. But they're kinda cool.'

Our host answers the door dressed in a pink dress and a red satin bra. Sometimes, I do wonder about these dress-up parties. Charles was previously married to Annabel, a rather snobby and not very popular expat. Since divorcing her, he has really grabbed life by the balls, as Gabriella would say, becoming a regular fixture at everything from Zumba to 'Therapy Through Art' classes. He has also fine-tuned his cooking skills and often entertains on a large scale. 'Come on in,' he shouts.

In the garden, a colourful cocktail party is in full swing. Both French and English guests have embraced the Bollywood theme with enthusiasm. I'm intrigued as to how they've managed to dress like extras from *The Best Exotic Marigold Hotel* with just a week's notice, until a friendly blonde woman in peach chiffon, tells me that everyone is wearing upholstery fabrics, picked up cheaply in the local *dépôt-vente*. Who knew that it was possible to look so glamorous wrapped in cushion covers or a sofa throw?

Someone on the terrace shouts my name. It's Zoe. I see immediately that she wins the prize for the most tasteful inter-pretation of the Bollywood theme. In a simple white tunic top – all the better to show off her Manuka-coloured tan – with subtly flared, cropped jeans and an armful of silver bracelets, she looks as if she is attending a different event to the rest of us, in our primary colours and curtains. I suddenly feel horribly overdressed, even if I am wearing Prada.

Her husband, Matt, who appears to have a small crowd of expats hanging on his every word, looks similarly understated in a white shirt with a Nehru-collar. There is no doubt about it: they make an attractive couple.

Zoe rushes over to greet me. At close quarters I can see that there is no trace of makeup on her beautiful, glowing face. When she wakes up in the morning, she probably looks this good.

'I'm so happy to see you,' she says, after the obligatory two kisses. 'I don't know anyone here.'

'But you know our host, Charles?'

'Matthew does. He met him in the Liberty Bookshop,' she says, referring to the internet café and bookshop in our village. Although she is friendly, I notice that she insists on calling her husband by his full name – at least when referring to him in the third person. This puts me in an awkward situation, as it seems presumptuous to call him 'Matt' when his wife doesn't. I suspect it is a subtle way of warning me to keep my distance.

'In case you're wondering,' says Charles, coming up behind and putting his arm around my shoulders, 'the main topic of conversation in Bonillet right now, is wind.'

'Ah, yes,' says Delphine. 'I know all about this.'

'What?' I ask.

'You mean you haven't heard about the local scandal?' says Matt, with a wry smile. I shake my head.

'The mayor and his councillors have given the go-ahead for a wind farm to be built in Bonillet,' he says.

'And it turns out that the mayor and four of the councillors who voted in favour of the project, had each been offered €8,000 a year for allowing a wind turbine to be built on their land,' says Charles.

'How could they have been so stupid as to think that they wouldn't be found out?' I say, laughing at the audacity of the move. 'It's not as if you can hide a wind turbine in the middle of the French countryside.'

'But surely a wind farm is a good thing?' says Zoe.

'Apparently, it brings a lot of disturbance to wild life,' says Delphine. 'And the owner of the monkey park is threatening to leave if the wind farm goes ahead, as it will be very upsetting for his monkeys,' he says.

'Why? Are the wind turbines noisy?' I ask.

'I don't know exactly, but apparently his monkeys will not be able to reproduce if windmills are built within a certain distance,' says Delphine.

'That's right,' says Charles, frowning. 'The owner has a dossier of scientific evidence to prove that it will disturb the mating cycles of the monkeys.'

Arianna giggles. I can guess what she is thinking. Having seen the bonobos in action, I'd have thought they could shag their way through a nuclear apocalypse. But a petition has been set up to ban the wind farm and keep the monkeys mating. And the British, who make up a high proportion of Bonillet's population, have been the most eager to sign it.

'Oh yes,' observes Delphine. 'The English can be very fired up when animals are concerned.'

'Thierry here, is going to lead our campaign,' says Charles, introducing a man who looks like a French version of *Top Gear*'s James May, but dressed in a shiny green tabard and silky blue harem pants.

Ari nudges me. 'Why is he dressed like Robin Hood?' she whispers.

'I don't know. He's French. Maybe he misunderstood the dress code,' I reply, as Thierry explains in faltering English, that he is planning to put himself forward as a candidate at the next mayoral elections, in order to lead the fight.

Matt, I notice, isn't saying much, but he's wearing the ironic half-smile, which appears to be his default expression. I suspect he is in favour of the turbines, even if they are a passion-killer for the monkeys.

'Dinner is served,' says Charles, marshalling his guests into the dining room, where tureens of curry and rice have been laid out on a trestle table, along with various dips and accoutrements. I estimate that Charles has been chopping vegetables for the best part of two days. Such is life in rural France, where being sociable invariably involves the ability to cater on an industrial scale.

'Gosh,' says Zoe, when we are standing in the buffet queue. 'I really struggled to keep a straight face when they were talking about those monkeys.'

'Me too,' I say. 'Have you seen the bonobos in action?'

'No, but I've heard about them. I noticed your niece giggling and it almost set me off. I expect there'll be a whip-round later, to help the monkeys carry on shagging.'

I laugh. 'So you design textiles?' I say, as she spoons a tiny amount of rice onto her plate.

'Yes, cushions, curtains, that sort of thing, for an online home furnishings company.'

'So will you be able to work from France?'

'I will but I won't be here full-time, as I do a lot of travelling with my job,' she says. 'But I guess, when it's finished, the house in France will be our base.'

'Sounds ideal. Like having two lives,' I say.

'Um, I guess,' she says, looking a little uneasy. 'But I'm so happy that we're going to be neighbours.'

'Me too.'

'Let's go and find somewhere to sit,' she says. 'Oh hang on. Let me get another glass of wine. Can I get you one?'

I shake my head. 'Unfortunately, I'm driving,' I say.

'*Zut*,' she says. 'Matthew's the designated driver this evening. We tossed a coin for it. If we'd known you were invited, we could have given you a lift.'

'Ah,' I say, suddenly seeing the advantages of having expat friends in the same village.

Outside, Delphine and Ari are sitting with Charles and his neighbour, a well-known French violinist, at one of a dozen tables. Matt is with them, chatting away as if he has been part of this social scene forever. For a new arrival, he seems to be making quite an impression on expat society.

'I'm thinking of getting a dog,' Charles says, as I sit down.

'A dog?' says Delphine, her eyes lighting up. 'What kind of dog?'

'I don't know. I'll probably go to the animal shelter in Poitiers and get one,' he says.

'What about a Rottweiler?' says Delphine, and I can see where she is going with this.

'Why?' says Charles. 'Do you know of one?'

'I know of two,' says Delphine.

'Hmm, Rottweilers,' says Charles. 'Well, I guess it would scare off burglars.'

'These two would scare off anyone,' says Arianna. 'I've seen the pictures.'

Zoe laughs. 'The vegetarian curry is excellent, by the way, Charles,' she says, although she has eaten very little of it. 'Did you make it yourself?'

'I did indeed.'

'Bravo,' she says.

Arianna also seems to be enjoying the dish, even though it contains chopped carrots and peppers. I've tried several times to sneak chopped vegetables into her dinner since she arrived in

Villiers, but with little success. She just picks them out as if they were ball bearings, which is annoying. Fortunately, Biff is not so fussy: as everyone files inside to help themselves to dessert, he moves silently around the empty tables, vacuuming up the curry leftovers from the paper plates. But even he jumps when the sudden sound of Tom Jones cuts like a combine harvester through the peace of the rural evening.

'OK, everyone,' says Charles, standing up and clapping his hands. 'Time to dance.'

'This I have to see,' says Ari, searching in her bag for her phone, no doubt to record the event for the entertainment of her friends back home.

In the sitting room, the furniture has been pushed back, and people are dancing in a large circle on the terracotta-tiled floor. In the middle is Thierry, hopping around like an ageing elf, in his green tunic top. When it gets to the chorus everyone points at him and shouts, *Sex bomb! Sex bomb!'*

Arianna watches, transfixed. Zoe is already dancing. Although I'm guessing that she is in her mid-thirties, she looks much younger. I can see why Matt thought we would get on: she is sweet and slightly mischievous, and it would be difficult for anyone to dislike her.

As for Thierry, he has gone from looking embarrassed to giving every impression of enjoying himself. I feel a sudden rush of love for rural France and the people who live here. You can say what you like about the expat community, but it knows how to enjoy itself. And despite the animosity that's said to exist between the British and the French, at ground level, deep in the countryside, the *entente cordiale* is alive and kicking... and dancing to Tom Jones.

When I go into the kitchen to get a glass of water Matt is leaning against the counter, arms folded, watching.

'That dog of yours is fun,' he says. 'Very mischievous.'

'Yup, he is.'

'And your niece is delightful. It can't be much fun for her being surrounded by so many middle-aged people.'

'As she keeps saying, everything in France is so old.'

He laughs. 'By the way, I hear that you write books?'

'Who told you that?' I ask, fervently hoping that he hasn't read any of them.

'I can't remember. Probably someone in the village. When we went for drinks in the Commerce and I asked you what you wrote about, you never mentioned books. You were a little cagey and mysterious.'

'Really?' I say. 'The one thing I could never be accused of is being mysterious.'

'Yes. You said that if ever you were invited on *Mastermind*, your specialist subject would be Victoria Beckham.'

'Yes, well… it was a joke about a piece I was working on at the time.'

Suddenly he becomes serious. 'Can I ask you something?'

'Yup.'

'What's it like living out here on your own?'

'That's a strange question to ask in the middle of a party,' I say, surprised by the sudden shift in conversational gear.

'Are you happy?' he persists.

'Yes. I am actually. I've got my dog and my work and my friends. That keeps me out of mischief. Why do you ask?' I say, while thinking, *what a patronising jerk*. 'Do I look miserable or something?'

But his answer is surprising. 'On the contrary, you seem very happy,' he says. 'The reason I ask is because I enjoy my own company, too. Quite a lot, actually. Some people don't, but I'm quite happy spending time alone.'

'Well, that's a little unfortunate, given that you're married.'

'Zoe is away a lot.'

There is an awkward silence, as I'm not sure what to say to this. 'But you must be pleased when she is with you in France,' I reply.

'Yes. And no,' he says, just as Zoe appears in the doorway.

'What are you two looking so guilty about?' she asks.

I am saved from having to answer, by my dog. 'Auntie Carrie,' shouts Arianna, from the dining room. 'Biff is helping himself to dessert.'

I rush in and find him taking full advantage of the distracted humans next door. Standing on two legs, with his paws on the table, he is about to stick his head into a pavlova.

'I'll say one thing for you, Biff-dude,' says Ari. 'You've got good manners. At least you wait until the humans have eaten before you make your move.'

I carry Biff outside and join Delphine, who is sitting by the fire pit – actually an old metal washing machine drum filled with wood – under a field of stars. She seems to be getting along marvellously with the French violinist, a rather debonair chap with a moustache and dark eyes. He is telling her that Charles's house was once owned by a pig farmer, Monsieur Bouffe, now sadly deceased.

'Imagine,' says Delphine, 'if old Monsieur Bouffe could see us in his garden now, dressed up in these clothes. He probably wouldn't believe his eyes.'

'I can't quite believe it myself,' I say, looking up at the sky, as opaque as navy cashmere, sprinkled with silver stars.

Zoe comes to say good-bye. 'We're off,' she says. 'I was wondering if you would you like to meet for a coffee in the morning? Or a drink tomorrow evening?'

'Ah, I would have loved to. But we're leaving for Spain the day after tomorrow, and I've got quite a lot to do.'

'How long are you going to be away for?' asks Matt.

'That depends on how lost we get,' I reply.

He laughs. Then, as Zoe is thanking Charles, he leans towards me and says, 'When you're back, I'd like to continue that conversation we were having in the kitchen.'

'Um,' I say. 'Which bit of it?'

'About liking your own company.'

'As the poet John Donne said, "Be thine own palace or the world's thy jail."'

'But no man is an island,' he shoots straight back at me. 'Donne also said that.'

'Impressed,' I say. And I am, as I don't know many people who can quote sixteenth-century poetry on tap.

Suddenly, Zoe is at Matt's side, sliding her hand around his waist, as if claiming a prized asset. 'Come on, darling; I hope you're not boring our new friend with stories about the barn,' she says.

'Not exactly...' he says. 'And anyway, she might be interested.'

'Oh,' says Zoe, looking at me. 'I forgot to get your contact details.' She rummages in her suede bag until she finds her iPhone and then taps my phone number and email address into it. 'OK,' she says. 'There will be no escaping me now.' Then with a cheery 'Ciao girlies', she grabs her husband's hand and is gone.

'Goodness,' says Delphine. 'He seems like a bit of a rogue.'

'Yes,' I say. 'He does.'

'By the way, are you serious about giving the Rottweilers to Charles? I honestly think they might eat him.'

'I will have to check the regulations,' she replies. 'I think they have to be certified as safe before I can rehome them.'

'Well, good luck with that,' I say. 'Though I suppose Charles would be the ideal match for a Rottweiler. He was, after all, married to Annabel.'

'And he seems to be good with dangerous dogs,' says Delphine. 'Don't you remember that he and Annabel had those two big dogs, Jenson and Button, and one of them knocked you over when you were looking after them?'

How could I forget? Billed as a black Labrador, Button had the head of a pit bull and the body of an ox, and when running towards you – even if it was just to give you a friendly lick – it was a terrifying sight to behold.

'If Charles could handle Jenson and Button, he should be able to handle a couple of Rottweilers,' I say.

It's 3.30 am when we finally leave, and almost light when we arrive back in Villiers, after dropping Delphine home. 'That,' says Ari, as she climbs the stairs to bed, 'was *so dope*.'

Googling the phrase before I go to sleep, I'm pleased to find that it is a term of approval.

I also type 'Chronic' into Google and discover that it is urban-slang for 'high-end' or extra-strength marijuana. That, I think, is not so dope, though one could argue that if you're planning to get high you might as well opt for the Waitrose of herbal leaves rather than the cut-price Lidl version. As for Arianna's bong-toting friend, her evening did not end so well. 'A night in the hospital is fine; a night in a police cell is not,' was the update that she posted on Facebook as we drove home.

Late the following afternoon, I phone Gabriella. 'What are you doing?' I ask.

'I'm in bed with my lover,' she shouts. 'I'm ninety-five. What do you think I'm doing?'

'Can I pop by and see you?'

'Yes. Do.'

Every time I go away, I worry that Gabriella might not be there when I get back. Although she is in robust health, at her age nothing can be taken for granted. Pinned prominently to the wall by her telephone are instructions written out in large letters and lists of telephone numbers to call 'in case of a crisis'. She has planned for every eventuality.

'Your hair looks nice,' I say, for she has obviously been to the hairdresser's. She gives a smile of such genuine delight that I'm touched. It occurs to me that when you're ninety-five you probably don't get many compliments on your appearance.

'My youngest son is coming from America, tomorrow,' she says, pointing to the piles of chopped vegetables on the table. 'That's why I'm preparing all this food. But tell me what you have been up to. How are you getting on with your niece?'

'She's adorable, and really easy to be around.'

'Very good. What else is going on?'

'We have some new people in the village,' I say, before telling her about Matt and Zoe.

'An architect?' she says. 'Is he charming?'

'Yes, he is charming. And quite flirtatious.'

'Herbaceous?'

'No, *flirtatious*. A flirt.'

'A squirt?'

'No,' I say, more loudly. '*A flirt.*'

'Just a minute,' she says, fiddling with her hearing aids. 'That's better. Now tell me about this architect.'

'There isn't a lot to tell. He has a wife called Zoe, who seems very friendly.'

'Well, if they're interesting and decent people, you should become friends with them. Who knows where it might lead?'

'Um, yes,' I say, thinking that's precisely what's worrying me. To change the subject, I ask Gabriella about her young optician friend, Marguerite. Six months ago, Gabriella invited

Marguerite to dinner, during which, it became apparent that she was not entirely happy with her fiancé.

'Then, leave him, you moron!' Gabriella cried.

'It's difficult. We just bought a house together.'

'Then sell it!'

Within weeks Marguerite had done exactly that, and last night popped by to tell Gabriella that she has a new fiancé.

'It gives me great pleasure to plant a bomb in peoples' lives,' says Gabriella, delighted by the news. 'I can't read or write or watch television, so I spend a lot of time sitting and thinking about my friends and their problems.'

'So Marguerite hasn't looked back?' I say.

'Of course not.'

'Is there anything in your life that you regret?' I ask.

'Regret? There is no point in spoiling your soup with regret,' says Gabriella.

'There must be some things that you wish you'd done differently?' I persist.

'I think my only regret is not thanking people enough,' she says. She tells me the story of the emergency doctor, called to her New York hotel in the middle of the night when she was pregnant with her first son.

'The doctor managed to prevent my son from making an early exit,' she says. 'Afterwards, my husband wrote him a cheque. But what we should have done is send him a case of good champagne, because he saved our son's life.'

Thanking people, I've noticed, is one of her favourite themes. Gabriella it was, who prompted me to write a thank-you letter to one of Luis's doctors, a few months before he died. This doctor, a psychiatrist, had been particularly helpful to me, providing updates on Luis's condition, and had even given me her phone number so that I call her at anytime, but it hadn't occurred to me to thank her.

I was grateful for the way in which Gabriella, no doubt seeing that I was too upset to think clearly, took charge of the situation. 'Fetch a pen and paper,' she commanded. 'And we'll write the good doctor a note, together.' Although I've earned my living from words for over two decades, I don't think I've ever composed any sentences more beautiful, succinct or sincere, as the three that Gabriella dictated to me in French, that evening.

I suppose that as a former diplomat's wife, she was well-practised in the art of the elegant thank-you, for she also advised me – a nice touch this – to send a single rose, to accompany the note. 'Don't bother with a bouquet or anything flashy; the simpler the gesture the better,' she declared. It was one of many lessons that she has taught me: a simple, thoughtful act can have much more impact than an expensive gift.

'So,' she says. 'Are you looking forward to your trip?'

'Yes, but I haven't packed yet.'

'Well then, why are you wasting time here? Get going, you moron! You've got much more important things to do than sit here with me.'

I laugh and kiss her cheek as I get up to leave.

'I want you to know,' she says, squeezing my hand, 'that I have a great deal of affection for you.'

'Well, I feel the same about you,' I say, touched. 'I really do appreciate all the advice that you give me.'

'Do you?' she says, beaming.

'Yes, more than you could possibly imagine.'

As I walk home in the July sunshine, I contemplate the truth of this. She might be physically frail, but mentally and emotionally Gabriella is stronger and happier than almost everyone I know. I smile at the thought of her ruling the world from her kitchen table. And, as usual after visiting her, I feel as if the world has just given me a great big hug.

Chapter 6

Breakfast in Biarritz

THE MORNING OF our departure arrives. My preparations – namely, buying a map of Spain and several weeks' worth of Biff's favourite dog food – are complete. I pack up the car with everything we need for a journey through three countries, and many more things that we don't, including half a dozen boxes of my books in various foreign languages.

Our road trip will culminate with a book signing in the Dordogne in August, when according to my friends Eileen and Wally who live there, the market in Eymet will be packed with international tourists. It will be a marvellous opportunity to offload the Polish, Mandarin Chinese and Taiwanese versions of *Tout Sweet* that have been lying under the bed in the spare room for several years.

When I've finished packing, there is just enough room for Biff to squeeze into his usual slot behind the driver's seat. My niece emerges wheeling a tiny suitcase behind her, and we are off. As we drive south listening to Lana Del Rey – Arianna likes this CD a lot, and so did I before I'd heard it forty times – all is sunshine and optimism.

I have even spun my lack of forward planning into a positive: no strict itineraries for us, I tell Ari. Instead, we will plan no further than one or two nights ahead. That way, we can freewheel around Iberia, but at least know that we've got somewhere for Biff to lay his doughnut bed each evening. For the first two nights, I've arranged for us to stay in Biarritz, thirty-five kilometres north of the Spanish border.

France is an excellent place to start a road trip, thanks to its superb motorways. And with the exception of certain weekends in July, when the French go on holiday en masse, you pretty much have them to yourself. Unfortunately, I *have* chosen one of the weekends in July when the French go on holiday en masse. When we stop at a service station, it is standing room only and looks like the aftermath of a national catastrophe.

It turns out that the authorities have chosen this weekend to dig up the car park. Dozens of people are standing around in the churned earth, looking dazed and displaced, while cars are parked at all kinds of crazy angles, with drivers sounding their horns because they're blocked in. I decide to skip the melee and drive straight through, forgoing the great pleasure of French service stations: the vending machine coffee. It's surprisingly good – the best I've had in France, where the trend for gourmet beans has yet to gain momentum.

We drive on towards surf, sangria and seafood. Somewhere south of Bordeaux, the sun becomes brighter and the light more luminous. In what seems like no time at all, the exit for Biarritz appears before us. On a Friday afternoon in peak season, there is a real buzz in the air as we follow the signs to the city centre. At the sight of so many cars with surfboards on the roof, I sense my niece almost trembling with excitement in the same way that Biff does when I'm cooking corned beef hash. Teenagers and dogs: they're not dissimilar.

'Wow, so many surfer-dudes,' says Ari, as a group of surfers in a camper van overtake us, waving. One of them turns to blow her a kiss. 'I think I'm going to love it here.'

'I can't think why,' I say.

Our stay starts auspiciously when our hotel looms magically in front of us – the very first building that we see. No need to figure out how that sat-nav works just yet, which is a relief. Our second lucky break is that we find the only remaining space in a nearby car park.

Clutching Biff's doughnut, a straw basket containing his food and bowls, various other bags and wheelie suitcases, we advance on the dog-friendly Ibis hotel, looking as if we're planning to stay until Christmas. The surfer-dude receptionist – he has the kind of highlights that money can't buy, even in John Frieda – appears unfazed when we deposit our little knoll of luggage in the lobby.

You've got to love a surfer and Biarritz is pretty much run by them: stuck behind hotel receptions, waiting tables, or working in bars, these aquatic hippies do their jobs with cheerful, laid-back charm, while counting the minutes – I imagine – until they're back in the sea.

Once our luggage is in the room, there isn't much space left to move around. Biff climbs into his doughnut and surveys his kingdom with shiny eyes and a grin, as does Arianna; and after some selfies, we set out to explore Biarritz.

My niece blends in perfectly – a surfer-dudette of the most authentic kind, in tiny denim shorts and with a slew of hippy beads around her neck. She makes a jangly noise as she walks, rather like the sound of goat bells, which means that I don't have to worry about losing her.

No sooner have we stepped out of our hotel than a camper van pulls up alongside us. A bronzed hippy with hair to his collarbone, winds down the window to ask directions, no doubt recognising in Arianna, a kindred spirit. She has, after all, spent a significant portion of her life, in and around the ocean.

The surfers are looking for La Grande Plage, the Bondi Beach of Biarritz, and I'm flattered that they think we might know, although the question is directed at Arianna, not me. Since she doesn't understand, I reply, pointing them in the direction of the resort's longest beach. The messy-haired driver gives us a salute of thanks and the surfer-dudes speed off in their sunshine-yellow van.

Biarritz is a somewhat bizarre mix of the well-heeled elderly, toting Hermes handbags and small dogs; and the young surfer set, padding through the streets in their flip-flops and board shorts, or emerging dripping from the sea. Somehow the combination of the two – the rich who have come to 'take the waters' in the glitzy hotels, and the lithe, bronzed folk who get their kicks less expensively, from being in the actual sea – seems to work wonderfully.

But if the French writer Victor Hugo had had his way, Biarritz would not be buzzing with well-preserved OAPs and cool surfer-dudes at all. In 1830 he expressed the wish that this wild and beautiful 'village' would never become fashionable. A couple of decades later, Napoleon III and Empress Eugenie arrived, built themselves a summer residence – now a luxury hotel – and put paid to Hugo's hopes of keeping it an insider secret of the literati. (The writers Ernest Hemingway and Emile Zola also loved it here.) Its fate as one of France's glitziest resorts, meanwhile, was sealed in 1915 when Coco Chanel chose Biarritz as the location of her third boutique.

I have been to Biarritz once before, to write a feature on thalassotherapy, the regime of seawater pummellings and algae-based beauty treatments of which the French are so fond. I stayed at a grand hotel overlooking the beach, where one treatment proved particularly memorable. The therapist wrapped me from head-to-toe in plastic and self-heating seaweed, and then left the room, supposedly for thirty minutes, to allow the algae to take effect. After enjoying a sneaky cigarette, or whatever it is that beauty therapists do when they ship out of the treatment room, she forgot about me and went home. I grew hotter and hotter in my snug-fitting layer of seaweed. The stuff was having an effect alright, but it wasn't the 'inner harmony and equilibrium' promised in the spa menu. Finally, when I couldn't stand the heat or the soundtrack of plinky-plonky music any longer, I managed to shuffle off the bed and out of the door like an ungainly mermaid.

As I stood in the corridor, trailing bits of seaweed and plastic wrapping like a distressed sushi roll, several white-coated spa attendants came running at once, offering glasses of water and apologies, shocked no doubt by the fact that my face was as red as a grilled snapper. It's fair to say that I sweated out quite a few toxins that afternoon.

Later, I topped them right back up again, enjoying a glass of white burgundy over dinner with colleagues in the elegant hotel restaurant, where the only fruits on offer were *fruits de mer* (sea food) and the calorie-controlled menu – I kid you not – included foie gras. For someone used to country house-style spas in the UK, where inmates shuffle to a low-calorie dinner dressed, depressingly, in slippers and towelling robes, this was a revelation.

People who had spent the preceding hours submitting to high-pressure jets, were now bejewelled and sparkling and downing bottles of wine. For the French, it was the natural follow-up to a day of 'detox'. And it had to be said, that they had a certain glow about them.

I duly wrote an article full of admiration for the French approach to detox. No arduous exercise regime or self-denial for our Gallic friends; for them, 'detox' means a sniff of ozone and extensive application of seaweed. My conclusion, despite being nearly braised alive, was that there might be something in it, for I left Biarritz feeling on top of the world.

'I want to live here,' Arianna declares, as we walk along the soft sand, throwing bits of driftwood for Biff. 'I'm going to learn French so that when I've finished school, I can come here and get a job.'

'Are you serious?' I say. This is the first time that I have heard Ari mention schoolwork with anything close to enthusiasm.

'Yeah,' she says. 'I love it here.'

'Well, that's excellent,' I say, feeling ridiculously pleased that, by bringing my niece to Biarritz, I might have motivated her to up the ante on the academic front. 'And you know what? I can see you really fitting in here.'

We climb up to the esplanade, and as we stroll along, eyes swivel towards Ari. It's what I call the rosé hour – the magical time between daylight and dusk when the world is cast in a golden-pink light. The surfers are still out in force, lined up in the sea or lying on the sand in small groups, drinking beers and setting up barbecues. One of them calls up to Arianna in French. Realising that she doesn't speak French, he and his friends try again in Spanish. Arianna starts to laugh.

'What are they saying?' I ask, although I can guess the general drift.

'They're asking me to go down and have a beer with them.'

'And?'

She hesitates. 'They want to know if you're my mother.'

'Oh,' I say, a little taken aback by the sudden reminder that nearly thirty years lie between us. In my head, I'm still twenty-two; in reality, I have just been mistaken for the mother of a teenager – albeit a lithe and beautiful one.

Arianna is laughing again. 'What?' I ask.

'I told them you are my aunt. And they said to invite you, too,' she replies.

'That's nice of them,' I say, though I'm relieved that Ari doesn't want to take up the offer. I have no idea what I would chat about with a group of twenty-something surfers.

'You know what? I can see you with an older surfer-dude,' says Ari later, when we are standing at the counter of a coffee bar, and a crowd of helpful surfers move in to offer their translation services, not realising that I speak French. 'You can find one here, for sure.'

'Gee, thanks,' I say.

It is obviously meant as a compliment, but I doubt that I'd have much in common with a surfer of any age, given that I don't like spending time on beaches and the only surfing I do, requires a broadband connection. That said, I can certainly see the advantages: they'd be good at barbecuing; could rescue you if you were drowning; and, if you were really lucky, they might own a camper van, which is not unappealing.

The following evening, we drive to Guéthary, a smaller surfer's paradise and fishing village not far from Biarritz, to meet up with a female surfer friend. Eliza, an artist, took up surfing in her forties after having three children, proving that none of us can take for granted the right to spend one's middle years relaxing on the sofa with a box set.

'God, your friend's gorgeous,' whispers Ari, before texting back to her friends in the Caribbean: 'Feeling quite jealous of all these amazing-looking older women.' She heads off to the beach with Eliza's daughter, while we sit at a terrace bar, watching the sea and sky merge in a shimmering metallic pink.

'So what's the plan?' asks Eliza, flagging up the fact that I don't actually have one. I produce my fold-up map of Spain. It's a portentous moment, as I haven't actually looked at it yet. Eliza once toured the Spanish coast in a camper van with her former husband, so I'm hoping that she can give me the edited highlights. But she doesn't seem to have particularly fond memories.

'Yeah, I seem to remember we had a terrible argument driving between here and here,' she says, grimacing as she indicates two points on the map. 'But Comillas is worth seeing.'

Eliza, I notice, does not offer the usual platitudes such as, 'I'm *so* jealous', or, 'You're going to have *such* a wonderful time.' Instead, she points to a place on the map and says, 'Ah yes, that's where we decided to cut the holiday short and come home.'

I wake up in Biarritz the next day, feeling quite shabby after too much rosé, and with a vague memory of shelling out the price of a transatlantic flight for a taxi back from Guéthary. There is only one antidote to a rosé hangover that I know of, and that's scrambled eggs on toast, so I lure Ari out of bed and we set off in pursuit of a decent breakfast. Although Biarritiz is buzzing with outdoor cafés, the choice is basically croissants, coffee and orange juice. Or nothing. We take the bus back to Guéthary, thinking we'll have more luck in the less glitzy establishments there.

We find Eliza in the market, where she sells her paintings on a Sunday morning. Like me, she is looking a little the worse for wear. I tell her that we're off to get breakfast and offer to bring her back a coffee. She looks at me oddly. As I should know, the concept of takeaway coffee, like the cooked breakfast, does not exist in France. A kindly bar owner does, however, let us have a *café crème* to take out, if we promise to bring the cup and saucer back. As we carry it through the streets on a tray, followed by some strange looks, Ari has an idea. 'We could open a café here,' she says, 'making breakfasts for surfers.'

By the time we reach the market stall, she has planned the interior (psychedelic), the furniture (wooden and distressed) and the china (floral and mismatched). My niece has also designed our logo: a tricolour turtle. I will make the cakes and she volunteers to do the cleaning, which gives me an idea of just how keen she is.

'Well,' I say, 'you're really going to have to pull your socks up at school, so that you can communicate with the customers.'

'I know,' says Ari. 'I'm going to call dad tonight and ask if he can find me an intensive French course, in Cayman.'

'And you might have to step up your effort with maths, because to run a café, you have to do accounts and spreadsheets and stuff.'

'Um, maybe that could be your thing.'

In the end, we realise that it will be neither of our thing. Eliza provides the reality check, pointing out that it won't be easy to find premises in Guéthary; there would probably be objections from other café owners; and that we would need various permits and licences if we wanted to serve hot food. And this being France, we are talking *a lot* of paperwork.

But by far the biggest obstacle, however, which Arianna and I eventually work out for ourselves, is not the paperwork, the hobbling taxes, or the barrage of licences that we would need, but the simple fact that, in order to run a café, you have to get up early. And since neither of us has much of a track record in this respect – I can imagine the arguments: 'Get up! It's your turn to do the early shift!'; 'No it isn't. It's yours!' – the Turtle Café won't be opening its doors anytime soon.

Chapter 7

When the Best Thing is Leaving

'AUNTIE CARRIE, STOP!' On the way back to Biarritz to collect our luggage, before leaving for Spain, we see a dog limping alongside a busy road. I am not sure what breed he is, but he's got a recognisable hairstyle (white and shaggy), which means that he must, until recently, have been cohabiting with a human, rather than living alone and off his wits.

'Look! He's really cute. Stop! Stop and pick him up,' shouts Ari.

Right at that moment, the dog, as if he can hear us, turns and looks directly at me. I hesitate for just a second too long, considering the implications of picking him up. What do we do with him after getting treatment for his leg? And how easy will it be to find a vet on a Sunday? In Biarritz, in peak holiday season, they've probably all swapped white coats for wetsuits. And if we pick up the little refugee, my instincts tell me that we'll be offering him permanent residency, which might not go down too well with Biff.

By the time I've run through the options and likely outcomes, we've passed the poor creature and I can't find anywhere to turn around. 'Go back!' says Arianna, when we reach a roundabout. 'He might get run over if we leave him trotting along that road.'

'This is what we'll do,' I say, feeling horrible that we drove past a dog in distress. 'We'll go back to the hotel because we have to check out in the next ten minutes. Then we'll find the number of an emergency vet and come back for him.'

At the hotel, we enlist the receptionist's help in phoning around local animal shelters but no one answers. Like everyone else in Biarritz, they've probably gone surfing. We write down the number of a local vet and set off to find the limping dog, but there is no sign of him, even though we travel up and down the road several times. 'Maybe he has been picked up by someone else,' I say, feeling guilty.

'Look,' says Arianna, pointing at two surfer types standing at the side of a roundabout with a sign saying 'San Sebastián'. 'That's where we're going, isn't it? Maybe we should pick them up instead.' The backpackers are wearing a hopeful expression similar to the injured mutt's and each time we drive by, it feels as if we are cruelly taunting them.

'They could be dangerous serial killers,' I say.

'They don't look like serial killers,' says Ari. 'They look like surfers.'

She's got a point. Surfing and serial killing are not natural bedfellows. But I am in charge of a minor and must, at all times, behave responsibly.

'I'm not sure,' I say, as we drive past them for the fourth time.

'Oh, go on, Auntie Carrie, pick them up.'

'It's too late,' I say, taking the turn off for San Sebastián. 'And look at the size of their rucksacks. In case you haven't noticed, we are not a camper van.'

Arianna falls silent. I feel like the world's biggest buzzkill. I worry that I will be remembered as the aunt who drove past a dog in despair, and who wouldn't give two impoverished surfers a lift to Spain.

'OK,' I say. 'We'll go back for them. But it's your fault if they murder us.' I'm pretty sure my brother wouldn't approve, but as his daughter likes to say, *What the hell?*

'Maybe someone will have already picked them up, like the dog,' says Ari.

But no one has. I stop the car on a grass verge and Arianna summons them over. 'Hey!' she says. 'We're going to San Sebastián.'

As they run towards us, my fears are allayed. They actually seem more scared of us than we are of them. 'You're stopping for us?' says one of them, with floppy red hair.

'Yes,' I say. 'But it will be a tight squeeze.'

'Trust us, we know how to pack a lot into a small space,' he replies, and after some skilled back-seat reorganisation, they are in.

We set off towards Saint-Jean-de-Luz, the view in my rear-view mirror entirely obscured. The hitchers sit with their rucksacks on their knees, pinned into place by several boxes of books, stacked in a tower between them. Ed, the red-haired hitcher, is forced to fold himself up like a half-open deckchair, his legs suspended at ninety degrees and his knees brushing his freckled cheeks, as Biff refuses to give up his space in the foot-well. Fortunately, it is only fifty kilometres to San Sebastián.

'We saw you go around the roundabout a few times,' says James, Ed's pal. 'We figured you were trying to decide whether or not to pick us up.'

'Actually, we were looking for a dog,' says Arianna, before explaining about the injured mutt.

'So are you going to Spain to surf?' I ask.

'No, we are woofing our way around Europe,' says Ed.

Woofing? Arianna and I look at each other, wondering if they are barking. But it seems that 'WWOOF', to use the correct spelling, is an acronym of 'Willing Workers on Organic Farms'. WWOOFers volunteer in return for food and accommodation.

Ed and James, originally from Surrey, have been picking asparagus in the Netherlands, and are now on their way to harvest onions in Spain. 'We thought it would be a good way to see Europe,' says James, although I wonder how much of a country you can see from an onion field? If you want to learn about organic farming, it sounds ideal. But it seems that not everyone that they WWOOFed for, actually had an organic farm. Or even a farm. One of their hosts, an elderly lady, just wanted company and someone to put up shelves.

'What's in all these boxes?' Ed asks.

'Books in Mandarin Chinese,' says Ari. 'And Taiwanese.'

Ed and James exchange looks in the back. I don't bother to explain that I'm a writer. After all, who isn't nowadays?

'Are you studying Chinese at university?' asks James.

'Actually, I'm still at school,' Arianna replies.

There is silence and then James asks, 'How old are you?'

'Sixteen.'

Silence again. In a strange reversal of roles, our hitchhikers seem a little scared of us. At some point we cross the invisible border into Spain – there are no signs to mark the event so I'm not exactly sure at what point we've left France behind – but suddenly we are on a motorway and the signs are in Spanish.

Eventually, we arrive alongside La Concha beach in San Sebastián, where our hitchhikers extract themselves from the car with unseemly haste. 'Wow,' says Ari, as they disappear into a side street. 'They were in a hurry to leave.'

'Well, at least they weren't serial killers,' I say. 'Perhaps they were worried I'd ask for a contribution towards the fuel.'

This seems like a good moment to familiarise ourselves with the sat-nav that my Portuguese cleaner, Carmen, insisted that

I borrow for the trip, presumably worried that we might not otherwise make it back. We unpack the device with due reverence but when we type in 'San Sebastián' it gives us half a dozen options – one of them in France, another in Brazil, but none of them, unfortunately, in Spain. It does not occur to me to search under 'Donostia', the city's Basque name.

Biff emerges from behind the seat to see what is going on, which makes three of us staring blankly at the screen. I put the disappointing device back into its box, where it stays for the rest of the trip. As ever, when faced with a problem, I find that the best solution is to procrastinate. 'I know! Let's give Biff a little walk and get some lunch,' I say. And so we set off in search of some delicious tapas, or *pintxos* as it's known in these parts, around the large curved bay of La Concha.

Like Biarritz, San Sebastián is also an 'encore' visit for me, and I'm hoping that it will be less stressful than the eight hours that I spent here in my twenties. I'd been holed up with Ben, my boyfriend at the time, and his extended family, in the guest wing of a château near Bordeaux, while the rain fell in relentless ropes outside.

After several days of Scrabble and Trivial Pursuits, tensions were running high. They peaked one evening in the Michelin-starred restaurant that Ben's foodie brother-in-law, Hugh, had booked for dinner. As Ben's staunchly vegetarian sister, Pippa, quizzed the waiter about the vegetarian options – basically there weren't any, but after some intense discussions with the kitchen, an omelette was produced – Hugh rubbed his hands together in gleeful anticipation of the calf brains.

The situation deteriorated further when Pippa discovered pieces of shredded ham lurking under the lettuce that accompanied her omelette – a culinary joke that French chefs often like to play on vegetarians. (In France, the assumption seems to be that if you shred animal products into small pieces, it somehow doesn't count.) Pippa was not amused. Possibly as a diversionary tactic, someone had the bold idea of driving down to Spain the following morning. It was only half a day's drive away and the weather was bound to be better there – and by implication, everyone's mood.

I had misgivings. The following day was Tuesday, a momentous day on the Sunday newspaper that kept me gainfully employed. The procedure went like this: at 11 am the section heads would be summoned into the editor's office to present their ideas for the next edition. A moment's hesitation, a quiver of nervousness in your voice as you described exactly why flesh-pink satin or the spacewoman look was suddenly *a very big deal*, and several thousands of pounds of photography and a week's work could end up in the bin. If the response proved positive, I'd return to my desk and thump out 600 words of ecstatic copy to present to the editor after lunch.

For this reason, it was pointless to write anything before going on holiday, and there was no one to step up to the wicket in my absence. This was the mid-nineties and mobile phones were still as big as steam irons and not yet in common currency, so I had good reason to stay behind at the château. There, I could use the owner's landline to dictate my finely-honed thoughts on safari suiting to the copytakers – a group of chain-smoking, hardened newspapermen, more accustomed to journalists phoning in from war zones than fashion editors dictating their thoughts on poacher pockets, from rural France.

Ben, however, was having none of it. 'You can easily find a public phone and call from San Sebastián,' he insisted. So the following morning, we set off in a little convoy – there were a lot of us on that holiday – for Spain.

At noon, while everyone else headed to a tapas bar, I roamed the streets in search of a public phone. I then had to exchange French francs into Spanish pesetas and find a shop where I could cash the notes into enough coins for an international call. This wasn't easy, as all the shops were closed – not just for lunch but for the rest of the afternoon, as appears to be the custom in Spain.

Finally, after one café owner took pity on me and swapped a note for the contents of his coin drawer, I got through to my assistant and received the good news that it was a green light for 'Go Wild for the Safari Look'.

Unfortunately, the copytakers had gone for their customary three-hour lunch, which meant that I would have to repeat the above procedure later that afternoon. Weighed down by my sack of pesetas, I went to the tapas bar to break this news to Ben. He was not pleased. 'Why do all holidays have to revolve around you and your work?' he asked.

He had a point. Earlier that year we had performed variations of this routine in Santa Barbara, San Francisco and Yosemite National Park, with the added complication of a seven-hour time difference. Our journey down the Pacific Coast Highway was punctuated by frantic calls from public pay phones and having to get up at 3 am to speak to the office. And somewhere near San Louis Obispo – or was it Big Sur? – the holiday was left in tatters after I discovered that my story on eco-conscious clothing had been dropped.

But for me, San Sebastián was the last straw. The heat, the stress and the fact that I hadn't wanted to go there in the first place, resulted in a loud public argument, although, in truth, no one noticed, as shouting and violent arm waving pass for normal conversation in northern Spain. I stormed out of the restaurant and sulked on a bench until it was time to call the copytakers again. To their credit, they took down my fashion words with the same world-weary gravitas that they'd treat a bomb going off at Buckingham Palace. Back in Bordeaux that evening, I packed my bags and left. With hindsight, I just needed some time alone after a surfeit of company.

So, San Sebastián: I'm hoping it will be better second time around. According to our guidebook, San Sebastián is home to an abundance of surfers. But, at first sight, it is mostly obese sunbathers, sitting in a bubble of cigarette smoke and Hugo Boss cologne, that occupy the long city beach.

'Look away, look away,' says Arianna, as our eyes alight on a man with a wobbly belly, in red thong Speedos. (And yes, I'm afraid you did read that correctly.)

He bends over to pick up something, demonstrating beyond doubt, that no matter how pressing a chap's desire for a pair of evenly tanned buttocks might be, the indignity of thong swim-wear is way too high a price to pay.

The city is known for its magnificent cuisine, so I'm looking forward to a decent lunch – ideally an al fresco café serving fresh seafood. But disappointingly, the only places that are open are dingy bars that smell of nicotine and deep-fat fryers. In San Sebastián, as in France, it seems that restaurants operate to strict timings and there is no possibility of lunch at 3.30 pm. Waiters look affronted that we've even asked.

Eventually, we decide to give up and go to our hotel. I remember from the website that it sits on a hill overlooking the city. 'I've got a feeling that it's over there,' I say, pointing to the other side of the bay.

'Cool,' says Arianna, unfazed by the idea of following a 'feeling' rather than a map, and probably just relieved that she hasn't been asked to read one. There's no doubt about it: as travelling companions, we are perfectly suited.

I should explain here, that rather than bother with maps, sat-nav or mobile phone apps, I prefer to find my way around by what I call 'intuitive driving', which means driving in the direction that 'feels' right, until a sign proves otherwise. You won't be surprised to hear that it has a high failure rate. Amazingly, on this occasion, it works. Fifteen minutes later we are driving into the hotel's car park, high above the city.

The hotel lobby is impressive: an expanse of white marble floor and a wall of windows looking down on the bay of La Concha. It's certainly more impressive than the online booking price led me to expect. But it soon becomes apparent that the hotel has made economies elsewhere, namely in staff charm. I greet the elderly receptionist with a cheery '*Hola*'. He gives us a hostile look and doesn't reply. We are made to feel as welcome as a trio of Colorado beetles in a field of King Edwards.

He doesn't speak English or French, or understand Arianna's Spanish, so I mime the fact that I've made a reservation, by signing a form in the air. He asks for our passports, stares at them for an age and then swivels round towards a computer. He types for so long, pauses so often, that I wonder if he is writing a novel and just fancies a bit of company. Tap, tap, tap, he goes, before sighing and then tapping some more.

At least three sets of guests arrive to drop off keys. He embarks on long, shouty conversations with them, before resuming the tapping and staring. The CIA recruitment process is probably quicker than the check-in here.

Eventually, he hands back our documents and just when it looks as if we're getting closer to the key... he's actually reaching for it... the phone rings. As he picks it up, I fight the urge to leap over the desk and wrap the phone around his neck. Did I mention that patience is not my strong point?

Finally, we get the key and, after ferrying our bags to the room, I take Biff for a sniff around the locale. A little further up the hill from our hotel, I find a restaurant in a delightful garden setting, its tables set with pink tablecloths, crystal and candles and with fabulous views of the city below.

It's the perfect place for an al fresco dinner, especially if you are travelling with a dog. I look at the menu, which features lots of fresh fish and traditional Spanish dishes, and know immediately that it will be perfect.

There is no one around to take a booking – the Spanish disappear in the middle of the day – but I figure that if we arrive early enough, we'll get a table. An hour later, Arianna and I present ourselves at the gate, dressed in our best swag – Ari is even wearing her belly rings – but the waitress gives Biff a pointed look, despite the fact that he too, is highly groomed and fragrant, and shakes her head. The restaurant is fully booked, she says, even though it is empty.

Cruelly taunted by the twinkling fairy lights in the trees and the scent of paella drifting from the kitchen, we drag ourselves away from this bosky paradise and back to our hotel to call a taxi down to the city. The receptionist greets us with a glare. Biff glares right back. He has stayed at the Plaza Athenée hotel in Paris, where he was given his own velvet chaise longue – they know how to treat a dog there – so he is not easily intimidated.

It seems that no request is too small or mundane to annoy our receptionist. You'd think that we'd asked for a glass chariot and a troop of dancing horses to take us to dinner, such is his barely concealed resentment at being asked to call a taxi.

When the cab arrives the driver looks at Biff and hesitates, but I offer an extra €10 (henceforth to be known as the 'Biff tax') and he reluctantly agrees to take us. With Arianna translating, I ask the driver to take us to a district with lots of good restaurants. He drops us in an area dominated by banks and office buildings. You have to hand it to the Spanish: they sure know how to wrong-foot a tourist.

We walk for a while but don't find any restaurants; just small, drab bars with standing room only. And displayed on the door of all of them, is the ubiquitous sign of a black dog struck through with a red line. Where, I wonder, are all the wonderful tapas bars? San Sebastián is regarded as a centre of gastronomic excellence – it boasts more Michelin stars per capita than any other city in the world – but we see no evidence of this.

I'm not looking for Michelin stars and all the prissiness that goes with them. I'm hoping for simple food and quality ingredients, cooked as unpretentiously as possible. Specifically, I'm imagining small, intensely flavoured tapas dishes of *patatas bravas*, calamari, fried whitebait and fresh seafood, served in a bustling restaurant – preferably with an outside terrace, jolly flamenco music and waiters that look like Joaquin Phoenix. In short, I am imagining the restaurant scene from Woody Allen's *Vicky Cristina Barcelona*.

Instead, we eventually find ourselves sitting in a grimy and narrow passageway staring at menus with pictures of unappealing food, and wondering: are there really people out there, who don't know what a burger looks like?

Dinner is sardines, served in an oil slick and eaten in a vale of cigarette smoke and sweat. I feel a deep sense of shame. How can it be possible that in a city that is known for its glittering gastronomy, I'm eating sardines, almost certainly from a tin, and sitting in an alley? I try not to think of the clinking crystal, the twinkling fairy lights and the paella that could have been. Instead, I pick up the guidebook and read a section aloud: 'It is said that, in San Sebastián, nothing is impossible. That is wrong. Everything is possible. [It is] cool, svelte and flirtatious by night, charming and well-mannered by day.' I am stunned, not just by the baffling non sequitur, but also the spectacular untruth.

'*What the hell*?' says my niece. 'Whoever wrote that must have been smoking crack.'

'Or else they were in a different San Sebastián,' I say, thinking of Carmen's sat-nav.

'I'll say one thing,' says Ari, as we walk back. 'It looks better in the dark. At least there are no men in thong-back Speedos.'

Back at our hotel, the receptionist is waiting. Needless to say, it is not with a smile and the the offer of a nightcap. Instead, he points to Biff and says something in Spanish. It's a good thing that Biff has high self-esteem, or he'd be developing a paranoid personality disorder by now.

'I think he's saying that you have to pay a supplement for the dog,' says Arianna.

'There was no mention of it when I booked,' I say, annoyed. 'Just keep walking.'

But the receptionist becomes more animated, waving his arms around and insisting that we come to the desk. He nods at Biff and shoves a piece of paper across the desk with '€30' scrawled on it.

'Just tell him that we don't understand.'

Later, I read some more of the guidebook: 'As the sun falls on another sweltering summer's day, you'll sit back with a drink and an artistic pintxo and realise that yes, you too, are in love with sexy San Sebastián.'

'Definitely on drugs,' says my niece, and I have to agree. There are many who will tell you otherwise, but the best thing about San Sebastián, is leaving. As we speed out of the sweaty, built-up city the following morning, I feel nothing but relief. From now on, I tell myself, it is going to be sweet little fishing villages all the way.

Comillas, 250 kilometres west of San Sebastián, is said to be one of the highlights of northern Spain. And certainly, getting there is (mostly) enjoyable. We follow the curving motorway, with a wall of lofty green mountains and limestone ridges to our left – these are the Cantabrian Mountains, which skirt the top of northern Spain, running parallel to the sea for about 300 kilometres – and the coastline to our right.

My spirits soar, along with the craggy peaks, as we fly along listening to the Red Hot Chili Peppers and Nirvana. (I've hidden Lana Del Rey in the boot.)

As we approach the port city of Santander, the mood changes. Several of our fellow drivers seem keen to be travelling in our car, so close to our bumper are they driving. Use of indicators is minimal. Instead, drivers samba and salsa around the various lanes, without so much as a glance in the mirror. I keep my cool, only shouting 'Bloody idiot' and thrusting my finger at the driver behind, about a dozen times, while my niece informs her friends back in Cayman that her aunt is 'totally raging'.

Our hotel, on the outskirts of town, is a Spanish colonial-style building with a mysteriously empty car park. The reason becomes clear when the receptionist manages to convey by sign language that the hotel car park costs €20 a day. Parking on the road outside, we subsequently discover, is free and readily available. While I sympathise with Spain's economic plight, there is a fine line between benefiting from tourism and treating visitors as cash dispensers with a missing microchip. Stand still for a moment too long in northern Spain and you might find that someone has stolen your trousers.

Our room, with its muted pink walls and dark wood furniture, is the perfect antidote to my bad mood and the midday heat. When I check my emails, I am surprised to see that Matt, my new neighbour in France, has tracked me down on one of my social media accounts. I hesitate over whether or not to 'follow' him back and I see that his 'updates' are mostly boring thoughts on architecture and the design of public spaces.

There is no meaningful comment on X *Factor*, or insight into what he ate for breakfast; there is nothing boastful and there are no angry rants – despite the fact that, by now, he must surely have had some dealings with Orange France. Annoyingly, he comes across as professional and sane. *What the hell?* I click to 'follow' him back.

Chapter 8

Raging in Comillas, Calm in Pechon

ARI AND I set out early for dinner, choosing a tapas bar near the central square. The terrace was packed when we drove into Comillas earlier, so I figure it must be good. But the lone waiter doesn't look thrilled to see us and appears strangely nervous, as he points to a table on the cobbled terrace.

I assume that it's because we're embarrassingly early – we skipped lunch – and are his first customers of the evening. The Spanish – and it *is* mostly Spanish holidaymakers in Comillas – don't even pick up a menu before 10 pm. At 7 pm, a good number of them are probably still sleeping off their lunch. Others are strolling around the town in the pre-dinner parade that seems to be the custom across Spain.

Despite the bleak experience in San Sebastian, I am full of hope, visualising fresh seafood and a glass of glacially cold cava. Ari, no doubt, is dreaming of burger and chips. I've given up on trying to get her to eat vegetables or salads, and I now know what arrogance it was to assume that I could. Never again will I judge a parent for feeding their offspring pizza and chips. Really, what did I know?

'Can you ask for the wine list?' I say to Ari.

'He says that there isn't one,' she replies.

'Ha, ha! Tell him that's very funny.' Then I realise that it's not a joke. I guess this should be the cue to leave, but, at this point, I am still giving Spain the benefit of the doubt, so I ask for a glass of red wine and hope for the best.

Our waiter, who does not look at all like Joaquin Phoenix, returns with a full-sugar Coke for Ari and a bottle of wine for me. He plonks it on the table and doesn't hang about to perform the normal waiterly duties, so I untwist the screw top and pour myself a small amount into a glass, to taste.

'Ari, can you ask if there are any other options?' I say, with a grimace. Our waiter replies in the negative. It's the same when we ask to see menus. There aren't any. Instead, the waiter points to the 'menu of the day' written on a blackboard.

Thinking that, although the choice is limited, it must be excellent – all those people dining here earlier, couldn't have been wrong – I order paella. It arrives almost instantly, having been reheated in a microwave and, by the looks of the flabby rice, not for the first time. Arianna's sardines are served with cold sliced potatoes in a slick of yellow oil, and let's just say that it's a long time since they saw the sea, and their journey to our table included a sleepover in a canning factory.

Bad though the food is, it's nothing compared to the scenario that unfolds when I ask for the bill.

The first problem is getting it. I ask for *la cuenta* four times and make the universally recognised sign of scribbling in the air, but the waiter ignores me. Eventually, he reappears and tells us that we owe €50. It feels like an ambitious figure for such disappointing fare, but I can't be bothered to ask for a proper bill. Instead, I hand him my credit card. He looks worried, as if I've tried to pay in magic beans or Venezuelan bolivars, or even red nightcaps and tin whistles, the currency with which Vasco da Gama tried to buy gemstones and spices on his travels around the world.

'He's saying that you have to pay in cash,' Ari translates. I point to a sign saying that the restaurant accepts credit cards. Our waiter says that he has to fetch the boss and eventually, a frowning man appears, his stomach spilling under his black waistcoat. He looks even less like Joaquin Phoenix.

He snatches my card from my hands and jabs his fat fingers at the credit card machine. He shakes his head and gives me a contemptuous glare. 'He's saying that your bank card has been refused,' says Arianna.

'That's not possible. Ask him to try again,' I reply. I have had a long and happy relationship with my Mastercard. During our travels around the world together, it has bought me everything from reindeer bells in Finland to six kilos of coconut and lime-scented body exfoliator in New York (a purchase I deeply regretted when one kilo broke free of its jar, marinading my clothes in tropical-scented oil on the flight home.)

Such is my card company's largesse that it once allowed a stranger to buy £600 of Agent Provocateur lingerie on my card, no questions asked. And when the purchase came to light, it refunded my account but declined to pursue the fraudsteress, as it wouldn't be 'cost-effective'. So I find it hard to believe that a €50 dinner bill in Spain has been declined. But the proprietor insists, in the least charming way imaginable, that it is so.

Now, I've gone a few gruelling rounds with French waiters in my time, and know that they excel at putting you in your place – slapping a plate of incinerated beef on the table when you've asked for it rare, for example; or stacking up chairs around you while you're still eating your main course, because they want to go home – but Spanish waiters are in a different class. This is the difference between a Chinese burn and waterboarding.

The proprietor rolls his eyes to convey that he's just about had enough of my outrageous behaviour – I mean, trying to pay by card! – and points at my bag.

'You have to pay cash,' says Ari.

When I refuse, because I don't have enough with me, he stabs away angrily at the credit card machine again, and before it could possibly have had time to process a transaction, he shakes his head vigorously like a spaniel emerging from the surf.

'Let me see,' I say, which he seems to understand as he yanks the machine away, but not before I've had chance to notice that he hasn't actually switched it on. He is *pretending* to process the transaction. It's as weird as it is frustrating, not being able to yell back at him in Spanish as he acts out this strange pantomime. He slaps my card back down on the table, shouting and pointing, as if ordering me out of the restaurant.

'He's offering to take you to the cash machine,' says Ari.

'I don't want him to take me to the cash machine,' I reply. I am, as my niece would say, 'raging' for the second time today, although unfortunately I lack the skills to do it in Spanish.

The proprietor waddles back inside, presumably hoping that I'll give in. Which is, of course, what I do. As I slope off to the bank across the road, under the forensic glare of the other dinner guests who've arrived on the terrace, I can understand how Napoleon felt as he limped back across the Pyrenees after his defeat in Spain.

The Spaniards, I remember from history lessons, fought a war of stealth and ambush against the invaders, much like the people who now work in its hospitality trade. Napoleon, who once said that an army marches on its stomach, described his conflict in Spain as his 'Spanish ulcer'. Based on what we've eaten so far, it certainly stacks up. Had I been the French emperor, I'd have turned around at San Sebastián and run back to France. William Beckford, meanwhile, wrote of 'the horror' of Iberian inns in the eighteenth century. It's fair to say that not much has changed since. The Spanish have failed to grasp that people go to restaurants expecting to be cosseted, not bullied and treated like convicts.

I hand over the cash, wondering how many other tourists will arrive here hoping for a jolly paella this evening, only to be served a dollop of abuse by this bruiser of a waiter.

'Maybe it's because they're in economical [sic] crisis,' suggests Arianna, as we walk back to our hotel. But, if a business is so desperate for cash, they should perhaps remove the sign that says credit cards are welcome. Hell, they could even trouble themselves to learn, 'We'd prefer cash please,' in a few other languages.

Back at the hotel, the receptionist uses sign language to remind us that there will be an extra charge for – you guessed it – the dog. We've only been here two nights, so perhaps it is unfair to judge, but I'm struck by how different northern Spain is to the south. In Granada when I visited, the food was edible, restaurants had wine lists – hell, the waiter even *poured* your wine – and the people were charming and multilingual. Based on our experience in the north, tourists are to be tricked, tolerated and marched to the bank.

When I look up the godawful restaurant on TripAdvisor, one review stands out among the many one-star reviews. 'POISONED!' is the title of the post, in which the reviewer details her own 'horror story' and 'the terrible pain in the stomach' that followed her dinner there. Her conclusion certainly strikes a chord: 'They don't care if you die, because you drive through their town and never return.' Funnily enough, this is exactly what I'm planning to do.

The following morning I pay the hotel bill using the credit card that caused such a ruckus the previous evening – as I suspected, it is not blocked – and we set out for Llanes, a former whaling port, less than an hour's drive away.

Hugging the coast, we follow a green and winding road, catching tantalising glimpses of deep-green sea and a golden, untouched beach. 'Let's try and get down there and give Biff a run,' says Arianna. The beach is in the direction of a place called Pechón. There is no mention of it in our guidebook, which is a point in its favour.

We follow the turn-off and find ourselves on a mountain road that corkscrews up and down through deep forest, thrilling us with the occasional glimpse of wild, empty beaches below. Just as we think we are getting near, the road climbs up again. 'It's like the road to Choroní,' says my niece, referring to a treacherous two-hour drive through mountains from Maracay in Venezuela, where my brother once lived, to the coast. Those of us who visited him there – he was collecting sandflies and stick insects for his PhD – invariably made the trip to the small coastal resort Choroní, which could only be reached by the narrow mountain pass.

Each of us had experiences of the bus trip that were exhilerating in different ways. My younger brother and his then girlfriend found themselves on a bus rolling backwards, seconds from a drop into green void, after the driver got out on a bend to inspect a tyre, without engaging his brain or, more importantly, the enormous handbrake. Only the fast action of a German backpacker, who raced forward to pull up the brake, saved them from being the main story on the BBC news.

My experience was less dramatic, verging on enjoyable. As my brother and I boarded the psychedelic-painted bus in Maracay station, I was much impressed by the on-board sound system. Blasting out cheerful salsa and merengue music, it was of a quality more normally found in nightclubs. The driver, I noticed, had a set of rosary beads hanging over his rear-view mirror, which seemed reassuring. My brother had told me that the bus to avoid at all costs was the one with a 'Master of Disaster' sticker on the driver's window.

There was a definite party mood as we sped up the mountain and into the mist, our skulls rattling from both the sound of the bass and the bumpy road. The only buzz-kill was the number of wooden crosses and floral arrangements that lined the route up the mountain pass, all marking the spot where someone had met an untimely, though possibly not entirely unexpected, death. That and the fact that the driver, along with several of my fellow passengers, would make the sign of the cross every time we approached another hairpin bend.

In addition to calling on divine intervention, the driver would also honk his horn to warn any vehicles that might be rocketing through the mountain mist towards us. This was important, as for most of the two-hour journey on the switchback road, there was only room for one vehicle to pass. However, as a warning system, it had one fatal flaw, namely that all the other bus drivers on the route were also playing salsa at ear-splitting levels, so that no one could hope to hear the horns of oncoming vehicles. It was an exercise in blind faith but, miraculously, we got to Choroní without any fatalities.

After a day on the beach marvelling at the force of the waves – the currents were so strong that if you went in deeper than your ankles, you could end up in Columbia – my brother took the bus back to Maracay, for a pressing engagement with some stick insects. I decided to stay on alone, and treated myself to a windowless cell in a backpacker hostel.

That evening, while wandering around the village, I met a British couple, Will and Tania, who told me about a 'secret' beach and lagoon that was perfect for swimming and snorkelling. They invited me along and told me to meet them and their Venezuelan friend, Mercedes, on the quay at 9 am the next morning.

I arrived to find that the tourist boat had been cancelled, as the sea was too rough. Undeterred, Will persuaded some fishermen to drop us at the 'secret' beach and pick us up later.

Within ten minutes of pulling away from the quay, we were in the open sea in a small rowing boat with an outboard motor, bouncing up and down on cliff-size waves. The sides of the boat were so low that each time it bounced into the air, there was no guarantee that you would land back in it; and with each sickening slap of wood on water, there seemed to be a real possibility that the boat might snap in two. By far the worst moment came when the engine cut out, and with walls of water rearing around us, the fishermen started shouting above the noise of the waves.

'They want to know if you can swim,' Mercedes yelled.

'Why?' I asked, which was a question that really did not need an answer.

'They have a problem with the engine,' she yelled back.

I convinced myself that she was joking – to this day, I'm not sure – as even Rebecca Adlington would not have survived the waves and currents around Choroní. I vaguely remember bailing out incoming water, while berating myself for setting out to sea without a life jacket, as the fishermen yanked a cord on the engine to try and restart it.

This is it, I thought. *The end*. I will never write a book, own a dog or learn how to poach an egg. I'm going to die at sea in a boat full of strangers, and wash up in Columbia.

Eventually we made it to the deserted beach and lagoon, where I sat on the sand, dry-mouthed and trembling like a dog on Bonfire Night, wondering if there was any way I could be helicoptered back. Only then did Will declare, 'Well, I've never seen the sea as rough as that before.' The clue, with hindsight, lay in the fact that the tourist boat wasn't running.

When I stepped back on the firm earth of the mainland that afternoon, I was ecstatic to find myself so wonderfully and unexpectedly alive. I felt invincible. With waves of pure adrenaline coursing through my body, I went to a bar with Mercedes and had a large, celebratory cocktail and a plate of lukewarm stew, thereby breaking the two rules that my brother had given me: to avoid ice in drinks, and meat dishes unless they were boiling hot.

I returned to the backpacker place with heaven knows how many poisonous bacteria multiplying in my stomach, and woke in the middle of the night with waves of pain cresting in my gut. I'd been spared by the sea but spent the next forty-eight hours thinking that being bashed to death on the rocks around Choroní might not have been so bad after all.

When I emerged from my backpacker cell two days later, I'd lost nearly a stone and had never looked so good. Every bout of staphylococcus poisoning has a silver lining, I discovered, as I headed to the bus station, in the shortest of shorts.

On the way, I bumped into a ravaged-looking Mercedes and discovered that I had gotten off lightly. She had been hospitalised for two nights by whatever microbes were lurking in that lukewarm stew, and had spent forty-eight hours on a drip. My tough northern genes had spared me the worst.

Fast-forward fifteen years and I was watching a TV programme about a bloke with long hair launching a posh chocolate business. There was something about him and his wife that looked very familiar. It all clicked into place when the scene shifted to their cocoa plantation in Choroní. It was Will and Tania, with whom I'd shared the intimate near-death experience. I did think of contacting them, but then I remembered how uncool I'd been – lying on the floor of the boat, possibly sobbing – and thought better of it.

Ah, yes, Choroní. Arianna and I have more shared references than I thought. Eventually, the road that we are on starts to descend and, although we are still not at the bottom, we spot a little café next to a campsite and decide to stop for lunch. The café, with its wicker chairs and paper tablecloths is basic, but the view is pretty. Our table overlooks a strip of remote estuary beach and the intense green-blue water of the inlet.

The food – chubby prawns in garlic, calamari and char-grilled tomatoes, courgettes peppers and aubergine – is our first encounter with fresh produce since arriving in Spain. It takes time to prepare, but the delicious smells and the sound of sizzling from the kitchen are all part of the pleasure. My niece even eats a tomato, which I notch up as a small victory in my campaign to get her to eat more healthily.

Biff, meanwhile, lies under the table and every so often gives a single bossy 'Woof' to remind us that he, too, is partial to prawns. This, after so many disappointments, is the Spanish lunch of my dreams: simple, fresh food served up with a beautiful view – and all for €22.

Afterwards, we walk through the campsite and down to a beach, where Arianna throws sticks for Biff. The two of them run in and out of the raging surf, while I sit on the beach with a cardigan on my head, in an attempt to avoid looking like 'a strawberry ice-cream sundae with sprinkles', as Ari so memorably described her father's freckled skin. Then we drive on to Llanes.

Chapter 9

Wrong Path, Right Path (Santiago de Compostela)

WHEN I PICTURED our journey across northern Spain, I imagined staying in secret coastal enclaves – the sort of places that have a single open-air tavern on the beach, a view of colourful boats, and some real-life fishermen bringing in the catch, or at the very least, unfurling their nets. But, in Spain, places referred to as 'charming fishing ports' in the guidebook, invariably turn out to be socking great big towns.

And so it is with Llanes. After circling it for an hour, trying to find our hotel, we seek help in the tourist office. Unfortunately, it is closed from 2 pm until 5 pm, despite it being the last week in July. This I find amazing. I mean, what are the chances, in a region where tourism accounts for ten per cent of the economy, that there might be one or two tourists out and about in the middle of the day, and in need of help?

We pass the time in a nearby café. When the tourist office reopens it is mobbed, such is the pent-up demand for its services. Some might see this as a sign. But not in Spain, where the locals and members of the tourism industry just seem bewildered

– and somewhat inconvenienced – by the arrival of non-Spanish speakers. When it's my turn, the official looks at me blankly when I ask if she speaks French or English – or even German, which I can manage at a (long) stretch.

As a guest in a foreign country, I work on the principle that the onus is on me to learn a few key phrases. Spanish tourism operates on this principle too. It's surprising how few of the people working on the frontline of its hospitality trade, speak English or French, despite the fact that a significant number of visitors to Spain come from English-speaking countries and neighbouring France. For my part, I have tried to learn Spanish, even going so far as Seville to do an intensive one-week course, at the end of which, all I could say was *'No hablo español'* ('I don't speak Spanish'). With hindsight, acting classes would have been more useful, given that mime seems the best way to communicate in northern Spain.

'She's saying that our hotel's not on their map,' says Arianna. To emphasise the point, the tourist advisor produces a large map of Llancs showing all its hotels except ours, and draws an arrow pointing off the far right hand corner. And that's as helpful as it gets. We leave the tourist office as we entered: with no idea of how to get to our guesthouse. It takes nearly two hours of intuitive driving before we find the elusive hotel, hidden in an alley on the outskirts of town.

Once there, we decide not to go out for dinner, as there is no guarantee that we'll make it back. Instead, we spend the evening responding to emails (me) and 'swellfies' (Ari) – a 'swellfie' being the word I've invented for the endless surf or swimming pool self-portraits that teenagers in Cayman seem to love.

When I log into my favourite social media account, I'm surprised to find a direct message from Matt. 'Are you OK?' he asks. 'You've been very quiet on here for a while.'

I'm touched by his concern; but also a little surprised by it. Does Zoe know that he is sending me private messages?

For this reason, I hesitate before typing back, 'All good, thanks. Hope all is well with you and Zoe.'

Almost immediately, he responds: 'Home alone. Zoe in London. Where are you?'

I'm flattered that someone should be so interested in my whereabouts, but, at the same time, I feel a little guilty corresponding privately with him. I tell myself not to read too much into it, as Matt is probably just being friendly, but I don't reply.

The following morning, stomachs rumbling after our enforced fast, Ari and I present ourselves in the dining room for breakfast. I'm hungry enough to eat any dried-up old fare that's on offer, and pay well over the odds for it – in this case, €12 each. I'm not a fan of the continental breakfast at the best of times, but in Spain it hits new lows. At least in France you get freshly baked bread and croissants. Here, you can expect bread rolls as hard as flagstones, along with hydrogenated-fat-packed pastries and biscuits, in plastic wrapping.

'How many more days before we arrive in Portugal?' my niece asks casually, as we pack up the car. I can see where she is going with this. I look at the map. We are roughly halfway across the top of Spain. We could skip the last section of the coastal route and head south from here, towards Santiago de Compostela, cutting out the top western corner of northern Spain. Alas, this will mean missing out on the Costa da Morte, or 'Coast of Death', so called because it is a place of many shipwrecks. According to legend, villagers along its rocky shores would put out lamps to deliberately lure ships onto the rocks. The locals sure are creative when it comes to shaking down the tourists.

'Desolate', 'lonely' and 'eerily beautiful' are the words that the guidebook uses to describe this shoreline, while another legend has it that the wind creates wild nightmares. Just as I'm thinking, *Could this sound any less appealing?* I read that the area is also the scene of several oil spills.

'If we step on it, we can be in Portugal by tomorrow evening,' I say. Arianna beams. I turn up the music. And in the back of the car, Biff gives a sigh, presumably of relief.

Our last night in Spain is spent in Ribadeo, a two-hour drive from Llanes. The guidebook describes Ribadeo as 'a lively port town', but in our, admittedly short, time there, we see no evidence of this. In the evening, we head to the harbour, which is deserted, even in July.

The restaurant that we choose is also empty, despite having the most commanding view of the harbour. I assume this is because it's only 8.30 pm, but it is still empty when we leave two hours later. I order 'a white fish' – that's how it's described on the menu; no further detail provided – and although I've no idea what it is, at least it is fresh, although served with the ubiquitous boiled potatoes and neon yellow oil.

The following morning, we leave the northern coast behind, turning inland on twisty mountain roads. It's a 200-kilometre drive from Ribadeo to Santiago de Compostela, and for most of it, we have no idea if we are heading in the right direction, as the road signage is infrequent and confusing. Where signs do exist, they are too small to be of any use, as you can only read them as you're driving past.

My niece doesn't trouble herself to look at road signs, but I enjoy the random nature of our conversations as we drive from one 'not-a-charming-fishing-port' to the next. Subjects range from, 'What do you think of Maroon 5?' to 'What's the craziest thing that my dad ever did when he was young?'

With regards to the former question, I have no idea whether Maroon 5 is a colour, a space station or a secret code, so I bounce the question right back: 'What do *you* think of Maroon 5?' A Google search later reveals Maroon 5 to be a pop band. (Having lived in rural France for eight years, I'm not up to speed on popular culture.)

As for crazy things that my brother has done, there have been quite a few.

'I can tell you the stupidest thing he ever did,' I say.

'Yasss!' says Ari.

'For years he had a crush on a girl who worked in a local bar, but he was never brave enough to speak to her. Then one Valentine's Day he sent her a really expensive bunch of flowers, but didn't include a message or say who they were from.'

'No way?'

'Yup.'

'Did he ever speak to her? Or tell her that he sent the flowers?'

'Nope. To this day, she has no idea who sent them.'

'Oh my God, my dad is a loser,' says Ari. 'That is *so* tragic.'

'By the way, what happened to your friend?' I ask.

'Which friend?'

'The one who was on the run from the police?'

'She's been grounded by her parents.'

'Are all your friends that naughty?' I ask, seeing the opportunity to slip a Gabriella-inspired 'bomb' – or at the very least a little squib – into the conversation.

'Not all of them.'

'Honestly, I can't think of anything worse than being addicted to drugs,' I say. 'They play havoc with your skin and your internal organs. Who wants to end up on a filthy mattress, lying in a pool of their own bodily fluids?'

'*What the hell*?' says Ari.

'I'm just saying, that drugs aren't glamorous. That's all.' Then seeing that I have her attention, I continue, 'My friend Gabriella says that we are each of us born with certain ingredients in life. Some people are blessed with wonderful ingredients, but create something lousy and inedible; others have very few ingredients but manage to make the most wonderful cake.' I turn to look at Ari. 'I think it would be sad for your friend if she wasted her ingredients, and ended up a drug addict. That's all.'

'Auntie Carrie?'

'Yes?'

'Where are those people going and why are they carrying sticks?' asks Arianna, no doubt hoping to steer the conversation away from hypothetical cakes. She points to the gaunt, weather-beaten folk straggling along the roadside, with rucksacks on their back and long staffs in their hand.

I explain that they are pilgrims, that they come from all over Europe, and that they are going where we are going: to Santiago de Compostela.

'Some look like they won't make it,' says Ari. 'Couldn't we offer them a lift?'

'They won't want a lift,' I say, before explaining that Santiago de Compostela is the Spanish equivalent of Lourdes, but with a long walk thrown in – in some cases hundreds of kilometres – to prove your level of commitment, and/or purify your soul.

People cycle or walk the *Camino,* or Path, sleeping in humble dormitories for €5 a night and eating simple food en route, I explain. Not all of the hundred thousand pilgrims who make the journey each year, do so for religious reasons. Many do the walk after a death of a relationship or a loved one, or because they have simply lost their way in life and feel that it will help – or at least distract them from their misery – if they get lost on Spanish roads instead. Others come because they fancy a good walk or want to lose weight, in which case, they will be greatly aided by the inedible local cuisine.

The unwritten etiquette of the *Camino* is that you do not ask your fellow walkers their reasons for doing it. This would be the very first thing I would want to ask, closely followed by, 'Are you sure this is the right path?'

The route is signposted with yellow arrows, thanks to a priest called Elias Valina Sampedro and his nephews, who marked out the path using leftover road paint, in the 1980s. I hope, for the pilgrims' sake, that they made a better job of it than the authorities have done with the road signs.

But I have the greatest admiration for the walkers. We are doing Spain in relative luxury, with each night's accommodation booked in advance, and that's proving challenging enough. How much less appealing to plod along busy roads – much of the route is on concrete – under a savage sun, with the added pressure that the beds in the *refugios* are allocated on a first-come-first-served basis.

A warning light flashes on the dashboard and I notice that the indicator on the fuel gauge has moved into the red zone. When we set off from Llanes this morning with the tank half full, I figured that there would be one or two service stations en route. Wrong. We seem to be travelling in a green hinterland, with little signs of civilisation, which was delightful at first, but has now become worrying.

Ahead of us, I see a sign for what I think is a motorway. (It's never clear in Spain as signs invariably bear a confusing range of numbers and letters such as 'A8/E70' or 'AP9', so that they read like an algebra test.) I decide to join it, in the hope that we will find a service station within the next thirty-five kilometres, which is how much fuel we have left.

After fifteen fraught kilometres, I'm much encouraged to see a sign for services. *Olé!* We are saved. But, after taking the exit, we find ourselves on a desolate roundabout, with no further signs to the service station. This happens quite a lot in northern Spain: the signs simply run out. I choose a random exit, and drive on, past lonely, parched farmland.

With perhaps the exception of the M25 in the rush hour, or one of the frozen highways featured on *Ice Road Truckers*, I can't think of a worse place to run out of fuel. At least on the M25, you'd be able to communicate the exact nature of your problem. Here, I imagine hiking for hours for help, and then attempting to mime the fact that my car that has run out of diesel. After a few more kilometres, we spot a lay-by in which a single lorry is parked. Normally, in such a situation, I'd be worried that the driver might be a psychopath or deranged killer; today that feels like a lesser evil than running out of fuel in northern Spain. So, I pull up next to the truck, wind down my window and ask, '*Hablas inglés?*'

'*Parlez-vous français?*' replies the potential serial killer.

'*Oui,*' I cry, more delighted than I could ever have imagined I would be, by an encounter with a French lorry driver on a lonely country road. In France, people often seem to enjoy imparting bad news, especially if you're already showing signs of anxiety. But here, on this desolate patch of land in Spain, there is a sense that we foreigners are all in it together.

'Turn around and about ten minutes down that road you will find a fuel station, a restaurant and everything you need,' he says, with noticeable empathy.

We make it with less than five kilometres of fuel left. After filling up with diesel, we celebrate with Diet Pepsi and some ham rolls at the nearby roadside café. It's second only to Pechón in terms of the best lunch we've had in Spain – that's telling you something – and it provides one of my better memories of the country: sitting in brutal heat by a busy road, surrounded by lorry drivers, but feeling happy because we have a full tank of fuel.

Our waiter tells us that if we continue on this road, it will take us all the way to Santiago de Compostela. There are even road signs – 'Spain you are spoiling us,' says Ari – but by this point, we could just as easily follow the straggly line of pilgrims.

The road we are on is less lively than the Spanish motorways – by which I mean that I don't spend my time cursing other drivers and shaking my fist in the rear-view mirror – so I take the opportunity to pass on another piece of Gabriella-wisdom to my niece: the importance of saying 'Thank you'.

This subject is close to my heart, since when Ari and her sister were younger, I would dutifully send presents on birthdays and at Christmas. A lot of thought and effort went into the gifts. On one occasion, I sent a poodle-shaped handbag stuffed with smaller, individually wrapped gifts – bracelets, nail polish, notebooks and sweets. It gave me joy to think of things my nieces might like, but when the gifts failed to elicit a response – not a phone call, let alone a handwritten note – the joy was eventually replaced by disappointment. The poodle was the turning point. Soon after, I stopped making the effort.

'There is more than one kind of intelligence,' I tell Ari. 'There is the sort that your dad values, that can be measured in exam results, and there is another kind: emotional intelligence. And sometimes that can get you further in life than passing exams.'

I seem to have Arianna's full attention – probably because her friends in Cayman are still sleeping off their hangovers and have yet to fire up their electronic gadgets for the day – so I push my point home. 'It really is very important to thank people properly – a phone call or a note. A small gesture can go a long way. People need to feel appreciated.'

'And I guess that if I send someone flowers, I need to remember to add my name, right?'

I laugh. 'Yes, that's one lesson you can learn from your dad.'

In Santiago de Compostela, we leave the car on a patch of wasteland purporting to be a car park and walk to the cathedral square, which is where everyone else seems to be heading. There is a definite buzz in the air, albeit of the religious kind.

The cathedral, with its lavish assortment of spires, statues and domes, is a suitable end point for an epic walk. Arianna slips into the cool interior first, while I wait with Biff on the steps outside, watching the arrivals. It's a mixed crowd. There are nuns and athletic-looking elderly couples; girls dressed in shorts and hippy jewellery, just like my niece; and gaggles of young guys with long hair and stubble, who could just as easily be attending a rock festival, if it weren't for their walking sticks.

Inside the main entrance, people stand in little groups chatting, pilgrims presumably reunited with other pilgrims that they've met en route. The scene resembles a cocktail party, minus the cocktails, and with a dress code best described as 'casual, not smart; bordering on hobo'.

What do the pilgrims do to celebrate their arrival, I wonder? A round of 'Hail Marys', for some; for others, a round of beers or sangria, I imagine. Later, I discover that many finish their journey by queuing for several hours to get the official certificate. To qualify, you must have walked at least 100 kilometres (sixty-two miles) of the route. I feel like an imposter, having walked less than a kilometre, and not even carrying a rucksack.

My niece is in the cathedral for a long time and when she emerges, she declares this to be her favourite place in Spain. I go in next, keen to see the famous Botafumeiro. The giant, swinging incense burner would have doubled up as a medieval version of an Airwick, sweetening the air around the unwashed pilgrims, many of whom slept and cooked in the cathedral. I imagine the scene would have resembled a religious version of Glastonbury, with a soundtrack of Gregorian chant rather than rock music.

Magnificent though the cathedral is, I'm keen to push on. Back under the burning sun, I pull out a map. 'Portugal is 153 kilometres from here,' I say. 'We could be there for dinner.'

'Let's go,' says Ari.

And so we do, flying past Pontevedra and the coastal port of Vigo. Like many of the pilgrims coming to the end of the *Camino*, I feel a mixture of relief and joy that the journey – at least the Spanish part of it – is done.

It wouldn't be fair to trash northern Spain on the basis of a five-day drive-by, much of that time spent on motorways which – crazy drivers aside – Arianna and I agree, was the best part of the Spanish trip. Perhaps we might feel differently if we'd had time to hike in its magnificent mountains, or had just one decent dinner, but based on our experience, I won't be in a massive hurry to revisit northern Spain.

Chapter 10

Little Balls of Pleasure in the Mouth

IT'S JUST AFTER 6.30 pm when we arrive at the Portuguese border. Before us, is an empty curve of motorway, bordered on both sides by mountains and dense forest. Finally, we've arrived on the Costa Verde, or 'Emerald Coast', in the northwest corner of Portugal. The air feels cool and sparklingly clean. Is it possible, I wonder, to get high on chlorophyll?

After the rigours of northern Spain, this feels like a welcoming hug. 'Inhale,' the scenery seems to be saying, 'exhale… and come on in.' The guesthouse I have booked, near Ponte de Lima, is less than thirty kilometres from the border, so we will be arriving in time for dinner. 'Please be sure to arrive before 8 pm,' the instructions said.

'I like Portugal already,' says Arianna, as we stop in front of the toll-booth and a sign saying, 'Please take a ticket', in English. How welcoming those four simple words seem, after Spain. The truth is that I am predisposed to love Portugal, because of Luis and my other Portuguese friends in Villiers. But how can you *not* love a country where people greet each other with the phrase *Bom Dia,* and where a high percentage of the men look like Joaquin Phoenix crossed with John F Kennedy Jr?

This is what I know about Portugal: it produces a large proportion of the world's supply of canned sardines, some truly excellent custard tarts, a sweet pink wine called Mateus Rosé and a tart 'green' wine called Vinho Verde, which is excellent with salty fish. Such are its attractions, I'm not surprised that Napoleon tried to invade the country three times.

As for the Portuguese, they are a happy, fun-loving people, who work hard and party even harder. This I know from first-hand experience, having lived next door to Luis and his builder friends in Villiers. (In the Poitou, the Portuguese are the second largest immigrant group after the British.)

Often they'd return from work at midnight, but the next morning they'd all pile into a van at 5 am and speed off again. Despite the gruelling hours that they worked, they always seemed to be laughing and having a good time.

At weekends, they would congregate in the tiny kitchen of Luis's house and cook lunch together, with much laughter and loud music. The conversation, which was always animated, would last until late in the evening. Sometimes, I tried to understand what they were saying, but it was impossible. There is a reason why Portúguese is said to be one of the world's most difficult languages, similar to speaking Spanish but with a custard pie in your mouth. But I get why they were so proud of their country and its products.

Portugal has some of Europe's best beaches, biggest waves – Nazaré, north of Lisbon, is the scene of some of the most spectacular waves ever surfed – and its worst drivers. It has the highest rate of accidents per capita than that of any other European country. Amazing but true: there really *are* worse drivers than the Spanish.

I'd be lying if I said that I wasn't nervous about driving here. I've read that the reason the Portuguese are so reckless on the road, is their belief in fate – the idea that nothing can alter the pre-ordained timing of your demise. I don't know if this is true, or whether it is plain old machismo that makes them drive like maniacs, but I do know that Luis was driving recklessly and without a seat belt, on the day that he crashed his car.

I remember too, the Sunday morning that he drove me to the airport, like the proverbial bat out of hell. True, I was late for my flight, but as we flew along the curved country roads at frightening velocity, in his white Renault Clio, I said a dozen heartfelt *Jesus Christ*s and vowed never to get into a car with him again. Unfortunately, I had to – for the journey home because, despite the speeding, I still missed my flight.

It wasn't my only experience of Portuguese driving. As a fledgling fashion writer, I was sent to cover a shoe trade fair in Lisbon. Before I'd even left the airport, I'd witnessed at first-hand the driving skills that earned the Portuguese their reputation as Europe's most dangerous drivers. To be honest, I don't remember much: my taxi took off at speed; there was a roundabout, a screech of brakes and the smash of metal and glass. Physically, I emerged unscathed, but then spent most of the weekend in my hotel room, goat-white and dazed, while a lovely woman from the Portuguese Trade Board tried to coax me out to see the latest in casual sandals and sling-backs.

It was fifteen years before I had the courage to return to Portugal – this time to the Algarve for a holiday with my friend Claudia. As we queued by the palm trees at Faro airport, for the car rental pick-up, she announced that she was a 'very nervous' driver and would rather not share the driving, thank you very much. This was a surprise, as Claudia, the publicity director of a well-known fashion brand, did not strike me as the nervous type, at all. But she was adamant. 'Anyway, you live in France, so you're used to driving on the wrong side of the road,' she reasoned.

At the check-in desk, we put Claudia down as the additional driver 'just in case', took out extra insurance and turned down the sat-nav, reasoning that if we turned right when leaving the airport, and travelled in an easterly direction, we'd eventually find ourselves in Olhão, a picturesque fishing port less than fifteen kilometres away. How difficult could it be?

'We can rely on intuitive driving,' said Claudia, as we wandered around in the soupy evening air, searching for our silver Peugeot among all the other silver Peugeots in the car park. As we set off, under a sky of ballet-slipper pink, we couldn't have been happier. But it took two hours to travel the fifteen kilometres to Olhão using 'intuitive driving'.

Let me say right here that getting lost does not bother me. A wrong turn in life can sometimes take you to a better place than the one you intended to go. But this philosophy wears thin when you've circled all the roundabouts in a town more times than you've had cold drinks in your life. I had printed out a map, but Claudia declared that she was 'absolutely hopeless' with maps, and perhaps we could just drive around a bit longer?

'It can't be that difficult. It says here that it's one minute from the sea, on Rua Vasco da Gama,' I said, as we performed yet another fly-by of the waterfront. And talking of Vasco da Gama, the irony that he found his way to India without a map, whereas we couldn't find a boarding house one minute from the sea, was not lost on me. To be fair, Olhão was more like a small city than the tiny fishing port I'd been expecting, but all the same...

By now the sky had darkened to a bruised plum and it was difficult to see the street signs, so Claudia suggested that we 'stop for a coffee' – a phrase by which, I came to realise, she actually meant a large gin and tonic – in order to get directions.

We parked the car outside a café with outdoor tables – and people actually sitting at them. (If you spend a lot of time in rural France, it's always a surprise to see people after 7 pm.)

Drink in hand, with a rattle of ice cubes, Claudia sat back to survey the nightlife, while I pored over a map and sipped a gin and tonic without the gin, since I was driving. I couldn't understand why we hadn't spotted the guesthouse when, according to the map, we'd driven past it at least twenty times.

Fortunately, the owner of the café, a compact, jolly fellow, who spoke perfect English, knew exactly where it was. We took our bags out of the car and walked the few hundred metres to a tiny street, not far from the waterfront.

I was a little nervous about the Pension Bicuar, as the rooms had been so cheap: £33 a night for mine, which had an en suite; and £24 for Claudia's, which didn't. As we arrived in the magnificently tiled entrance, we were hit by the overwhelming smell... of clean sheets. The place spoke of multiple floor scrubbings and the Portuguese love of soap.

My room, with its tightly tucked white sheets and headboard carved of dark wood, was simple, clean and radiantly sunny, with a view over the orange-tiled rooftops. It was perfect.

In the days that followed, I chauffeured us the entire length of the Algarve. We followed the coastal road to the beautiful town of Tavira. (Oh, the tiles – how I loved all the elegant houses with their brightly patterned facades!) I drove us in the opposite direction, to Lagos, where we watched the expats eating a full English breakfast under the palm trees, and counted the signs for 'Happy Hour' – nearly a dozen in a five-minute walk along the sea front. I'm not knocking this – in France, I've often dreamed of finding a café that serves a cooked breakfast – but it seemed a bit of a comedown, for the town responsible for launching some of Portugal's famous voyages of discovery, to be earning its living by selling bangers and beans and Sex on the Beach (the cocktail, not the act) to tourists. Still, I figured, better that than African slaves, the commodity for which Lagos was once known.

As the trip progressed, I began to wonder if Claudia's fear of European driving was just a cunning ploy. With me to chauffeur her around, she was free to partake of all the lavish refreshment that the Algarve had to offer. 'Let's stop for a coffee,' she would say. Then as soon as we'd sat down, she'd cry, 'Oh, we're on holiday, I think I'll have a glass of wine!' while I ordered yet another glass of sparkling water. But in return she was the ideal holiday companion, finding something to appreciate in everything and complaining about nothing.

And now here I am at the opposite end of Portugal, but once again relying on 'intuitive driving'. I did print out directions to the rural hotel but an extra roundabout seems to have popped up since the map was drawn.

'Let's follow this road,' I say. 'It sort of feels the most likely.'

'Sure,' says Arianna, 'but what happens if we don't get there by 8 pm?'

'I don't know. But don't worry. We've got loads of time.'

After half an hour of following the twisty country road, we stop at a petrol station to ask directions. It turns out that we are near Braga, forty kilometres south of where we want to be.

'All the men here seem to have big noses and unibrows,' observes Arianna, as I frown at the map.

'That's a bit of a generalisation,' I say, looking up to see a man with a larger-than-average nose and eyebrows that meet in the middle, peering through the window.

'Excuse me, can I help you?' he says in perfect English, before providing precise and complicated directions as to how to find our hotel when we arrive back in Ponte de Lima.

'Is it far?' I ask, fearing that I know the answer.

'About forty minutes,' he replies, with a cheerful grin.

My niece checks the time on her phone. 'We've got ten minutes,' she says.

The roads become narrower and dustier as we approach the hotel. So it's a pleasant surprise when a cheerful hacienda-style building suddenly appears before us, in the evening sunshine. And despite its secluded rural location, its veranda is packed with people enjoying a drink. I assume they are locals, as our arrival seems to attract some interest. 'Breetish,' I hear someone say, in a not unfriendly way.

A dark-haired woman in jeans and a checked shirt appears. Edite, as she introduces herself, greets us with a smile even though it's well past the 8 pm deadline, and leads us through double iron gates at the side of the guesthouse, into a private green paradise with a swimming pool.

A footpath takes us across an immaculate green lawn and through a garden well stocked with tropical plants and lemon trees, the unwaxed fruits of which lie dotted across the lawn and around the pool. I make a note to salvage one to squeeze into a glass of water in the morning. Several days of cellophane-wrapped Spanish breakfasts have left me feeling like one of Vasco da Gama's scurvy-ridden sailors, craving vitamin C.

Edite shows us to a simple but clean room with a terracotta floor, at the end of a narrow pathway. When I ask if there is any possibility of dinner, she replies – without hesitation – that she can make us some Portuguese-style chicken with rice. I have no idea what 'Portuguese-style' chicken is, but it sounds promising. Before disappearing to make our dinner, Edite indicates that I should park the car behind the iron gates.

As I manoeuvre into the space, there is a loud bang and the sound of something smashing into pieces. I'm gutted to find that I've driven into an enormous terracotta pot and there is now a significant depression in the front of the car. It's ironic that I've driven over a thousand kilometres, dodging dozens of demented drivers in the Iberian Peninsula, only to damage the car in a collision with a pot of geraniums.

I know from previous experiences – yes, there have been a few – that the bill for repairing the damaged bodywork will run to at least four figures. But at least no one comes rushing out with a bill for the damaged pot, as I'm pretty sure would have happened in Spain. Instead, several people appear and pace around my dented car, shaking their heads in a form of group commiseration, as if the pot were somehow to blame. I shrug to acknowledge their concern, while thinking, *What the hell?* and channelling my niece's freewheeling approach to life. No one died and Edite is cooking us dinner.

The orange tables on the veranda are all taken – this place is popular – so Edite indicates for us to follow her into the restaurant, which she has opened especially for us. 'I think it will be better for you in here,' she says. I ask if it would be possible to have a glass of Vinho Verde. 'But of course,' she replies and returns with a full bottle in an ice bucket.

'Is it sparkling?' I ask.

'Yes, it will create little balls of pleasure in your mouth,' she says, which is quite the nicest way of describing a sparkling wine that I've ever heard.

Edite's chicken and sausage casserole also creates much pleasure in the mouth. Biff lies peacefully under the table, Arianna has her Coke and I have the chilled glass of wine I have been dreaming of since Santiago de Compostela, which already seems like a lifetime ago. Our first evening in Portugal exceeds all expectations, made all the more perfect by the fact our beds are just around the corner.

The next morning I take Biff out early while Ari is still sleeping. We follow the dusty orange road out of the village, Biff's ears pricking up at the sound of a cockerel crowing and the bleating of unseen beasts. I drag him to one side as a herd of horned goats is driven towards us, bells tinkling, by a lone herder. This is the real rural deal.

The path takes us down to a wide river, edged by a band of blue-green mountains. I free Biff from his lead, hoping that he won't dive into the water as it looks deep and it's a long way to the other side. 'If you jump in, you're on your own,' I tell him.

I stop for a moment to take in the scenery – the lavish fringe of reeds along the riverbank, the vines and the stalks of beet in nearby fields and the purple-green of the mountains in the distance. I've always thought of Portugal in terms of three colours: the white of the churches; the hard blue of a hot sky; and the scorched orange earth of the Algarve. But the Costa Verde gives you the full gamut of greens, from forest to frog and every shade in between. I'll take northern Portugal with its mountains and its green fronds, over the glare and the beach-front bars of the Algarve, any day.

Gazing at the silver river, I wonder how many people have stood at this spot through the centuries? And how many people will stand here after me? Suddenly, I'm hit by a wave of *saudade* (pronounced *sah-ooh-dah-jee*). This Portuguese word is almost impossible to translate, but relates to a deep-felt longing for something that you cannot quite put your finger on; a form of melancholy for opportunities lost, roads not taken, or a moment that cannot ever be recaptured – the kind of enormous feelings that are impossible to pinpoint.

Arianna is still asleep when we get back, so I take Biff to sit on the veranda at the front of the hotel, which is empty apart from two Portuguese men, who wish me '*Bom Dia*'. I am mesmerised by their style: one is dressed in lemon-yellow trousers that have been meticulously ironed; the other, in a crisp green and white shirt that perfectly matches his emerald eyes and mint-white teeth. They are not young but they are still rakishly attractive and there is something about them that reminds me of Luis. Had he lived, he probably would have looked like them one day, smoking on a café terrace in his beloved Portugal.

Inside the café I notice a bottle of Ginja, a Portuguese liqueur made from Morello cherries, and remember the winter afternoon that I first tasted it. Luis was hosting one of his all-male Sunday lunch gatherings while I worked next door. Towards the end of the afternoon, his boss came to invite me to join them for a drink. I went, fearing I'd have to drink whisky or port to be polite, but instead they produced a bottle of Ginja.

It amused me greatly to find myself squeezed around a kitchen table with half a dozen macho builders, all drinking a sweet cherry liqueur. I remember too, how pleased they were that I liked it. 'You see, *chérie*, we make some good things in Portugal,' said Luis with a wink.

So true, I think, noticing the *pastéis de nata,* or custard tarts, on the counter. I order two and a large espresso. (Total cost: €1.40 – Portugal is astonishingly cheap.) Then I sit on the veranda for half an hour, pleased to be in a corner of Portugal that feels authentic, untainted by Ryanair flights and full English breakfasts. I booked it because it was the only dog-friendly guesthouse near Ponte de Lima that I could find, and, although the rooms are basic and there is no wifi, it has turned out to be unexpectedly wonderful.

I return to the room just as Arianna emerges from the bathroom dressed in tiny denim shorts and a green T-shirt, a slew of beaded necklaces around her neck. She tears open a Snickers bar and chugs it down with half a litre of Coke. I contemplate a little discourse on the benefits of good nutrition, but then remember that the two main ingredients of my own breakfast were caffeine and sugar, and think better of it.

Outside, Biff is lying among a pile of lemons in the shade, a look of patient forbearance on his face. 'OK, dudes,' I say. 'Let's go and explore Ponte de Lima.'

Chapter 11

One Poppy in Winter

PONTE DE LIMA, Portugal's oldest town, is perfectly charming. We walk down to the riverfront, passing sugar-pink buildings and several *pastelarias,* their windows piled high with almond biscuits and Portuguese pastries. Everything, from the white mosaic pavements to the pristine white telephone boxes, looks so clean and well maintained.

The people seem friendly too. On the low Roman bridge over the river, a small child stops to pat Biff, encouraged by smiling Portuguese parents. I don't remember a single person looking pleased to see him in Spain. There is a lovely holiday atmosphere as we cross the river to the sound of jaunty Peruvian pipe music from concealed speakers.

On the other side of the bridge there is a pottery studio, where a simple white vase, hand-painted with two crimson poppies, immediately catches my eye.

I guess it is to be expected, given that I'm so close to the region where he was born, that Luis should keep popping up in my thoughts. Most of those thoughts can be now be filed under the category 'fond memory' – the raging grief has long subsided

– but the vase triggers a flashback to something curious that happened a few months after his death.

It was late November and I was walking Biff on a farm track about five kilometres from the village. The track turned and meandered, past fallow fields and the occasional lonely farmhouse. I had no idea where I was going but I kept following it, because whenever I find a path that I haven't explored, I have to know where it goes.

Eventually, the muddy bridleway widened into a dusty orange track and I could see a road in the distance that I did not recognise. Suddenly, I was hit by a feeling of absolute foreboding, of a kind that I had never experienced before.

An air of mourning hung over the churned brown fields and I sensed immediately that something terrible had happened here. Biff must have sensed it too, as he stopped dead, reluctant to go any further.

I kept walking towards the road, hoping to spot a sign to a small hamlet or a landmark that I recognised, so that I could work out where I was. And then I saw it. About twenty metres before the dirt track met the tarmac road, the ground was glittering. I looked more closely and saw small pieces of glass and fragments of mirror ground into the orange earth, forming a sinister mosaic. Nearby, there was a piece of a wing mirror and small pieces of metal with white paint. My stomach lurched. This couldn't possibly be...?

Surely the *sapeurs-pompiers* would have removed all traces of debris? I stood under the sorrowful winter sky, thinking that I was imagining this awful scene. Maybe, I told myself, the glass was from a tractor accident. But then I saw the coins, about half a dozen of them scattered on the ground. I picked one up, noticing that it looked subtly different to a French euro.

When I turned it over, it was stamped with the word 'Portugal'. The other coins, a mixture of silver and copper centimes, were also Portuguese in origin.

I remembered that the friend who was in the car with Luis – he was wearing a seat belt and survived unscathed – had just arrived from Portugal. With a painful jolt, I realised that I was standing at the scene of Luis's crash.

My first thought was a strangely prosaic one: I was surprised at how far into the fields the car had travelled, after Luis lost control of it. My second thought was: *what are the odds?* Although I knew the road, the D741, where the accident happened, it is a long road that runs for over twenty kilometres, bordered on either side by identikit fields. Until now, I had not known where exactly the accident took place and I would never have guessed that the twisty track I started out on today would lead here. To stumble over fragments of debris from Luis's car and the precise scene of the crash, while walking my dog, seemed like a coincidence of the most freakish kind.

I stood in the flat, sombre landscape for a while, feeling viscerally shocked and shaken. I remember thinking how sad it was that only fragments of windscreen and mirror marked the spot of the tragedy. Usually, in France, the scene of a fatal accident is made into a memorial by loved ones, with a makeshift wooden cross or a bunch of flowers tied to a nearby tree. But no one had done that for Luis.

I don't know how long I stood there, lost in my sad thoughts, but as I turned to go home, I saw something extraordinary. Growing in the churned brown earth nearby – in late November – was a single, thriving poppy. It was as if nature had provided its own memorial.

'Auntie Carrie, you should buy that vase,' says Ari, pulling my thoughts back to the sunny artist's studio. 'It's cute.'

'Yes,' I say. 'I was planning to.' I take it to the counter where the potter takes his time wrapping it. 'I hope you enjoy it,' he says, as he hands it over.

'It's not for me,' I reply. 'But thank you.'

Walking back over the bridge, the jaunty Peruvian pipe music suddenly changes to 'Auld Lang Syne'. It's bizarre to hear the song associated with New Year's Eve and funerals, being sung in the bright sunshine. I half expect the people around us to start linking arms or showering each other with drunken kisses and cries of 'Happy New Year!'

As we stop in the middle of the bridge to admire the view of the river, I remember Gabriella's theory that so much of life is down to fate and coincidence. And then I remember another of her favourite sayings: 'There is no point in spoiling your soup with sadness or regret.'

'Shall we get some lunch?' says Ari.

'Good idea. Let's go.'

We find a restaurant close to the river, serving 'traditional' Portuguese cuisine, though I have no idea what that means. I pop my head round the door and bid the waiter '*Bom Dia*', before pointing hopefully at Biff. Sensing that his presence might be a problem, Biff assumes his most winning expression, eyes full of hope, his head cocked to one side. The waiter says something in Portuguese, which I assume means '… blah, blah, health and safety… regulations… no way José…'

But wait… it seems that we are not being asked to leave. 'He wants to know how many we are,' says Ari.

Minutes later we are seated on the terrace of a packed restaurant and our Portuguese neighbours are smiling at Biff and asking if we need any help with the menu, even though we've been given an English version. Once again, I am brimming over with love for Portugal and its lovely people. Meanwhile, Arianna is busy with her phone, tapping out a status update to friends in Grand Cayman. 'Waiter's hot,' she writes, with admirable concision. (He is.)

We order 'two doses', as the menu so delightfully puts it, of the Portuguese fish pie. When it arrives, it looks more like four doses and just in case we haven't eaten for a couple of weeks, it comes with a large platter of rice. I glance around the restaurant – many people seem to be having the same dish – and marvel that no one has passed out in a carbohydrate coma.

But our second experience of Portuguese cuisine is as good as the first. 'The Portuguese have really got their shit together,' declares my niece, and I agree.

Driving back to the guesthouse, I suggest that we extend our stay for another two nights. I love the relaxed rural vibe and I'm enjoying the break from packing and unpacking the car each day. Arianna is keen to stay too, despite the lack of wifi and phone signal. Edite says that it is no problem. Although this is good news for us, I'm a little sad for her, and for northern Portugal, that hotel rooms are so readily available in peak season. The Emerald Coast deserves to be full to bursting, with people queuing to get in.

The following morning, after another walk along the silver river, I leave Biff behind with a sleeping Arianna and drive into Ponte de Lima in search of breakfast supplies and a launderette, as we're running out of clothes. Or rather, *I'm* running out of clothes, having packed in my usual manner (badly and in a hurry). Arianna seems to have an endless supply of shorts and tiny tops in bright colours.

I find a supermarket that goes by the rather charming name of Pingo Doce. (It's pronounced 'pig-uh dose' and means 'Sweet Drop', as far as I can tell.) Even more charming are the cream canopies that are suspended like yacht sails over the parking bays – a simple and stylish way to prevent customers' cars from turning into slow cookers. It's the small but thoughtful touches that make me love Portugal so much.

I wander around Piggo, as I decide to call it, fascinated by the produce on display – great hunks of ham and salted cods, fat figs, blueberries (for me, a particular delight as you can't find them in French supermarkets), fresh oregano (ditto) and rows and rows of Vinho Verde.

I could spend hours looking at the wall of pale green wines and trying to figure out the subtle differences between them, but I figure it would be unseemly to linger in the alcohol aisles so early in the morning.

Instead, I address myself to the tasks in hand: Pop-Tarts, Clearasil and Coke. Life is certainly surprising. If you'd told me six months ago that I'd be roaming a supermarket in search of such items, I'm not sure I'd have believed you. I further surprise myself by feeling disappointed that I can't fulfil my niece's request for the sugary snack.

'Nothing makes me so happy as Pop-Tarts,' she declared last night, when I mentioned that I was planning to visit a supermarket. No pressure then. Hating myself for doing so, I buy her some sugar-laden cereal bars instead, and stock up on bottled water, fresh figs and flattened white peaches, which look deformed but turn out to be the Premier League of peaches. On the way back, I keep my eyes peeled for launderettes. But like Pop-Tarts, they just aren't happening in Portugal.

Over the next few days Ponte de Lima starts to feel like home. We drive into the town at least once a day to visit our favourite café, which has free wifi, a limitless supply of custard tarts and toasted sandwiches, and a lovely view of the bridge. Unlike rural France, where the café-bars only serve coffee, canned drinks and alcohol, Portuguese cafés offer a full range of snacks. And they are happy to serve you, no matter what time of day.

Ironically, given that the slow pace of life is supposed to be part of the appeal of the French countryside, I spend much of my time there rushing to meet deadlines. The post office, the banks and most of the shops, close at noon for two hours. If you want lunch in a local restaurant, you're pushing your luck if you arrive after 12.30 pm. Should you wish to send a letter, the deadline for dispatch is 2.30 pm. And if you want to go out to dinner, there are two deadlines: many restaurants will refuse to seat you after 8 pm and, if you haven't finished eating by 10 pm, you can expect the staff to start stacking chairs and switching off the lights around you, even in the better establishments.

In Portugal, everything is open for business – and pleasantly so. In restaurants, waiters look pleased, rather than pained, to see you. It helps, too, that so many Portuguese people speak English. (The cashier in Piggo spoke English, French and Spanish, in addition to her native language.)

On our last evening in Ponte de Lima, we decide to join the locals for drinks on the hotel veranda. I'm curious to know more about these happy, attractive people, who all seem to know each other. They are so beautifully dressed that we could just as easily be in a chic metropolitan bar as sitting on a terrace in a rural backwater. As usual, Biff is the icebreaker. One chap brings his toddler over to stroke 'the pretty little dog', and strikes up a conversation. Are we enjoying Portugal? he wants to know.

Ari and I assure him that we couldn't love Portugal more. I ask about the hotel and its customers. He tells us that his parents own the hotel and that most of the people chatting on the veranda are family, who live nearby. His parents still live on the first floor of the hacienda, but now lease the bar and the hotel to Edite. What a convivial arrangement.

The following morning, after thanking Edite, who is hard at work as usual, watering the garden, we leave our rural retreat. It's the first time since our trip began that I am sad to be leaving somewhere.

We head into Ponte de Lima one last time, to visit the Monday market. Set up along the side of the river in the shade of the plane trees, and taking up most of the town, it is one of the oldest markets in Portugal. The knock-off Prada wallets and fake Louis Vuitton bags, however, are a twenty-first-century addition. And although there is a lot of local produce – eggs, cheeses, live poultry, breads as big as cushions, and cakes – most of the non-edible merchandise appears to have been shipped in from China.

Arianna, bless her, couldn't be more excited. She phones her father – waking him up in the middle of the night in Cayman – to ask if she can withdraw money on the debit card that he has given her. He tells her that she can withdraw €100 and we discover just how far that will go in a Portuguese market, as she wanders down the avenue of plane trees, buying items in multiples. The haul includes three plaited belts for €5, two pairs of shorts, five T-shirts and a Portuguese flag. The flag, she tells me, is going to be displayed prominently in her bedroom back in Grand Cayman, as a reminder of the trip.

Chapter 12

Holy Smoke

THERE IS NO denying that Portugal has excellent, state-of-the-art motorways – great empty swathes of them snaking through the countryside, rolling over rivers and viaducts, and coiling around mountains. The reason there is no one on them? Portuguese motorists can't afford the tolls, introduced to pay back the €96 billion awarded by the EU since 1986.

Those who *can* afford the tolls seem to be suffering from a bad case of motorway megalomania. For most of the three-hour journey from Ponte de Lima to Leiria, we have the road to ourselves. But every so often, a glance in the mirror reveals a slab of metal hurtling towards our rear window, the driver waiting until the last moment to brake.

Despite empty lanes on either side, he (for it invariably is a 'he') will then hug our bumper for several kilometres, travelling close enough to listen to our conversation, before overtaking. Then – the ultimate insult – he will shave back in front of us with millimetres to spare, and, get this... *slow down*.

Why? After such an assertive display of being in a hurry, they could at least have the decency to speed off into the distance, leaving us to crawl along at 130 km/hr, in peace. 'Maybe they're Spanish,' says my niece, since it's a form of driving that we first witnessed near Santander. 'And desperate to get away from Spain.'

I have mixed feelings as we approach Leiria, which is halfway between Porto and Lisbon. I'm excited to see it, having heard so much about it from Luis, but it also feels strange to be visiting a place that is so linked with him.

Our first glimpse of his hometown reveals it to be a city of pretty white buildings, their orange-pink rooftops quivering in the late afternoon heat. Our hotel, in the centre of town, is a fetching pastel blue, which makes it easy to find.

Our room continues the colour theme – lagoon blue walls and bed coverings and, in the bathroom, every surface apart from the loo seat, tiled in blue and white. No one could accuse it of being bland. And, better still, it has French windows on to a small balcony which, unlike most hotel windows in European hotels, actually open. I love it.

Keen to avoid a repeat of our experiences in San Sebastián and Comillas, I book a restaurant after doing some internet research. If we want to eat somewhere decent, Biff will have to stay behind in the hotel room, so I turn on the Euro news to keep him company. But I can tell by the look on his face that watching the German chancellor Angela Merkel battling to save Europe from its latest meltdown, is a poor substitute for a night out in Leiria with his bitches, which is, I'm sure, how he thinks of Arianna and me.

We find the restaurant in a narrow alley in the old town. First signs are good: dim lighting and a stylish, dark-wood interior. The waiter is friendly, speaks English and doesn't look like the type to pick a fight with his customers. I order the cod and banana curry, out of curiosity – it's the house speciality – and steak and chips for Ari. The waiter returns to our table with two shot glasses containing a frosty green substance, which turns out to be cucumber in cunning disguise.

'Oh,' says Ari, who never knowingly eats salad ingredients, even when they're masquerading as a sorbet.

We eat them to be polite and before we know it, the waiter is back with two small plates of slippery eel. We manage to eat those too, hoping it will be the last of the complimentary hors d'oeuvres. But no, the little delicacies keep on coming.

'It's a shame that Biff-dude isn't here,' says Ari. 'He'd enjoy this.'

'Um,' I say, tackling a terrine of something exceptionally salty. This amuse-bouche bombing strikes me as odd, since the more a restaurant fills up its customers with free terrines and tongues of eel, the less likely they are to order from the menu.

Ari and I keep eating and our waiter seems thrilled, which I put down to pride in his national cuisine. By the time our main courses arrive, we can't eat another thing. Discreetly, we wrap a piece of Arianna's steak in a napkin for Biff and ask for the bill.

It contains over a dozen items that I don't recognise. It turns out that we have been charged for the 'complimentary' appetisers that we ate out of politeness. This, I later discover, is the custom in Portugal. The hors d'oeuvres are never free. And if you allow the waiter to leave them on the table, but don't eat them, you will still be charged. So you just have to butch up and send them back. I pay the bill, thinking that at least we are doing our bit to help Portugal out of its economic crisis.

Walking back across the plaza, Leiria reminds me even more of a mini-version of Paris, full of life and light. The fountains in the central square are lit up and the castle glows like a pile of gold bullion on the hill above the town.

I can easily imagine Luis here, sitting outside one of the many bars and restaurants, laughing with a crowd of friends and, almost certainly, flirting with the waitresses.

Back at the blue hotel, the receptionist looks at me accusingly. 'After you left, your dog cried for five minutes,' she says. 'He was very upset.'

'Oh dear. I'm sorry.'

'It's OK. After five minutes, he gave two woofs and was silent,' she replies. 'I hope he hasn't made any mess in the room.'

I reassure her that trashing hotel rooms isn't his style. 'He was probably just practising his fado,' I say, referring to the tortured Portuguese singing style. She gives me a strange look.

Far from making a mess, Biff has actually done some tidying up, collecting our shoes and clothes into a little pile on his bed. He flashes me a withering look and doesn't bother to come and greet me, thus failing in the key dog duty of making its human feel loved and missed.

I feel as if I've committed an act of unspeakable cruelty. Biff is a good little traveller, accustomed to climbing into his doughnut wherever it is laid, but it must be upsetting to find yourself excluded from the evening's excursion and left alone in strange surroundings. 'At least we brought you a treat,' I say, waggling his ears, as he wolfs down the steak.

Checking one of my social media accounts before I go to bed, I'm surprised to find another message from Matt. 'I'm half way through your first book,' he has written.

I cringe. Normally, I'm thrilled when someone tells me they're reading one of my books. But it makes me feel uneasy to learn that Matt is reading about the roll call of disasters that constitutes my private life. Still, I can't resist replying, 'And?'

'I now know quite a lot about you,' he replies.

'But not everything,' I type back.

The following morning, I walk Biff around the old town while Arianna is still sleeping. The cafés in the arcades around the square are just opening up and the waiters are sluicing down their respective patches of terrace.

I wander the narrow back streets, admiring the faded elegance of the buildings with their wrought iron balconies and French windows – untouched by UPVC – and imagining the possibilities. They are crying out for renovation.

I'm also quite taken by the sudden, joyous bursts of tiling – over an archway, on the walls of an old-fashioned pharmacy or the facade of an elegant old house. Why, I wonder, has the concept of treating building exteriors as if they were shower cubicles, not taken off all over the world? It's a genius idea – eye-catching and requiring minimal maintenance.

Leiria, I discover, is a good base from which to explore some of Portugal's most famous sites, including the abbey of Batalha and the pilgrim site of Fátima, both less than a twenty-minute drive away. I also have to make an important pilgrimage of my own before we leave Leiria, so I decide to extend our stay by a couple of nights.

The blue hotel is fully booked, but the receptionist says that we can move to its sister establishment, a country hotel in Cortes, just outside Leiria. And so, the following morning we decamp to the 'country hotel', which turns out not to be in the country at all, but two kilometres from a busy main road and next door to a construction site.

Our room is in a modern annex and it's perfect in every way, if you're about to go down with a migraine.

The window is the size of a crisp packet and just to emphasise the crepuscular gloom, the walls are painted the colour of cocoa powder. It's not even possible to stick your head out of the window to snatch a glimpse of the riverside setting. Thanks, no doubt, to EU health and safety regulations, it only opens an inch, presumably to stop guests from throwing themselves out of windows. Frankly, I've no idea how common a phenomenon the suicide tourist is, but it strikes me that in certain circumstances – fire, roving terrorist attack to name but two – sealing people into their hotel rooms is not very safe at all.

On the plus side, the hotel has a nice terrace overlooking a river – indeed it is built on the river, with the deep green water rising up against the hotel walls – and the restaurant has an excellent reputation. People travel from miles around, it seems, for the signature dish of rooster-in-its-own-blood stew.

Batalha, or Battle Abbey, rears up suddenly from the motorway, so close that it appears to be sitting on it – a sudden and unexpected merging of medieval architecture and EC development fund. The travel writer, billionaire (by eighteenth-century standards) and bon viveur, William Beckford, would have met with an entirely different view when he rocked up with his baggage carts, servants and 'famous French cook', a couple of centuries ago.

The poor monks, he noted, looked on 'rather enviously' as his lackeys carried in his gauze-curtained bed, exotic carpets, and picnic hampers overflowing with pies, hams and sausages. My entourage, a niece and a small dog, is more modest. Standing before the colossus of a Gothic monastery, which consists of several buildings, I do wonder how Beckford found his way in without a trickle of tourists to follow.

I imagine that dogs will not be welcome. But the guard indicates, by way of a little mime, that Biff can come in if I pick him up and carry him. And so I do, warning my furry pal that he must be on his best behaviour as I carry him into the Founder's Chapel. He seems to understand, as he doesn't try to wriggle free, but gazes up in awe at the stained glass windows, the whites of his eyes widening at the splendour of it all.

The long, narrow panes of coloured glass dazzle like Pucci scarf prints against the pale limestone walls, while in the church next door, the light bounces off the stained glass to create an effect like disco lights on the stone floor.

Biff is not allowed in the monastery itself, so I buy Arianna a ticket and wait outside. My niece goes in reluctantly, but half an hour later emerges looking strangely animated. Has some kind of Damascene conversion taken place in the cloisters, I wonder?

'Yo, I smelt weed in there,' she declares. 'And it was pretty strong weed too.'

'Well, I hope you didn't inhale,' I say, handing her Biff's lead.

As I stroll around among the spires and soaring fir trees in the quadrangle, I try to imagine what life must have been like for the brothers who lived here. What made a good or a bad day for a monk? Or do the days all merge into one when you devote your life to God, in a never-ending round of fasts, Mass and choir practice?

And then, every now and again, the arrival of a wealthy and flamboyant traveller, such as Beckford, would have livened things up, especially if their entourage included, as Beckford's did, a renowned French chef whose omelette provençal apparently sent the abbot into paroxysms of delight.

As I leave, I catch the scent of incense drifting across one of the cool stone passageways, and I wonder if it was this that my niece mistook for pot.

'Did you smell it too?' she asks, as I emerge from the monastery.

'It was incense,' I reply. 'And it doesn't make you high.' If it did, I would have spent a large chunk of my Catholic childhood giggling like an idiot and talking gibberish.

Ten minutes later, sitting in one of the cafés opposite the monastery, I wonder what the monks would have made of twenty-first-century innovations such as Trufo Plus ice creams. And I feel sure that Beckford would not have approved of the yellow plastic seating and parasols (advertising Lipton Tea), which cast everyone's face in an unhealthy, liverish colour.

Arianna is furiously typing a Facebook update on her phone. I look over her shoulder. 'Man, the amount of ganja I smelt on holy ground today. This cannot be right!' she has written.

'Come on,' I say. 'Time for another religious experience.'

Our first impression of Fátima, just fifteen minutes drive from Batalha, is that it is an excellent place to stock up on the many accoutrements of the religious life. The town's shops and market stalls are bursting with rosary beads, prayer books and statues of the Blessed Virgin. 'According to the guidebook, this is one of the most important places of pilgrimage in the Catholic world,' says Arianna. '*No kidding.*'

A sign near the entrance to the holy shrine indicates that everything you can think of – and some things that you can't – is forbidden at Fátima. Unacceptable pilgrim behaviour, indicated with pictures of the offending activity struck through with black crosses, includes playing football, the trombone and dancing. There is a lot of stuff that is banned at the religious site, some of it inexplicably so. If, for example, you have made the journey to Fátima with your family, you might want a photograph to commemorate the occasion. Well, tough chips. Posing for a picture with other people is also forbidden. *Verboten. Interdit. Prohibido. Proibido.*

'Ugh,' says Ari, looking at the board of banned activities, her face contorted in disgust. 'The trombone.'

'Sorry?'

'It is literally the elephant of musical instruments,' she says. 'I was forced to play that thing at school. It ruined my childhood.'

I start to laugh, which is almost certainly forbidden in Fátima. Dogs I notice, are also *proibido*, although as Arianna points out, God made them too, so surely he would be happy to see his furry friends? In any case, it's too hot to leave Biff in the car, so he too will have to enter as a pilgrim and abstain from playing football, wearing headphones or listening to loud music. I give him The Talk, as I always do when I require him to be on his best behaviour. 'You've got to be a good boy here,' I say. 'God is watching. So bear it in mind if you want to go to heaven.' (The current Pope, incidentally, has declared that dogs can, indeed, go to heaven. As if it were ever in doubt.)

The field where the Virgin Mary is said to have appeared to the three shepherd children in 1917, has long been concreted over to accommodate the millions of pilgrims who visit every year. The site consists of a long concrete strip – Ryanair lands planes on shorter runways than this – leading to the Sanctuary of Our Lady of Fátima, a basilica and a church that rises up like a stiffly iced cake, against the brilliant blue sky.

For a mecca of religious devotion, it feels strangely soul-less. To be fair, it is low-season in the religious calendar and at peak moments such as Easter, I imagine that to witness a night procession by candlelight or a round of 'Ave Maria' sung en masse here, must be, well... a religious experience. But in comparison to Santiago de Compostela, with its laid-back, 'everyone welcome' hippy vibe, Fátima feels intimidating. It's for the truly devout, not gawkers or day-trippers or people with bare legs, like Arianna and me.

In the Chapel of Apparitions, which looks like an open-sided bus shelter, a Mass is in progress and pilgrims are shuffling around a statue of the Virgin Mary, on their knees.

'So let me get this straight,' says Ari. 'All of this was built because three kids claimed to have seen the Virgin Mary in a field.'

'Yup. That's pretty much the sum of it,' I say.

'And everyone believed them?'

'Not everyone, but many people, yes.'

'Oh boy,' says my niece, shaking her head in wonder.

'But it wasn't just the three children who saw things,' I say, before relaying what I've read in the guidebook.

In October 1917, the crowd that had gathered in the field in anticipation of another vision, witnessed what became known as the 'Solar Miracle'. Some saw spinning solar discs, others a multi-coloured 'fire wheel'. (I've seen similar things myself, after drinking one too many champagne cocktails.) Some saw nothing at all. In the absence of smart phones, Instagram and selfies ('Me plus #miracle!'), witness statements are the only clue as to what might have happened.

The sceptical might say that the reports of multi-coloured flashes of light could just as easily be a description of sunstroke as a celestial visitation. Another explanation is that those present had had their retinas bleached by staring directly at the sun; or mass hallucination, fed by religious fervour. Others have claimed that it was a UFO.

Whether or not you believe in miracles, there is some truth in the phrase, 'Once a Catholic, always a Catholic', just as when you sign a broadband contract with Orange France, you will find that, despite your best efforts, you cannot break free. Although I cannot claim to be fully signed up to the faith, I do show my face at key moments in the Catholic year – notably Midnight Mass on Christmas Eve, and Easter Sunday – and I do love a beautifully sung 'Ave Maria' and the smell of incense.

One of my favourite Catholic rituals is the practice of lighting candles to honour the dead, or summon divine help for someone who needs it. Here in Fátima there seems to be a game of candle one-upmanship going on. A pilgrim appears with a candle the size of a rolling pin; another comes along with a wax column as big as a postbox. Then, just when you think that the candles can't get any bigger, a super-sized rod of wax appears, towering over the person carrying it. It's like a Monty Python sketch. Except no one is laughing.

I buy two medium candles and we follow the crowd to the area dedicated to candle lighting, where we are greeted with a roar of flames. A fierce wall of heat shimmers in front us, making it difficult to get close enough to put the candles in the holders. Most of the offerings have keeled over, resulting in a tangled mass of tan-coloured wax.

After we've risked maiming ourselves by reaching through the wall of heat to stab the candles into slots, Ari offers to sit on a bench and wait with Biff while I take the first turn at looking around the basilica. I notice a family of pilgrims – two small children and their father, led by a pious-looking mother – performing a circuit of the holy ground, and our bench. The mother glares at us as she walks by. We are not killing it in Fátima.

When I return, the family is still performing circuits of the bench where Arianna and Biff are waiting. The children and the father look as if they are flagging, but the mother marches grimly on, powered by religious fervour and mouthing silent prayers. It's a shame, I think, that they cannot be wired up to the national grid, to harness all that energy.

Arianna looks miffed. I imagine it's because she'd rather be hanging out with surfer-dudes than holy-dudes. But it seems that while I was in the basilica, the matriarch of the family stooped to pick up a cigarette packet next to the bench and scowled at Arianna, as if to imply that she had dropped it. 'So much for love and peace,' my niece declares.

Before we leave Fátima, we visit the largest of the religious emporia in the town. Never one to miss a consumer opportunity,

I buy some church candles in red plastic holders for €2 each. We also do a tour of the market, where the *artigos religiosos* on offer include everything from Virgin Mary snowdomes and key rings, to hair ornaments decorated with scenes of the apparition. Then, feeling that we have well and truly 'done' Fátima, we head back to the car. I later regret not buying a job lot of the candles, which burn for hours.

Later that afternoon, I leave Ari reading in our truffle-coloured room with Biff lying at her feet. 'I'm going out to get fuel for the car and to stock up on bottled water,' I say, putting the vase that I bought in Ponte de Lima in my bag.

'Sure,' says Ari, without looking up, no doubt relieved that I'm not about to drag her around another religious monument. Tomorrow we are leaving Leiria, so the time has come for the part of the journey that I have been most dreading, but also anticipating. I want to go to Amor, but I don't.

First, I drive into Leiria to buy some flowers. I'm looking for a bunch of plain roses or a mass of just one type of flower, but the shop sells only ready-made bouquets – fussy combinations of flowers decorated with tinsel, feathers, crystal drops and sequinned birds-of-paradise. To send a rose out into the world naked is not the done thing in Portugal, it seems. Luis was a man of good taste, so better to arrive without a floral tribute, I figure, than one that is dripping in crystals and sequins.

I drive on, and twelve kilometres from Leiria, I see the sign for Amor, or 'Love' in Portuguese. How marvellous for its inhabitants to be able to say, 'I live in Love'. (Legend has it that the town got its name because a Portuguese king staying in Leiria, fell in love with a beautiful peasant girl that he saw in a field of poppies and daisies, while out riding his horse. He would then gallop over each day 'for love'.) I can't help thinking

143

of the contrast between my melancholic mission and that of the king, riding over for some fun in the fields.

I feel increasingly nervous the closer that I get to Amor, but also curious. I know it is going to be a sad experience but I want to see where Luis was born and where he now lies. I've imagined a small hilltop village with a few houses around one main street, maybe some goats being herded down a dusty road, and a humble, radiantly white church with a small cemetery attached. But Amor is not what I expected.

It is more of a small town than a village, surrounded by rural flatlands and factories, an uneasy mix of agriculture and industry. This, I figure, is 'deep Portugal' or the equivalent of *la France profonde* – the phrase used to describe 'authentic' and hidden pockets of the French countryside. Not many holiday-makers, I imagine, come here.

It feels as if I'm driving into the set of a spaghetti western. Dark-eyed men sit outside a café on the dusty street, smoking and looking moody. I feel conspicuous, as my arrival seems to be attracting some curiosity. I guess it's not often that someone rides into town with British number plates.

The area feels poor, although its pale-coloured bungalows look as neat as pins. There is a lot of poverty and unemployment in the French countryside, where many people live on the breadline, but Portugal is even poorer. It is for this reason that so many Portuguese go to France in search of work, just as Luis and his friends did.

I notice a cream-coloured church rising up majestically from the sunburnt terrain. I park the car by a lone palm tree and climb the steps, thinking that it will be locked, but when I push the door, it opens. Inside is a surprise, like cracking open a plain egg to find that it is Fabergé – all jewels and lavish decoration – on the inside. Instead of the simple wooden benches and whitewashed walls that I was expecting, there are crystal chandeliers and wall sconces and extravagant displays of fresh flowers – shamefully, it flashes through my mind that no one would notice if I took a few for Luis – and an abundance of gilt.

The walls are cheerfully decorated with patterned tiles, creating a joyous, almost carnival atmosphere, far removed from the sombre decor of most Catholic churches. You have to hand it to the Portuguese: they know how to decorate a church.

The splendour is in stark contrast to the humble neighbourhood outside. But it feels like a fitting place for Luis to have returned to, since everything about him – his personality, his clothes, even his bed linen – was colourful, too.

With a heavy heart, I drive back along the main street until I find the cemetery. It looks clean and well kept, its pathways paved in white mosaic. I unwrap the porcelain vase that I bought in Ponte de Lima and walk through the dove-coloured iron gates, into a landscape of white marble and bright flowers. I notice several other visitors tending to graves and feel a little stupid to have come here with nothing but an empty vase.

The cemetery is bigger than I imagined. For the first time, it occurs to me that I have no idea where to find Luis. I wander towards the back of the walled cemetery, away from the ancient gravestones, and find him in the last row, his grave marked by a grey granite headstone. I am surprised to see that there are fresh flowers on his grave – a mixed bunch of humble pink, purple and white blooms. Someone has been here recently.

This I wasn't expecting, as Luis was estranged from his parents, and his close friends are hundreds of kilometres away in France. I figure it is probably his mother, who lives in Amor. If so, it is ironic that she visits her son in death, but had little to do with him when he was alive.

Clutching the porcelain vase, I stand under the hot sun, feeling again the full force of *saudade* – that deep melancholy yearning for people and eras that are gone forever. The word was probably invented for moments like this.

But it is consoling to know that Luis has been laid to rest in a pleasant spot, a place of peace and light, with sunbeams bouncing off the white marble tombstones around him. And, because he was always surrounded by people, when alive, it gives me comfort to know that someone comes here to visit him and tend to his grave.

I place the vase in front of the headstone. Maybe, I think, his mother will fill it with flowers and be happy to know that someone else loved her son enough to come here. I stand at the graveside for a while, thinking of how Luis threw his life away so carelessly, yet fought so hard to hold on to it at the end.

And then I walk away, back through the pale grey gates, to my car. I pass an elderly man, clutching a bouquet of flowers and dressed up for his visit, in a pale, crisply ironed shirt and trousers. We acknowledge each other with a respectful nod. The cemetery feels oddly alive – a reminder that for the well loved, death is never the end.

I drive back over the viaduct, away from Amor, feeling sad but pleased that I've kept the promise I made to myself a year ago. I always knew that I would come here one day. And now that I have, it feels as if an important part of my journey has come to an end.

Arriving back at the hotel, I hear shrieks of laughter and shouting from the nearby bridge, where some local schoolboys have gathered. Nut brown and dressed in colourful shorts, they dive into the deep green channel of water that runs parallel to our hotel, and then resurface like seals, their black hair glistening in the sunshine.

In the dark hotel room, Ari and Biff are watching a movie, *Ted*, on my iPad. Ari is giggling and I swear Biff is grinning too.

'Ted reminds me of you,' says my niece.

'What, a swearing, pot-smoking teddy bear? Thanks a lot,' I say, kicking off my flip-flops.

'He drives like you,' Ari replies.

'You spoil me with these compliments,' I say. 'Why don't we go for a swim?'

'What, now?' says Ari. 'It's almost time for dinner.'

'Yes, why not?'

Biff, of course, is already at the door, his tail wagging and ready to go.

We run down to the river, in swimsuits and sarongs, as other hotel guests are arriving on the terrace for dinner. Ari dives fearlessly in from the bridge, while I edge my way in, over pebbles that are as cold and slippery as ice cubes in a glass of water.

Beside me, Biff scrambles across the mossy stones, before pushing off with his paws and swimming smoothly towards the middle of the river. He turns around as if to say, 'What are you waiting for?'

I brace myself and push into the water, the shock of the cold, as painful as a slap in the face, bringing the present into sharp focus. I don't stay in there long, but it's worth the pain for the pleasure of getting out.

Later, sitting on the terrace with a glass of wine, as a curtain of orange-pink light draws the day to a close, I drink a silent toast to Luis. It is, after all, thanks to him that I found this beautiful backwater of Portugal.

Chapter 13

Puke

OUR LAST NIGHT in Portugal is spent in the university town of Coimbra, a forty-five-minute drive north of Leiria, where I am hoping to meet up with my Portuguese friend, Magda.

Magda, the world's most glamorous wielder of a mop and duster, was a lynchpin of my life in France until she decided to move back to Portugal to be with her boyfriend (who was actually someone else's husband at the time).

Naturally, I'm keen to know how things have worked out for her. I called her several times before leaving for Portugal, but her mobile appeared to have been cut off, which is pretty typical of Magda, who always had trouble paying her bills.

However, all is not lost. Carmen, our mutual friend in Villiers, has given me Magda's address, which is apparently next door to a convent. The nuns, I think, are probably in shock. I picture my friend, tottering past in her tight white jeans, shattering the silence of the cloisters, or livening up evening prayer, by yelling and swearing into her phone.

Just as Luis led me to Leiria, it was Magda who made me want to visit Coimbra. She had always been lavish in her praise for the city, speaking fondly of the nightlife, the nearby beaches and the fact that it was possible to have cake with your espresso. Magda couldn't understand why the bars and cafés in rural France served only alcohol and coffee and no snacks. I couldn't understand it either, until I realised that the French look down on *le snacking* and believe that eating should be restricted to proscribed hours.

I've booked us into a French chain hotel on the riverbank, mainly because it is dog friendly. But there are different inter-pretations of 'dog friendly' I discover, when the receptionist hands me a three-page contract to sign, listing all the things that four-legged guests can and cannot do. Biff is not allowed to loiter in reception or enter any of the public rooms. He must be muzzled in public at all times and a €100 deposit will be deducted from my credit card to cover cleaning, if he leaves behind any visible signs of his stay. I'm tempted to cover his ears as the receptionist runs through the possible infringements of the contract, as I know he'd be mortified.

The pet liability form turns out to be a bit of a cheek, given that when we get to the room, the carpet is already alarmingly stained – whether by guests of the four-legged or the biped kind, I do not know. But since I don't want Biff to be blamed – he looks as horrified as I am by the carpet – I ask the receptionist to send someone up to record the damage. Such is life when you are travelling with a dog.

Coimbra, which is twinned with Aix-en Provence in France, is a city of white buildings and red roofs, climbing up in layers from the Mondego River. It is home to one of the oldest universities in Europe, along with a profusion of convents and monasteries, two cathedrals and some apparently lovely botan-ical gardens. But all of this will have to wait for a future visit, as we have arrived too late in the afternoon to do Coimbra's attractions justice. In any case, having visited so many holy places in the last few weeks, I think both Ari and I might be suffering from cloister-fatigue.

As we wander towards the centre of town, I'm convinced that we will bump into Magda wobbling over the cobbles in her high heels, preceded by her magnificent cleavage and raucous laugh. Even when she came to clean my house, she dressed as if for a nightclub in plunging tops, tight jeans and gold hoop earrings, with her lips and nails painted dahlia-red. In Coimbra there are many girls who look like her, with long dark hair and tidily fitting clothes, but none of them is Magda.

Her apartment is in a modern block on the other side of the river, but there is no reply when I press the button on the intercom. Eventually, an older Portuguese woman appears at the window of an adjacent apartment and tells us that Magda does not live there anymore. 'She did not stay very long. And she leave in a hurry,' she says. Oh dear.

Over dinner at a café in the main square, I plan our journey home. The idea is to spend as little time as possible in Spain. My initial thought is to breathe deeply, hold tight to the steering wheel, say some Hail Marys and race across in a day, but, since driving in Spain requires a state of hyper-alertness, I decide to break the journey in Salamanca.

The next morning, we leave beautiful Coimbra feeling that we have barely made its acquaintance and follow the road signs for Fuentes de Oñoro, close to the Spanish border. En route, I stop at a Pingo Doce supermarket and buy more bottles of Vine Verde than is seemly for a Sunday afternoon.

'Gifts for friends in France,' I explain, feeling conspicuous as the bottles roll past the multi-lingual cashier.

'You have made some very good choices,' she replies, confirming my belief that the Portuguese are not only blessed with impressive language skills, but also buckets of charm. As

I cram the bottles of wine into the boot of the car, it occurs to me that taking wine back to France is a bit like taking corals to Queensland. But I leave Portugal a committed Lusophile – a label that sounds as though it ought to carry a prison sentence, but in fact denotes someone who loves Portugal and its people.

As we cross the invisible border back into Spain, there is one thing that I don't understand: how can a country that produces so many excellent products – from leather sandals to ceramics, textiles and wines (as well as the cork for bottling them) and a significant proportion of Europe's organic vegetables – possibly be the third most indebted country in the EU? Portugal, unlike the UK, still makes things, lovely things that people want to buy. I just don't get it.

'Maybe the people who run Portugal are just really crap with money,' suggests Ari. I don't know the answer, but the people are hardworking, charming and educated. Portugal deserves to be sitting on piles of national cash, rather than going cap-in-hand to its European neighbours for financial help.

Our hotel in Salamanca is the most elusive of our trip. It is bang in the centre of the city, but there is no car access unless you're in the kind of four-wheel-drive vehicle – I'm sure I've seen Jeremy Clarkson in one – that can climb over bollards and bistro tables. So we park in Barcelona, or that's how far away it feels, and make our way on foot, dragging our various pieces of kit across a large plaza and assorted cobbled streets. I like to think that one of the many things that I've taught my niece on this trip, is the importance of travelling light.

Our hotel room, when we get to it, boasts one arresting feature: a transparent bathroom door, which appears to have been precisely designed and positioned to showcase... the loo. *What the hell?* says Ari, eyes wide.

I log onto a review site to find out how this feature has gone down with other guests. Answer: not well. As one traveller, who had a romantic break spoiled by the transparent door, complained, 'It put quite a strain on things.' Well, quite.

Otherwise, Salamanca proves to be a pleasant place to spend an evening, its streets buzzing with people in beautifully pressed clothes, taking part in the pre-dinner parade. Ari and I watch them from a café on the Plaza Major. It feels as if we are in the classic postcard shot of Salamanca, which shows the eighteenth-century square – apparently one the most beautiful in Spain – lit up and golden, against a cobalt sky.

I'm a little nervous when I hand over my credit card to pay our bill, but the waiter doesn't throw up his hands in horror or try to march me to a cash dispenser, so in that sense Salamanca is a definite improvement on Comillas.

The following morning, we drag our stuff back across the cobbles to the car. I'm relieved to find that no one has stolen my Taiwanese copies of *Tout Sweet* or bottles of Vinho Verde, which gleam like pale green stones of peridot, in the boot. And then we set off on the remaining 450 kilometres of our journey across Spain, towards the border with France.

On Spanish roads, just five kilometres can seem like a lifetime. But the first half of our journey passes without incident. We even find a service station where, mindful of our experience in northern Spain, we stock up on diesel, Diet Coke and... an Eminem CD. I know this is a bad idea – I will, after all, have to listen to it – but Arianna convinces me to buy it as it contains one of the rapper's most iconic songs, 'Puke'.

What the hell? I think as I add it to the pile of chocolate bars and bottles of Coke on the counter. (My standards have really fallen; when I get home, I'll have to do a year-long detox to recover from this trip.) When I produce my card to pay, the assistant pulls a face and asks if I can pay for the fuel and other goods in cash. I don't know how Spain got itself into an economic mess – though it cannot help that a significant proportion of the nation goes to sleep for several hours in the middle of the day – but it's not a good sign when even petrol stations are desperate for hard currency.

And so I find myself driving across a particularly flat and arid stretch of Spanish motorway, listening to Eminem pretending to throw up, interspersed with such lines as 'I f***ing hate you'. Arianna explains that some believe that he wrote the song – if one can call it that – about his childhood sweetheart and mother of his child.

'What do you think, Auntie Carrie?'

'It's pretty… sick,' I reply.

'You mean "sick" as in "cool"?'

'As in, I don't think it's good karma to hate people or rant about a former girlfriend like that,' I say, before embarking on my favourite theory, namely that everything you do in life, good or bad, eventually comes back to you with double the force. It's far from an original train of thought, but Ari makes a decent show of being interested.

'The thing is Ari,' I say, warming to my theme. 'In life, you are going to meet many people who will be jealous of you, or who for no apparent reason feel bitter towards you, or try to do you harm. But you must not take it personally, as you don't know the inner demons or turmoil that makes them act that way.'

'What if they act like a real jerk?'

'Wish them love and peace.'

'Seriously, Auntie Carrie?' says Ari, pressing replay on 'Puke'.

'Yup. We are all of us, on this journey through life together and… *what the hell*?'

My lecture is cut short by an alarming development: in front of us, the motorway has been coned down to one lane with a speed limit of 50 km/hr. But as I glance in my mirror before braking, I see a truly terrifying sight: a black BMW coming down the fast lane at around 160 km/hr, which pretty soon will have nowhere to go, other than into the back of my car. The additional peril is that a slip road joins the motorway just where the cones begin.

I immediately switch on my hazard lights to warn him to slow down, but the BMW driver makes no attempt to slow down. The f***wit is, I realise, planning to shave into the single lane ahead of me. I have a split second to weigh up the options: accelerate into the coned lane at double the restricted speed limit to (hopefully) stop him crashing into us, or slam on the brakes so he that he can overtake before the cones.

Panicked, I opt for braking hard, which allows him to cut in front of us with millimetres to spare. Shocked at his reckless stupidity, I blast my horn and stab the air with a furious two-digit salute. There are no words to describe the anger I feel.

'F*****g, f*****g idiot,' I shout. 'You could have f*****g killed us, you MORON.'

'*What the hell*?' says Ari, eyes and mouth wide open. 'I cannot believe that he did that.'

I am shaking with rage. This idiot driver, in aviator shades and too much hair gel, has endangered some of the most precious things in my life: my dog, my niece and my cache of green wine. As the sound of Eminem puking fills the car again, I totally get how the rapper felt when he wrote those lyrics. I feel visceral hatred towards the moron in front.

But oh my God, it gets worse. Far from feeling remorse at having almost killed us, he decides to have another go, slamming on his brakes and forcing me to stop abruptly for a second time, with no time to check if there is a car behind me.

'Oh my God,' cries Arianna. 'What the hell is he doing?'

Answer: using his car like a dangerous weapon. Now he is alongside us, driving down the hard shoulder. He winds down his window, menacing us with his fist, a time bomb of testosterone and grotesque stupidity. I can see that he is young and dressed in a black T-shirt and leather jacket. I'm pretty sure he will be wearing copious amounts of Hugo Boss aftershave and that he's got a small... brain. (My other assumptions about him are not fit to print here.) He then pulls back in front of us and stops abruptly, so that I'm forced to hit the brakes for a third time.

'Oh boy. He's trying to kill us,' says Arianna.

'Take down his number plate, so that we can report him. And try and find the emergency number for the Spanish police,' I shout. In the UK this kind of behaviour usually earns a prison sentence and lead story in *The Daily Mail*. In Spain, it probably passes for normal driving.

But the ordeal is not over yet. When the motorway returns to two lanes, the maniac proceeds to play a dangerous game of undertaking and overtaking, driving alongside us, then pulling in front and forcing me to brake sharply, oblivious to the pile-up he could cause, should someone come flying around the bend of the curving motorway behind us.

Fortunately, no one does, or else I would not be writing this. Eventually, he tires of this terrifying game of motorway roulette and drives on, ready to ruin someone else's day or, possibly, their life. His reckless, macho driving has left me shaking with rage. It's a few minutes before I can speak.

'I think he might have been a drug dealer,' says Ari. 'He looked like one. And he was driving a brand-new BMW.'

'I don't give a f**k what he is. If we find him with his BMW wrapped around his stupid neck further up the motorway, I won't be stopping to call an ambulance,' I reply.

Arianna types furiously into her phone, probably something along the lines of, 'Aunt is raging again. This time almost got us killed.' I can imagine her friends lying by their pools in the Caribbean, 'LOL-ing' and waiting for the next exciting instalment of our trip.

'Perhaps you could take a break from Facebook and try and find the number for the police,' I say, while realising that even if we could get through, the chances of them doing anything are non-existent. In fact, Spanish police seem non-existent, per se. Probably Spain can't afford them. In France, the gendarmes descend in squads on key tourist routes and are often to be found lurking behind bushes with speed cameras – how fondly, I think of them now – but in Spain we haven't seen a single cop.

'So,' says Ari, looking up. 'What were you saying about karma and sending out love and peace?'

'They should bring back the death penalty for tailgaters and morons who endanger the lives of others,' I rant. 'Ideally, public disembowelling. And in the case of that moron in the BMW, I'd like to do it myself.'

We continue in silence, counting down the kilometres back to France, while I replay the incident over and over in my head. But our nightmare is not over yet. The final 200 kilometres of our Iberian trip coincide with the Spanish lunch hour. At around 2 pm, presumably as blood sugar levels on the motorway start to fall, the driving starts to get even more lawless and unpredictable. It's a dizzying mix of under- and overtaking and tailgating. It feels as if everyone is taking part in some crazed dance, with a ton of fast-moving metal as a dance partner.

And then, in the hour after lunch – possibly because alcohol has been added to the madness – it ramps up to a whole new level of crazy. At one point, we see an ancient Spanish petrol tanker pelting along, comfortably over the speed limit, while straddling two lanes of the perilously curving motorway.

'Wow,' says Arianna, eyes shining with excitement as she captures it all on her phone for the enjoyment of her friends in Cayman (complete with soundtrack of her aunt 'cussing and swearing'). 'This is insane.'

The day when cars drive themselves cannot come too soon. Compounding the misery of the Spanish motorway experience is the lack of signage. You'd think that France might deserve a mention as we approach San Sebastián, but no. As far as the Spanish are concerned, France does not exist. So I follow instead the signs to Irun, a Spanish border town, pronounced 'I run' – as in 'I run from Spain'.

By now my nerves are so taut that they could be plucked with a plectrum. The fact that we decided not to stop for lunch – yup, we're *that* keen to leave Spain – does not help the situation. I leave the motorway too soon, but when I see the tollbooth ahead, I figure that someone should at least be able to point us in the general direction.

'France?' I say, hopefully, as I draw up at the kiosk to pay. The man inside looks at me blankly. Arianna tries in Spanish, but he really, truly, staggeringly, does not know where France is.

'You know, that big blob on a map of Europe, right next to your country?' I mutter.

It's the last straw. Could the Spanish authorities really not field someone at the border with a few language skills, or a grasp of basic geography? It's not as if we are asking the way to Belarus or Moldova.

And so I'm forced to rely on 'intuitive driving' to get us back to France. Stopping at a petrol station to establish where we are, I don't bother asking. Instead, I buy a bottle of water and look at what is written on the receipt: Irun.

For the record, France is within spitting distance of here, but after performing several circuits of the Spanish border town, we cannot find a single sign for it. In Irun, the McDonald's is better signposted than the country on its doorstep.

Eventually, we come to a roundabout and see a small sign – no bigger than an A4 sheet of paper, and of the makeshift kind that normally advertises car boot sales – that says '*Francia*'. It sums up everything that is frustrating about northern Spain. Could the authorities really not have found the wherewithal to put up a road sign saying 'France', the name by which a significant portion of the world population knows it? Maybe when Angela Merkel has finished dealing with Europe's other problems, she can organise a whip-round to buy some decent road signs for Spain? And maybe even a traffic cop or two.

Finally, we limp across the invisible border. We are towed into port by signs for the McDonald's in Saint-Jean-de-Luz, where I fall upon a Filet-O-Fish, fries and a bucket of Coke with an enthusiasm that terrifies me. Not only have I failed to teach my niece to love kale and quinoa, but I seem to be turning into a teenager, eating junk food, listening to Eminem and calling Biff 'dude'. Before I know it I'll have spots, and a poster of Harry Styles on my bedroom wall. Arianna, meanwhile, perks up noticeably as we head to Biarritz for the night. Me, I'm just glad that we made it out of Spain with everyone alive.

One of the things that I've learned during our road trip – apart from a full set of rapper insults and swear words – is to appreciate just how dog-friendly France is.

We spend the night before my book signing in Eymet, in a hotel just outside Saint-Émilion, which is super-prime Dordogne. It is a real relief, as it was in Biarritz the night before, not to have to sign a dog-disclaimer form before Biff can put his paws through the door. Nor are we hit with an unexpected 'Biff tax', as I nicknamed the surcharges levied at every possible opportunity in Spain, for travelling with a pet.

Saint-Émilion is a pretty hilltop village surrounded by vines – neat rows of them for as far as the eye can see. Its cobbled streets are filled with shops selling Bordeaux's best-known product – for which, incidentally, you pay a premium of around ten per cent for buying so close to source – along with everything you could need for the professional care and consumption of the fermented grape.

Given that Saint-Émilion is known for producing some of the best wines in the world, I'm certain that the cuisine will be of an equally high standard. After all, if you can't count on getting a decent dinner in the most famous wine village in France, where in the world can you?

A little later, tucking into a piece of grey, factory-farmed flesh – which on the menu masqueraded as chicken in a fancy-pants sauce – I realise that it was a mistake to choose one of the restaurants on the main square. The assumption by local business owners seems to be that the first-rate setting will blind customers to the third-rate food.

It feels frankly disrespectful that Saint-Émilion can serve up such poor quality fare, no doubt gambling on the fact that tourists can't be counted on for repeat business. Given the French love of regulations – for everything from line dancing to the start and end dates of the January sales – it seems to me that the authorities are missing a trick here. They should send a crack team of inspectors to Saint-Émilion, *tout de suite*, to supervise the restaurants that are doing so much to trash the reputation of French cuisine.

Despite the beautiful setting my niece looks bored. I put this down to the lack of surfers. Our fellow diners are mostly young

French families and the affluent sixty-plus set. I'm heartened to see a significant contingent of Chinese, which bodes well for the possibility of offloading the Cantonese and Taiwanese versions of *Tout Sweet* in Eymet tomorrow.

Back in our hotel room, I open the window and gaze out at the vines swaying softly in the gloaming, while Arianna calls her father. I try to imagine my brother's reaction when she tells him that I almost got us killed in a bout of road rage on a Spanish motorway yesterday.

The incident has been playing on my mind. I have always, if I'm honest, been an impatient person with a low tolerance for incompetence, injustice and stupidity. And while I'm not quite in the league of Jeremy Clarkson – I have never lamped anyone – I can see that I do have anger issues. I couldn't have prevented the encounter with the speeding maniac, but in my uncontrollable rage, I made matters worse with an angry, two-fingered gesture, further endangering the lives of my niece and my dog. Yesterday, I earned my epithet, 'the dangerous aunt'.

I close the window, the better to eavesdrop on Arianna's conversation. Instead of relaying the details of the motorway incident, she is making the kind of promises that I imagine any parent would be overjoyed to hear.

'Dad, when I get home, I promise I'm going to ditch most of my friends, especially the ones you don't like. And I'm going to work really hard at school...' she is saying.

There is obviously a stunned silence at the end of the phone because she continues, 'Really, Dad. I mean it. I'm going to work my ass off when I get back, and learn French so that I can come and live in Biarritz.'

I allow myself a silent pat on the back. *Job done*, I think, proud that our tour of Iberia's churches and burger bars has had such an inspirational effect (though I suspect that this turnaround is mostly attributable to Biarritz – and specifically, its bronzed surfing community).

'Dad said to say "Hello",' says Ari, putting down her phone.

'Was he pleased when you told him that you are going to work hard?' I ask.

'You bet. He said that I sounded like a different person. And that the trip was money well spent.'

Hmm. It was mostly *my* money that was well spent but I refrain from saying so. Instead, I feel grateful to my niece for keeping the road-rage episode a secret between us – and her 500 or so Facebook friends.

'What was your favourite part of the trip?' I ask.

'Probably driving around trying to find our hotel each night.'

'You're kidding me?'

'No, it was fun. I really enjoyed it. That and being in the car with you, driving between different places.'

I scan her face for signs of sarcasm but can't see any. It seems that for my niece, the old adage that it is better to travel than to arrive holds true.

'I'm like a dog,' Arianna is saying. 'I loved being in the car and driving along with my head out of the window.'

Ha! It seems that my initial theory, that teenagers are just like dogs, was spot on.

'What was your favourite thing?' she asks.

'Well, it wasn't the food or the Spanish driving,' I say.

With hindsight, my favourite part of the journey was stuffing the various boxes, bags, suitcases and baskets into the car each morning, ready to depart. I am never happier than when I'm packing up to leave, I've realised. This was particularly the case in northern Spain.

It is the drive to the hillside town of Eymet the following morning, however, that provides my best memory of the trip.

We opt for the scenic route; travelling up through the vineyards of the Dordogne in the early-morning sunshine, the windows down and the air filled with the sweet, green scent of the vines. It takes just over an hour, as we roll through the back roads, singing along to Rihanna's 'Man Down'.

I enjoy the drive so much that I am almost disappointed when we reach Eymet, which is possibly the prettiest medieval town that I've visited in France. Many of my compatriots think the same, for one-third of the population of the *bastide* (fortified) town, is British.

We park as close to the square as possible and ferry boxes of books to the organic wine store, whose lovely Irish owner has agreed to let me and another local writer, Peter Hoskins, set up a table in the covered walkway outside her shop. Peter, a charming man and ex-RAF pilot, is already there. Although there is no obvious link between our works – he writes about the battles of the Black Prince; I write about the battles I've fought with French artisans – this is the second signing that we've done together.

Our mutual friend Eileen who lives in Eymet, whose idea it was for us to do a joint signing, arrives with cappuccinos. (It seems that an enterprising Brit has imported the concept of takeaway coffee – even better, made with fresh rather than UHT milk – to the medieval town.) Peter, meanwhile, has persuaded the neighbouring pizza restaurant to lend us a couple of tables. We lay out our respective books as people start to pour into the market, and then sit back and wait for the buying frenzy to begin.

The only problem is that no one comes… at least not for my books. Peter, on the other hand, is attracting quite a crowd. Pretty soon he has a line of people wanting to talk to him about the 2000-kilometre walk that he did for *In the Steps of the Black Prince*. More to the point, some of them are buying, even at €25 a pop. I can only watch in awe. Under the table, Biff gives a loud 'Woof' as if to remind people that it's not all about Peter and his Prince, but also, I suspect, because he would rather be roaming around the market with everyone else, sniffing the cooked meats and pies, and other tempting products.

Where, I wonder, are the hordes of Chinese customers (or indeed any customers)? I flatter myself that the people of the Dordogne have already bought my books. Or maybe they are just not interested in the goings-on in the Poitou. Despite the lack of sales, it's not all bad news. Two lovely readers have travelled from the coast to say 'Hello'; others arrive with copies of books that they have already bought and would like me to sign.

By lunchtime, I have sold a total of three books, which barely covers the tip that I leave in the pizza restaurant for the loan of the tables. In terms of sales, it is my least successful signing ever. In terms of memories, it is one of the best. After saying goodbye to Peter and Eileen, and thanking the owner of the organic wine shop – which also involves buying a case of wine to add to the collection in the boot (any excuse) – Arianna and I ferry the boxes of unsold books to the car one last time.

The final leg of our journey feels like the longest. It is less than 250 kilometres, but takes over five hours since, once we are north of the Dordogne, the route crosses one of the most desolate patches of France. We pass through characterless towns and villages, bereft of shops, cafés and all signs of human life.

It is early evening when we pull into the square in Villiers. It feels as if we have been away forever. Among the little crowd of people enjoying aperitifs at the café on the corner, I see two familiar faces: Matt and Zoe. They both look browner and fitter than when we left: Zoe in a pale green sundress and over-sized sunglasses; Matt in a dark T-shirt and matching stubble. They are perfect snapshot of 'the good life' in France.

'Wasn't that your friend?' says Ari, as I look away.

'I didn't see,' I lie, driving past Pierre-Antoine's boutique, and thinking how weird it is that Matt and Zoe should be the first people I encounter. It is almost as if they were waiting for me. Once home, I throw open the shutters at Mason Coquelicot, unpack the car and water the plants in the courtyard. Then just as we are about to switch on the TV and catch up with the news, the sky above Villiers explodes.

I've no idea why fireworks are being set off in August, but we drop everything and run across the square and down towards the river and the municipal park, where all outdoor celebrations take place. I follow my niece's long brown legs, as Biff's paws pound the pavement beside me. Standing in the crowd gathered by the lake is Pierre-Antoine, who seems delighted to see us. He and his shop have had a good summer it seems, and the pastel-coloured biker jackets have sold out several times over.

As for the fireworks, they're from the cache that the *mairie* had bought for the cancelled July 14th celebrations. And so, Ari's last night in France culminates in sparkles and bangs – glittery bursts of palm fronds, chrysanthemums, waterfalls and willow trees, and trails of silver and gold stars in the sky. It seems like a fitting end to our trip.

*

'Got time for one last Coke?' I ask. Arianna shakes her head. We are standing in the departure hall at Heathrow, having checked in early for her flight. The truth is that she has plenty of time, but armed with some leftover dollars from the money her father gave her, my niece wants to go. And who can blame her? Who knows what shopping possibilities lie on the other side?

I throw my arms around her. 'It's been wonderful,' I say. 'Sorry about the road rage.'

My plan was to broaden my niece's mind and leave a lasting impression. Unfortunately, the impression left, after nearly two months in my company, is that of a mad woman.

'Thank you, Auntie Carrie. It's been a fantastic summer,' she says, avoiding the subject of road rage. 'I'm really going to miss you and Biff.' And then she is gone.

I linger as she heads through passport control, wondering if she will look back. She doesn't. And why would she? At her age, the only place to look is forward. But I like to think that she will never forget the summer that she spent with her godmother and a little black dog, raging around the roads of Iberia.

As I wait for the Heathrow Express to be swept for incendiary devices by a team of stern-looking people in high-vis jackets, I have a small insight into how a parent must feel when their child leaves home. But I cheer up at the thought of Biff waiting for me back in France. The beauty of a dog is that they are never going to pack up their belongings and head off to a new life without you. Nor do you have to worry that they'll fail their exams, fall in with a bad crowd or start smoking pot.

As the train pulls into Paddington Station, I'm checking a social media account and responding to a comment that a reader has jokingly made. 'I hope you don't think I am stalking you,' she has posted on a public forum.

'I don't flatter myself that anyone would stalk me,' I type.

This is followed almost immediately by a private message from Matt: 'I would,' he has written.

'You can't be serious?' I type back, for even I can see that this counts as flirting of the most overt kind. 'You're married.'

'Yes. And yes,' he replies.

Chapter 14

Chased

I ARRIVE BACK in France in time for a heatwave. When I step out of the house with Biff in the morning, it feels as if I am walking into a wall of heat. It presses down from a stark blue sky and seeps into the house through the thin glass windowpanes. In the afternoon, with the sun at its most potent, the village is as still and silent as when it snows.

But late in the evening, Villiers comes alive, thanks largely to the Café du Commerce, which is pulling in quite a crowd, most of whom seem to be friends of Basile, the owner. Guy, the waiter, however, has disappeared. His replacement is a skinny chap with a goatee beard, who is much more efficient. He's there when I go for coffee in the morning; and late in the evening, he sits with Basile on the balcony above the café, smoking.

A couple of days after my return, I bump into Zoe, who is coming out of the Intermarché. 'Hurrah, you're back!' she says, putting down her straw basket for the obligatory kisses.

'Yes,' I say, thinking of the 'stalker' message that her husband sent, and feeling a horrible mix of guilt and embarrassment, even though I have done nothing wrong.

'Where are you off to?' she asks, hands on slim hips.

'I'm taking Biff down to the lake for a walk,' I reply.

'Do you fancy an aperitif?'

'What, now?'

'Why not? *Carpe diem* and all that. We had good news while you were away. We got the planning permission for the barn.'

'Congratulations. So how long before you move in?'

'Oh, ages. We've decided to extend the lease on the house in the village for another six months. Hey, why don't I drop this shopping home and I'll meet you in the Commerce for a glass of wine? I want to hear all about your trip.'

'Well, actually...'

'See you in five minutes,' she says, with a grin.

'Alright then,' I say, but she is already walking away.

I wait for Zoe at a table outside the café. She is much longer than five minutes – her timekeeping is on a par with mine – but I entertain myself by reading the new English version of the menu, which appears to be the work of Google Translate rather than an actual English-speaking person. How else to explain dishes such as 'lamb nuts' (presumably medallions of lamb) and 'a slut, slow-cooked in its own juices'?

I look up and see Zoe walking across the square, followed by several admiring glances. She is dressed in the shortest of denim shorts and a ruffled blue top, and as she sits down, I notice that her toenails are painted a coordinating arctic blue.

'Matthew wanted to join us but I told him that it was girls only,' she says, placing a large carrier bag on the table.

'Ah,' I say, though I fear it comes out as, 'aagh'.

'Sorry, not to have been in touch while you were away. I've been wrapped up in ribbons,' she says. For a second, I think that she means it literally. She is, after all, a textile designer. Or maybe she means it in a *Fifty Shades of Grey* way. Then I realise that it is just a delightful way of saying how busy she is.

How clever, I think, to make yourself sound like an expensively wrapped gift. I file the phrase away for my own future use, while thinking that there are probably quite a few men who would like to see Zoe tied up in ribbons.

'I've been going back and forth between here and London for work and it's all been... exhausting,' she explains. 'Oh, and before I forget... a little present for Biff.'

She hands me the big carrier bag. Inside is a woollen dog blanket, mink-coloured with white paw prints. 'Oh, how fabulous,' I say. 'Did you design it yourself?'

She nods.

'But what has Biff done to deserve this?'

'Oh, it's just a factory sample from a new range of pet furnishings. I thought he might like it.'

The waiter arrives to take our order. When Zoe asks what white wines they have by the glass, he runs through over half a dozen of them, briefly describing their attributes and principal notes, all from memory. He is way more on the ball than his predecessor.

'Goodness,' says Zoe, once we've ordered. 'They have more wines by the glass than most London restaurants would offer. And who'd have thought that a little village like ours would have its very own gay bar?'

'A gay bar?'

'Don't say you haven't noticed?' she says. I glance around. There is an elderly English couple on the terrace and a French family with two young children.

'I don't understand.'

'I mean in the evenings,' says Zoe. 'You probably haven't noticed because you've been away, but the clientele is almost entirely male.'

'But why would Basile be running a gay bar in Villiers? There isn't much of a target audience. And anyway, he's married.'

'Married, yes,' says Zoe. 'But how often do you see his wife? I'm pretty certain Basile sleeps in the apartment above the café most nights.'

'I think the new waiter lives there, now that Guy has gone.'

'Exactly, and Basile is usually with him,' she replies.

'Guy certainly seems to have disappeared quickly.'

'Lover's tiff, *peut-être?*' whispers Zoe, as the waiter returns with two glasses of Sancerre.

'Maybe he was just sacked for being hopeless?' I say, remembering the haphazard way that he served customers and the argument that I overheard on Bastille Day. 'Anyway, I don't really care about Basile's private life. I'm just glad that we've finally got a fabulous restaurant in the village.'

'*Absolument,*' says Zoe clinking my glass. 'Cheers!' She leans towards me, looking conspiratorial. 'There certainly seems to be a lot of latent passion simmering in the French countryside,' she says. 'Have you noticed how badly some expats behave out here, ditching their husbands or wives and having affairs? It's as if people lose their inhibitions on the ferry over. And the over fifties are the worst.'

'Yes, I've noticed that some people hit fifty and go… slightly wild,' I say, nervous as to where the conversation is going.

'Matthew turns fifty next year,' says Zoe. 'Perhaps I should be worried?'

'Um,' I say, unsure how to reply. 'How long have you been married?'

'Five years.'

'Did you meet through work?'

'No, his ex-wife was a friend of mine.'

'Oh,' I say. 'Awkward.'

'Yes. It was.'

'Are you still friends with his ex-wife?'

'Of course not. Though Matthew has to keep things civil for the sake of their daughters.'

'I can imagine,' I say, slightly taken aback by her candour.

'At least his daughters are grown-up. And anyway, things will change when we have a child of our own.'

'Oh, you're...?'

'Pregnant? No not yet, but we're working on it.'

'Well, fingers crossed,' I say. 'And how's the barn?'

'I think Matthew's putting the foundations in at the moment, but I must admit I switch off when he starts talking about the nuts and bolts of it. I'm only interested when it gets to the fun bit – choosing the colours for the walls and fabrics.'

'Ah, I miss all that,' I say. 'It's so much fun doing up a house.'

'So tell me, I'm dying to know. How was your trip?'

'Well, Portugal was great; northern Spain, not so great.'

'I can't wait to read about it. It's for a new book, right?'

'Um, yes.'

'Matthew, who rarely reads anything other than architectural magazines, loved your books. He couldn't put them down.' She pushes her sunglasses back on her head, and looks at me. 'I'm not a big reader myself, but I'm taking your first book on the plane back to London next week. By the way, I hope you don't mind my asking but I was wondering if you would be a darling and give me a lift to Poitiers airport on Monday?'

'Yes, of course. Is Matthew away?'

'No, but he has to be on site because some building materials are being delivered, so I thought it would be easier if I asked you. And of course, anytime you need to go to the airport, I'd be happy to return the favour.'

'No problem. Just let me know what time to pick you up.'

When we go inside the café to pay, Basile is behind the bar chatting with a group of friends and barely acknowledges us. 'Is he ever in the kitchen?' whispers Zoe as we wait for the waiter to reappear and give us the bill.

'I'm beginning to wonder that too,' I reply.

'Well, thanks again for Biff's blanket,' I say, when we reach the *boulangerie* at the corner of my road.

'You're welcome. So which house is yours?' she asks.

'It's the one with the pale blue shutters.'

'Coolio. Speak very soon.'

I head home having learned quite a bit about Zoe. She is open, gossipy and prone to over-sharing – all the qualities that I love and admire in a friend. The fact that she is a self-confessed husband stealer is something that I decide to overlook. After all, it's not as if I have anything to fear on that front.

The next day, a Saturday, I drive over to the Intermarché in the blazing heat of mid afternoon to buy some diesel. Everyone is behind closed shutters, slumped, I imagine, in a post-lunch torpor; and the streets around my village are deserted. But as I pull out of the square, a blue police van appears in my rear-view mirror, its blue light flashing and siren wailing. 'Must be pretty serious,' I think, slowing down so that it can overtake.

But it doesn't overtake. It stays right behind my car. Jeez, I think. I was tailgated around Spain and Portugal; now here I am in France, being tailgated by the police. I turn right, and the police van does likewise, driving really close to my rear bumper. Irritated, I turn into the petrol station, hoping to lose the screaming blue vehicle.

To my great surprise, it swings into the petrol station, too. The police van, I realise to my horror, is chasing *me*. As three stern-faced gendarmes jump out and surround my car, I assume that it's a case of mistaken identity. Perhaps an *Anglaise* in a nearby village has tried to murder her husband – it has been known – and is now on the run. Terrified, I get out to face the French cops, while Biff cowers behind the driver's seat and refuses to leave the car.

As the gendarmes come running towards me, I even consider throwing my hands in the air, in surrender. 'Madame,' shouts one of two robustly built female cops, both barely out of their teens. 'You have just committed a serious offence.'

'Really?' I say, incredulous. 'What have I done?'

'You did not stop at a white line.'

I am dumbfounded. 'Which white line?'

'Madame, you know perfectly well which white line,' sneers the younger and scarier of the two female cops, who has badly dyed red hair and multiple nose piercings.

Eventually, I realise that she is referring to a minor junction next to the florist on the square. No one ever stops there, mainly because the road is so badly designed that you have to advance beyond the line, in order to see what is coming.

'If I didn't stop completely,' I say. 'I would have slowed down long enough to see that nothing was coming.'

'Madame, how long have you lived in France?' says the other female gendarme, with a derisory snort. It's a rhetorical question, which suggests that she knows exactly how long I've lived in France. (The rural gendarmes are surprisingly well informed as to who is living in their communities, be it naughty expats or convicted wife-murderers.)

'It was a solid white line, not a broken 'Give Way' line. You must be *seen* to stop, even if nothing is coming.'

Now it is my turn to sneer. 'I must be *seen* to stop even if nothing is coming for miles around? How long exactly must I be *seen* to stop?'

She hesitates, and then says, 'For a minimum of three seconds, Madame.'

'OK, well I'm very sorry. In future, I will stop for at least three seconds,' I say, eager to pay the fine and be done with it. But from the expressions on the gendarmes' faces, you'd think I'd been caught sneaking into the Louvre with an incendiary device. I guess I should be grateful that I'm not in handcuffs, spread-eagled on the ground.

Suddenly, I'm struck by the absurdity of the situation, not to mention the irony that I drove over 2000 kilometres to Portugal and back, with no sign of a cop when I needed one; now, here I am, enjoying the company of several on a quiet village road. Obviously, on a sleepy summer afternoon, the gendarmes have nothing better to do.

I start to laugh. 'You chased me through the village and are treating me like a terrorist because I did not stop at a white line?' I find myself saying.

Now it's the gendarmes' turn to look incredulous. The golden rule when dealing with *les flics*, as most expats know, is to smile apologetically and be as obsequious as possible.

'I'm sorry but that is absolutely ridiculous,' I continue. 'You were far more likely to cause an accident than I was. Using a siren was totally unnecessary and excessive.'

The red-haired gendarme stares at me open-mouthed. But I'm on a roll now. 'Don't you have better things to do? For example, you could stop the many drivers who tailgate on the N10 while talking into handheld mobiles?'

'Please show us your documents,' says the other female gendarme. I produce my driving licence from my wallet and then search the glove compartment of my car for my insurance certificate. Unfortunately, it is out of date.

'I'm sorry but I don't have the insurance forms with me,' I say.

'Are you saying that you haven't insured your car,' the red-haired cop says, almost quivering with excitement at the possibility of escalating the affair.

'No. That's not what I'm saying at all. Why are you putting words in my mouth? The up-to-date document is at home.'

At this point, the male gendarme intervenes, and presumably tells his colleague – whom I later discover is a trainee – to back off, because she goes and sits in the van in a sulk.

I am then sent home to fetch my insurance note. When I return, I hand over my documents and they get in their van and pore over them, while I simmer on the forecourt, in the glare of the August sun. The male gendarme eventually hands back the documents and tells me that I can look forward to a fine of €90 in the post.

That evening, I've arranged to have dinner with Delphine in the Café du Commerce.

'The ambience is lovely and the food is fantastic. You're going to love it,' I tell her, as we walk across the square. But when we arrive, the restaurant is empty apart from one table that is occupied by Basile and three male friends – this at 8 pm on a Saturday.

Basile barely raises an eyebrow as we enter. It seems a little odd for a restaurant proprietor to be so blasé about his customers. And on that point, where are the customers? The Commerce appeared to be thriving before I left for Spain. What has happened in the interval?

There are just two choices of main course: one pork dish; the other a 'butcher's cut', which is vague enough for me to worry that it might be horsemeat. The waiter is evasive when I ask what kind of animal it came from, but we both order it anyway.

'I saw your friend, Matt, in the Liberty Bookshop a couple of weeks ago,' says Delphine, as the waiter whispers something in Basile's ear. Reluctantly, the proprietor gets up and goes to the kitchen. 'He was asking about you.'

'What exactly did he ask?' I say, skewering an olive.

'He wanted to know if I'd had any news from you and did I know when you would be coming back? He was very friendly.'

'Yes, he is... very friendly. By the way, I was chased by the gendarmes this afternoon.'

Dephine's eyes widen as I recount my run-in with the police. 'Ah yes, white lines,' she says, knowingly. 'The gendarmes take them very seriously. They probably thought that, by not stopping, you were trying to escape from them.'

'Travelling at less than 25 km/hr?'

'Yes, I'm sure that this is what they thought,' says Delphine.

'I was so shaken that I think I was quite rude to them,' I continue. 'I suggested that rather than wasting time in an empty village, they should get themselves on to the N10 and monitor some of the dangerous driving there.'

Delphine's eyes widen again. '*Mon dieu*, you really said that? You were lucky they didn't arrest you.'

'For not stopping long enough at a junction?'

'No, for disrespecting the gendarmes.'

'Oh dear,' I say, suddenly seeing how much worse the situation could have been.

'Well, I have some good news,' says Delphine. 'I managed to find new homes for the Rottweilers.'

'Really?'

'Yes, I took the advice of the animal shelter and called in a dog behaviour specialist to see if it was safe to rehome them. He did some psychological tests and concluded that they are young and boisterous, but not aggressive with humans. So he said it would be OK to rehome them, so long as the new owners agreed to muzzle them in public and take them to training classes.'

'So have you found them new homes?' I ask.

'Yes. One has gone to a single lady in my village, Célia, who wanted a guard dog; the other is now living with Charles.'

'Just as you planned,' I laugh. 'You are the dog matchmaker!'

'Yes. And this story gets even better. Charles decided to take his dog, a female, to animal training classes with a company called Animal Solution.'

'Yes, I know them. I thought of taking Biff there once.' (I remember the name because it sounded alarmingly like 'final solution'.)

'So Charles went along with his dog, Betty; and at the class he met Célia, who was there with her dog, Alphonse. And of course, the Rottweilers knew each other. And now Charles and this lady have become good friends.'

'What a wonderful story.'

'It's early days yet, but I have seen them together and they both look so happy, Célia especially as she has been on her own for over ten years. She and Charles walk the Rottweilers together every morning and often have dinner together in the evenings. It is almost as if these dogs brought them together.'

'And the Rottweilers have been reunited, too,' I say. 'How lovely.'

'I'm very happy for Charles and Célia because they did a good deed in taking these dogs,' says Delphine. 'And that good deed led them to one another.'

'Life works in mysterious ways,' I say, as the waiter delivers our 'butcher's cut'. Even though we ordered the steak rare – always a good idea in France, as if you ask for it 'well-cooked' you'll be given the oldest, toughest cut in the kitchen – it looks as if it has been incinerated and comes with a big dollop of custard-coloured sauce on top.

I'm immediately suspicious when I see the thick yellow gloop. In rural restaurants, it is nearly always designed to conceal meat that's as tough as old bikers' leathers. The *frites*, meanwhile, are so limp and pale, it's as if they've had a fright. For €18.50, surely Basile could have rustled up something better than this?

'I'm so sorry,' I say to Delphine. 'When I had lunch here with Pierre-Antoine, the food was amazing.' I look around the empty restaurant and wonder what happened. This restaurant started so well and had so much promise. Where did it go wrong?

The answer soon presents itself. Basile reappears from his brief labours, holding a bottle of wine. He sits down at the next table with two of his friends. It's a little too close for comfort, to be honest. At least he doesn't ask how the food is, which is a blessing, as I'd be obliged to tell him.

Few things in life leave me speechless, but I'm staggered by what happens next. The waiter follows him out of the kitchen with four plates of delicious-looking, perfectly cooked steak and a pile of golden chips. No custard yellow sauce for Basile and his chums. The waiter then sits down to eat with them. It is quite something to see your chef and his staff tucking into something considerably superior to what they have just served you – especially at such close quarters.

As I scrape away the yellow goo, I look pointedly at Basile, but he doesn't notice. We don't bother with dessert or coffee, as we are both so taken aback.

'Zoe thinks he is running the Commerce as a private club for friends,' I say, as we leave. Delphine says nothing, but I think we both know that we won't be returning.

Back home, I log onto my social media account and find a direct message from Matt: 'Zoe in London for work next week. Would love to be invited into your courtyard! Mx'

This is so strange. Why on earth is he chasing me when he has a lovely wife? Flattered though I am, I type back: 'Sorry, v. busy. And not sure Zoe would like it.'

From today's events I draw three conclusions. Firstly, Matt is a *dragueur* – a rather fabulous French word that has several meanings, including 'minesweeper' and 'womaniser' – and to be avoided from now on. Secondly, something has gone badly wrong at the Commerce. Thirdly, and most importantly, I have to do something about the volcanic anger that flares up in me so suddenly, especially in and around moving vehicles.

I think of the passive-aggressive cab driver that drove us to the garage in Twickenham, the moron who almost killed us on the Spanish motorway, and today's run-in with the gendarmes. There is a common denominator, I realise: most of these 'raging' incidents involve cars. 'It's so funny,' Arianna observed towards the end of our road trip, 'you're this sweet little writer, but then you get behind the wheel of a car and go crazy.'

'I only get mad when dealing with morons,' I replied. But we all have to deal with morons in life; raging is not the answer. I need to 'find my chill' as my niece would say.

I subsequently learn that in France, a great deal of importance is attached to white lines. When I tell friends about my run-in with the gendarmes, they shake their heads knowingly. It seems that most of them, French and British alike, have at some point, fallen foul of the unbroken white line. One French friend stopped at one before exiting a supermarket car park, but was slapped with a €90 fine anyway, because according to the gendarmes, his wheels 'had not entirely ceased moving'.

I'm reassured to know that I am not being singled out, but it does not lessen my fear of the French police, or of the raging anger that I felt, after the chase. I have to find a way to control it before it controls me and I end up picking up litter in a high-vis jacket, just like Naomi Campbell.

Chapter 15

Guru in the Garden

ON MONDAY AFTERNOON, as agreed, I drive over to Zoe's house to take her to the airport. Nothing happens when I sound the horn, so I get out and knock on the heavy oak door. No response. I try to phone but her mobile goes to voicemail, so I send her a text – 'Hi, I'm here' – and then sit in the car growing increasingly anxious as time creeps on.

After a while, I knock on the door again, exasperated. To my surprise, Matt opens it.

'Hi,' he says, looking even more rakish than usual in a dark, long-sleeved T-shirt and jeans. His feet, I notice, are bare.

'Is Zoe there? I'm supposed to be taking her...'

'To the airport. I know. Here she is.'

Zoe appears behind him, in a pale green smock dress and silver flip-flops. Her face, tanned and glowing, is so open and guileless that it is hard to be cross with her.

'I was just about to drive off,' I say, with a frown. 'I thought you'd left already.'

'No, I'm just a little... disorganised.' She slings a canvas travel bag over her suntanned shoulder and turns to kiss Matt.

'Ciao baby. Be good,' she says, looking back before she slides into my car. He stands in the doorway, smiling as we drive off.

'You're cutting it a bit fine,' I say, annoyed that she hasn't apologised for being late.

'I always do,' she replies, with a smile as white and fleeting as a snowflake. 'I can't bear hanging around airports.'

'Well, let's hope we don't get stuck behind a tractor or a combine harvester.'

'I know. There are so many of them at the moment, rolling around the countryside and slowing everyone down while they harvest our porridge oats. How bloody dare they!'

I laugh and she reaches around to pat Biff, who is curled up behind my seat. 'Hello, lovely boy,' she says, deflecting my annoyance – but not entirely.

'I thought Matt had to be on site today?' I say.

'He did. But the delivery arrived early, so he came home for lunch,' she replies. 'He offered to take me to the airport, but I wanted to go with you so that we could have a girly catch-up. How was your weekend?'

'Eventful,' I reply, before telling her about my run-in with the gendarmes.

Gratifyingly, she laughs in all the right places before concluding, 'Tossers! It's probably because of your English licence plates.'

'More likely, it was because there was no one else around to chase,' I say. 'So how about you? How was your weekend?'

'Nowhere near as exciting as yours,' she replies. 'Matthew took me out to dinner on Saturday night, for our anniversary.'

'Anywhere nice?'

'A lovely place in Usson-du-Poitou, called the Auberge de L'Écurie. We must go some time.'

'Oh,' I say, thinking back to the night of the party at the Commerce, when Matt asked about good restaurants in the region and I recommended it. 'Well, I'm glad you liked it.'

'We loved it,' says Zoe. 'It's our new favourite restaurant.'

It's my favourite restaurant, I think, feeling suddenly protective of it.

'So, have you got lots of work meetings in London?' I ask.

'One or two, but that's not the reason I'm going back.' She turns to look at me. 'Can you keep a secret?' She doesn't wait for a reply. 'I'm going to see a fertility specialist.'

'On your own? Shouldn't Matt be going with you?'

'He's too busy. And anyway, I wouldn't want him to. Men hate that kind of stuff.'

'But surely, he's got to... play his part,' I venture.

'It's just the initial consultation. This specialist takes an holistic approach, advising on diet and stuff like that.'

'Well, good luck,' I say, glancing at my watch. We've got less than half an hour to get to the airport, before her flight closes and we're still at least twenty kilometres away. Once again, I feel a surge of annoyance. While Zoe sits there calm as a pond, in apple-coloured cotton and a bubble of candy scent, I am the one getting stressed.

'You know, there's a chance you might not make your flight,' I say, as the traffic slows on the N10.

'*Que sera, sera.* If I miss it, I'll just have to go tomorrow instead,' says Zoe, running a brush through her hair.

'There isn't a flight tomorrow. The next one is Wednesday.'

'Well, I'll take the TGV to Paris and get the Eurostar.'

'What about your appointment with the specialist?'

'It's not until Thursday.'

'Damn,' I say, as the last set of traffic lights before the airport, switches to red. 'We've got four minutes.'

'It'll be fine,' she says, casually checking her phone.

Finally, I pull up in front of the airport, where a couple of other late arrivals are rushing in with their bags. '*Merci mille fois*,' says Zoe, kissing my cheek. 'See you very soon.'

I watch as she heads towards departures, her canvas bag brushing against her bare legs. I wait a few minutes in case she is turned back at check-in, but through the glass windows I see her, the last to go through, showing her passport to the customs officials. Even if the gate had closed, she would probably have persuaded them to reopen it. She and Matt seem to have a way of getting what they want.

Gabriella calls. 'Is that you?' she shouts.

'Yes, it's me,' I shout back.

'Do you know anyone with ailments?'

'What?'

'Afflictions. I'm looking for someone with problems as I have a naturopath staying with me; a very good one. And an Indian guru,' she replies. 'They have come from their commune in California and are staying in my *gîte*. Do you know anyone who would benefit from meeting them?'

'OK,' I say, marvelling, not for the first time, at the number and breadth of her acquaintances. 'I'd like to meet them. When should I drop by?'

'Now! Come over now, as we'll be having dinner in half an hour. I'd invite you to join us but it will be lousy.'

'Lousy?'

'Yes. They only eat plants.'

As I arrive at Gabriella's house, Dolores, her housekeeper, is leaving. She grabs my hand. 'Oh my goodness, *Ka-renne*,' she declares. 'These people are amazing. They have helped my son with his spots,' she says. 'In just two days, they've disappeared.'

In the kitchen, Gabriella is preparing a salad, helped by a small blonde woman in a pale blue tunic, who radiates an enviable degree of serenity. Gabriella introduces her as Barbara, and tells me that she is a naturopath, but is also trained in conventional medicine. Looking at her beautiful, calm face I suddenly know what I'm going to consult her about: my anger. Since the confrontation with the gendarmes, I've been searching, without success, for a decent yoga class, but there is nothing within half a day's drive of my village. So if there is a naturopathic solution to rage, I'd like to hear it.

Gabriella suggests that I go into the garden to chat to Barbara. Sitting on wicker chairs in the wisteria-wrapped pergola, she listens and nods as I divulge the boiling anger that I felt on the Spanish motorway. I have always been short-changed in the patience department and had a low tolerance for stupidity and incompetence. And, in truth, I'm often a little too direct in my dealings with others. (On the plus side, I don't bear grudges and have a short memory where slights are concerned.) But where, I wonder, has this anger come from? And what can I do about it?

Barbara looks concerned, which worries me. She tells me that anger is one of the stages of grief and insists that I come back at 9.00 pm to meet Babaji, the Indian guru. 'I think you would really benefit from talking to him,' she says.

I return at the appointed hour and Barbara leads me along the path, past the rose bushes, to the *gîte* at the bottom of Gabriella's garden. An Indian man of indeterminate age – he could be late forties or he could be early seventies – is waiting for me in the doorway. He shakes my hand and pats the top of my head, as if I were a pet. His calm, wise face immediately puts me at ease.

'Let me take Biff,' says Barbara. I hand over Biff's lead and Babaji leads me into a room of simple decor, with a terracotta-tiled floor and a bed with a plain white cover.

'Please,' he says, indicating the wicker chair opposite the bed. I feel a little embarrassed, as I have no idea what I am going to say to this stranger, pleasant though he seems. It turns out that I am not required to say anything. I am here to listen. Barbara, no doubt, has prepped him, but as Babaji starts to talk in a calm and compassionate way, I am certain that he is going to tell me something useful – and possibly life-changing. He looks at me intently, as if opening all the locked filing cabinets of my mind.

There is a quiet intensity to his words and, although he speaks in general terms, everything he says seems to relate directly and powerfully to me. Afterwards, I can remember little of what he said, but the general gist is that everyone has *merde* to deal with in life, even if it is not always evident.

After about twenty minutes, he offers some specific advice. 'OK,' he says. 'This is what I would like you to do. Get up with the sun, or as close to it as possible. Then, when you are showered and dressed, I'd like you to sit on the floor in a quiet place and light a candle. Look into the flame, then close your eyes and hold the image of the flame in your mind.'

He tells me that I should practise emptying my mind of all thoughts or, as he puts it, 'Give yourself a break from the daily rosary of misery.' If any thoughts do present themselves, I am to acknowledge them and then push them gently away.

He also gives me a one-word mantra to silently repeat. (When I google it later, I discover that it is an Indian word for 'peace and integrity'.) I nod, relieved that this is all that's required and that I don't need to convert to a plant-only diet or start wearing hemp clothes, or worse.

'I want you to do this every morning before going out for a walk with your dog,' he says. 'If you can do this, everything will be fine.' And just like that, almost casually, in Gabriella's garden, I've been taught to meditate.

'Is it a religion that you practise?' I ask, as I get up to leave.

'No, it's not about religion,' he says. 'It's about humanity. Religion is like a marriage; spirituality is love.'

Suddenly, I hear the sound of howling outside. 'Ah,' says Babaji. 'That's your little dog calling to you. He is saying that it is time to go. I can see that he is very tuned into you.' He pats my head again and hugs me.

Outside Barbara is waiting with Biff. Babaji pats him on the head too, and says something to him that immediately stops the wailing. Biff looks as awed and humbled as I feel. As I walk back up the hill, I feel as if I've been given a key to a room containing a potentially fabulous gift. I feel a huge surge of gratitude to Babaji and Barbara and above all, to Gabriella, who led me to them.

Zoe pays me a surprise visit. '*Coucou*,' she shouts. 'Anyone at home?' Dressed in a yellow cotton skirt and a grey cashmere jumper, she looks carelessly chic, her legs bare, despite the sudden hint of autumnal chill in the air.

'Hope I'm not interrupting anything?'

'Yup, the washing-up. Come on in.'

She hands me a box of handmade chocolates from Fortnum and Mason and a bag of dog treats for Biff. 'A little thank-you for running me to the airport,' she says.

'Anytime. It feels as if you've been away for ever.'

'Yes, I stayed longer than planned. A few things came up at work that were... unexpected.'

'Sit down and I'll make you a coffee,' I say, pointing towards the kitchen table and feeling hugely guilty when I think of her husband. Zoe seems so... innocent.

'Actually honey, I've given up coffee,' she says. 'Sorry to be a bore, but have you got any herbal tea?'

'Yup, I have several kinds. How did your appointment go?'

'Fine. I've got to give up caffeine and alcohol, which is a bit of a bitch, and make some changes to my diet. Then I guess Matthew and I will be going at it like monkeys.'

'Well, let's hope that no one erects a wind turbine near your garden,' I say, rummaging in the cupboard for herbal teas. 'What about camomile?'

Zoe pulls a face. 'Have you got anything else?'

'Ginger? It boosts stamina and energy levels and is said to have aphrodisiac properties,' I say, reading from the box.

'The last thing Matthew and I need is an aphrodisiac.'

'Too much information,' I say, brightly.

She laughs and then throws a curve ball into the conversation. 'Did you see Matthew at all, while I was away?'

'No. Why would I?'

'I don't know. You're both at home alone, in a small village. I thought you might have bumped into each other or met up for a drink or something,' she says.

'No, I haven't seen him,' I say, grateful for the fact that I haven't. 'Would you like a cookie? They're homemade.'

She screws up her face. 'Sugar,' she says, as if I were offering campylobacter. 'I can't. By the way, Matthew and I are having some people round for supper on Saturday and wondered if you would like to come?'

'Ah,' I say, thinking how much I dislike the word, 'supper' and its smug, middle-class pretentiousness.

'I think I'm already invited to dinner on Saturday,' I reply, my voice rising noticeably, as I'm a terrible liar.

'Oh,' says Zoe. 'That's a shame. We've invited quite a few people that you know. And Matthew is cooking his pumpkin and sage risotto, which is scrummy. He'll be terribly disappointed that you can't come.'

I can't deny that the offer is tempting, not least because I don't actually have anything planned for Saturday; and I would love to sample Matt's 'scrummy' risotto. But all things considered, it is not a good idea. I don't want to feel like a cuckoo in Zoe's beautifully decorated nest. (At least I'm assuming that it is beautifully decorated, as I haven't actually seen the interior of their rented cottage.)

'Well, thanks for the invite all the same,' I say.

'Can't you wriggle out of whatever it is that you're going to?' says Zoe. 'I'm sure that our little supper will be much more fun. Matthew even grew the pumpkin, himself.'

'I'm sorry, I can't,' I say, impressed that Matt can find the time to plant pumpkins, while building a house.

'Well, if you change your mind, we can always squeeze you in at the last minute. Oh, and that reminds me, we need some extra dining chairs before Saturday. You once mentioned a fabulous junk yard hidden away in the countryside?'

'Ah, the secret *dépôt-vente*. I don't give that address away to just anyone, you know.'

'You have such fabulous taste,' she says, getting up from the table and gazing through the window into the courtyard.

'Flattery will get you everywhere,' I say, thrilled to have my interior decor choices validated by a professional.

'I mean it,' she persists. 'Your house is lovely. Is it very far away, the *dépôt-vente*?'

'Not that far; it's near Douhé; literally a barn in the middle of nowhere. It's hard to find, but if you promise to keep it a secret, I'll take you there sometime.'

'That would be amazing,' says Zoe. 'What about tomorrow?'

'Tomorrow? I don't think I can …'

'Oh, go on,' she says, tilting her head to one side, just as Biff does when he wants me to take him for a walk. 'It'll be fun looking at vintage furniture together.'

'I really should be doing some work,' I say. 'I try to be at my desk during the day. But I suppose I could be persuaded.'

'Wonderful. Do you mind driving? I could come to your house around 2 pm?'

'OK,' I say, marvelling at the way in which Zoe manages, via a few well-chosen compliments, to twist people around her manicured finger and get them to run to her timetable.

The following afternoon, she arrives early for our excursion to the *dépôt-vente,* displaying her usual flair for colour, in cropped, flared jeans and a pea-green sweater, a violet scarf wound around her neck. As we drive through the country roads in the coppery autumn light, she uses her phone to take photos of the trees and hedges, glowing like precious metals, rose-gold and bronze, along the route.

'The countryside is so pretty at the moment,' she says.

'Maybe an inspiration for a fabric design?' I venture.

'Yes,' she says, with a wink. 'Like you, I'm always working.'

When we arrive at the *dépôt-vente,* a small crowd is already waiting for the gates to be opened at 2.30 pm. I pull up on a grass verge in the narrow lane.

'Wow,' says Zoe, eyeing the wooden tables and benches, along with the rusty garden furniture and various unidentified clumps of metal, dotted around the yard.

'Don't worry, it gets better inside,' I say.

'Oh, I'm already impressed. Look at that lovely old barn ladder,' she replies, throwing her bag over her shoulder.

'What would you do with that?' I ask, intrigued.

'You could use it in a bathroom as a towel rail, or lean it against a courtyard wall and hang plants from the rungs.'

'What a lovely idea,' I say, inspired.

Once inside, Zoe doesn't hang around. To my surprise, she heads straight towards the enormous wardrobes in unfashionable dark woods. Most of these items have been languishing in the barn for years, as they are too big and too brown to fit into a modern interior. But the sight of them sends Zoe into raptures.

'Ideal for storing bed linen,' she declares, opening the door to one vast wardrobe. 'And this cupboard would be perfect in the kitchen, for storing crockery, just as the French do.'

She acts swiftly and decisively, calling over the owner of the *dépôt-vente* to assist her. He trails around in her wake and whenever something takes her fancy, there is a short period of negotiation, during which Zoe tilts her head and smiles a lot, before the owner gives a curt nod and sticks a '*vendu*' sticker on the item. As usual, Zoe gets what she wants, helped by the fact that she smiles a lot and her French is excellent.

Once she has bought enough furniture to furnish Versailles, she moves on to accessories, snapping up old green wine flasks, earthenware jugs and piles of vintage French linen, which she pronounces 'ideal for making curtains and sofa covers'.

I notice that we have spookily similar tastes. At one point, we both find ourselves standing in front of an antique mirror with tarnished glass and peeling paint.

'I rather like that,' I say. 'It would be perfect for a wall of my courtyard.'

'It would look fabulous stripped and repainted,' says Zoe.

It's only €30, but I hesitate, put off by the idea of having to get busy with a paintbrush. 'I'll think about it,' I say, heading over to look at a barn ladder. When I go back to buy the mirror, five minutes later, I'm annoyed to find that it has gone.

'All done,' says Zoe, appearing beside me, with a brisk smile. 'I just have to pay for everything.'

Two members of staff are busy moving her purchases to one side, for collection later in the week. I watch as Zoe conducts one last negotiation to reduce the collective price of the goods.

The owner of the *dépôt-vente*, a gentle chap of Romany lineage, who clearly knows a fellow professional when he sees one, does not put up much of a fight.

As Zoe counts out a slab of euros, I am miffed to notice that the mirror I wanted to buy, is among her pile of purchases. She has bought up half the *dépôt-vente;* she could at least have left me one lousy mirror. I'm about to make a comment to this effect – albeit jokingly – but something stops me. Rather than reacting, I bite my lip and remain silent.

'That place was amazing,' says Zoe, as we drive home.

'All that brown furniture that you snapped up, I wouldn't have thought it was your thing.'

'Oh, it won't stay that way. I'll either strip it or paint it,' she says. 'Good job that I specialise in breathing new life into old things, eh?' She turns and gives me a wink. 'I am, after all, married to Matthew.'

'He's not that old, is he?' I say.

'He's fifteen years older than me,' she replies. 'It's funny, before I met him I preferred men of my own age or younger. Never in a million years did I think I could be attracted to an older man.'

'So what *did* attract you to him,' I ask, as I'm certain that Zoe could have taken her pick from an entourage of suitors.

'I don't know. I like the fact that he's so intelligent. He makes me laugh and he challenges me all the time. And he's a brilliant architect. It's always a turn-on, don't you think, when someone is good at what they do?'

'Um,' I say, unable to comment. My last relationship was with a builder and I have no idea how good he was at laying floors or putting up scaffolding.

'If I had to say the single most attractive thing about him, it was his persistence,' Zoe continues. 'Matthew was so determined, in his pursuit of me, that in the end I gave in, even though he was my friend's husband and I felt guilty about it.'

'I know what you mean,' I say. Zoe turns to look at me. 'I mean with regards to the persistence. I've been in a similar situation myself,' I quickly add. 'Most of my boyfriends chose me, rather than vice versa. It's probably where I've gone wrong.'

'I think it's important to ask yourself what you really want.'

'"I want", never gets.'

'Really?' says Zoe, raising an eyebrow. 'It's always worked for me. But you have to know what you want. If you could write your spec for the perfect man, what would it be?'

'I don't know. Someone who is clever and funny, calm in a crisis, a good conversationalist, is generous, reads books, and is a little bit mischievous. And if they can cook, so much the better.'

Suddenly, Zoe looks thoughtful. 'And what about deal-breakers?' she asks.

'Infidelity, custard-coloured cords, being too clingy and not liking dogs,' I say. 'How about you?'

'Having different goals or wanting different things,' she says, without missing a beat. 'And definitely custard-coloured cords.'

'Here we are,' I say, pulling up in the square.

'Well, that was a revelation,' she says, blowing me a kiss. '*Merci beaucoup.*'

'You're welcome.'

I don't want to be judgemental, but as Zoe slings her bag over her shoulder and walks away, I can't help thinking of the mirror that she snaffled before my eyes. Maybe she just got carried away with the excitement of the *dépôt-vente*. Or could it be that Zoe is actually a ruthless, rather selfish operator? Husbands or antique mirrors, if she wants something, she takes it, regardless of the feelings of others. Why, then, do I like her so much?

Chapter 16

Flames

I GLIDE INTO late autumn doing as Babaji taught me, sitting quietly and imagining a flame for ten minutes every morning. I begin to look forward to the ritual of unfurling my purple yoga mat and lighting a candle. As I sit cross-legged on the floor, silently chanting the magic word, I find that my breathing slows, my shoulders drop and a feeling of peace descends. Biff appears to join in, sitting next to me and staring into the flame.

Often the thoughts that pop into my mind while I am trying to silence it are the most important of the day – reminding me of something I must do, or someone that I forgot to thank. Intrigued, I do a little research and discover that the benefits of meditation, which many people dismiss as hippy-dippy nonsense, have been established by reputable studies. As one psychologist puts it, temporary silencing one's inner chatter, interrupts 'the normally unnoticed flow of impulse and reaction that feeds the way we are in the world.' More simply, it means that you think before you fly off the handle.

When I ask Gabriella about Babaji's background, she tells me that he was teaching poetry and philosophy at New York University when he realised that he wanted to help people in a more direct way. It seems that the writer Jack Kerouac and poet Allen Ginsberg attended his meetings in New York, though whether they, too, started their day by rolling out a yoga mat and gazing at a candle flame, I do not know.

A week or so after our visit to the *dépôt-vente*, Zoe drops by one afternoon, looking as colour-savvy as ever, in a shaggy fern-green coat and an ink-coloured bobble hat. Hovering behind her is a guy in a plaid shirt and a hoodie, carrying a barn ladder over his shoulders, that appears to have been freshly painted in pale grey.

'A little thank-you, for taking me to the *dépôt-vente*,' she says, nodding towards the ladder and presenting me with a large bubble-wrapped item. 'It's for your courtyard. And this is Pascal, my neighbour. He's been doing some stripping for me. Can we come in?' She doesn't wait for an answer.

'Wow,' I say, as they follow me through the kitchen and into the walled garden.

'Global warming, eh?' says Zoe, nodding towards the geraniums, in valiant late autumn bloom. 'The polar bears might be pegging it, but it's not all bad.'

She motions to Pascal to lean the pale grey ladder against the far wall. '*Et voil*à,' she declares, before turning to thank her handsome helper, in fluent French. 'I'll see you back at the house, Pascal. If you could start on the blue chest, that would be marvellous,' she says.

She then removes the bubble-wrap to reveal the mirror that I had admired in the *dépôt-vente*, now transformed by a coat of the same pale grey paint used for the barn ladder.

'Wow, that is so completely fabulous,' I say, blown away by the stunning generosity of the gesture. Heaven knows how long it took to strip and repaint the unloved items.

'Did you do this yourself?' I ask.

'With a little help from Pascal,' she says with a wink. 'May I?' With a brisk confidence, she moves a few planters and terracotta pots around, and enlists my help to move the blue bistro table, as if professionally styling my outdoor space. The transformation is immediate and amazing.

'I think the mirror will look best, here,' she says, holding it up against the stone wall, so that it reflects the dining table and chairs. 'And the barn ladder... here. It will look fabulous with pots of herbs or flowers hanging off the rungs.'

She stands back to admire her work, her skin glowing in the coppery autumn light. 'And maybe in the spring, you could add some trailing geraniums or ivy, to create a sort of vertical garden,' she says.

'Zoe, I really don't know what I've done to deserve this,' I say.

She shrugs. 'You're my best friend in France. It's nothing.'

'Will you stay for some aphrodisiac tea?'

'I'd love to, but I've got to get back to my stripping before I pick up Matthew from the airport, later. He's been in London for a client meeting.'

'Another time, then. Thank you so much for this.'

'My pleasure,' she says. 'If you like, I'll send Matthew around tomorrow to hang that mirror for you.'

'NO... I mean, that's fine, thanks,' I say. 'It's the sort of thing that my friend, Pierre-Antoine, loves to do.'

'Isn't he away on a safari holiday, at the moment?'

'Er, yes but I can wait until he gets back.'

'Well, let me know if you change your mind and I'll send Matthew around with his power drill. Ciao bella.'

As she leaves, my overwhelming feeling, as is so often the case with Zoe is one of guilt. I'm deeply ashamed that I assumed the worst of her when she was, in fact, planning such a generous and elegant gesture.

*

As winter arrives, I am on fire. Literally. I am so busy responding to messages on a social media account one Sunday evening, that it takes a while to notice the burning smell emanating from the kitchen. Even then I don't panic. I just assume that the rice for Biff's dinner has boiled dry. But when I go downstairs to investigate, there is a field of flames covering the oven and the dishwasher, where a tea cloth has caught fire on the hob. The toaster meanwhile, has melted in a fug of noxious fumes.

Using a wet cloth, I throw the toaster into the courtyard, then run back inside and throw pans of water over the hob and the dishwasher until the flames are out. *Panic over*, I think, although my heart is still in sprint mode. But then I look outside and see that the toaster has set fire to the barn ladder and the flames are now licking their way up the wall, towards my neighbour's woodpile on the other side. *Panic so not over.* I run upstairs to my office and call the emergency services. The operator asks an endless list of questions. Where is the fire? How did it start? How big are the flames?

'I'm very sorry but I think I should go and take a look,' I say, imagining mountainous flames engulfing the courtyard. I run downstairs and throw pans of water at the wooden ladder until, finally, the fire is out. But when I run back upstairs to speak to the operator, she tells me that the fire brigade is already on the way and that I should cut the electricity and stand in the street. Shivering, I cool my heels in the moonlight while reflecting on the irony of the situation. After years of struggling to get a log fire going, I have managed to set the house alight without any effort at all. If Biff could speak, he would no doubt be saying, '*Merde! Putain!* My human is a MORON!'

A few minutes later, the truck arrives on the square, its blue lights flashing. My road is too narrow for it to pass down, so two firemen run towards us, unfurling a big hose, the blue lights of their torches advancing like large sapphires in the darkness.

I am mortified. I apologise profusely as three more fire-fighters arrive and crowd into the sitting room. A quiet Sunday evening has suddenly turned into a party. After surveying the damage and opening the windows, they leave as quickly as they arrived, telling me that I did well to get the burning toaster out of the house, as it could have been so much worse.

Ten minutes later, the doorbell rings. It's Matt and Zoe.

'Are you OK, hun?' says Zoe, her eyes big and concerned, under her bobble hat. 'We saw the fire engine arrive on the square and the *sapeurs-pompiers* run down your road.'

'We thought we'd walk down and take a look,' says Matt. 'And saw your windows open.'

'Yes. All fine,' I say, though all evidence points to the contrary and little specs of black plastic are falling from the ceiling, like sinister snow.

'Why don't you come and spend the evening at our place?' says Matt, frowning as he takes in the singed surroundings. 'We've got a spare room, haven't we, darling?'

'Absolutely,' says Zoe. 'I was just about to suggest the same thing. In fact, we insist on it.'

'Really, I'm fine.'

'At least let us help you clear up,' says Zoe.

'No, honestly. I'd rather leave it until tomorrow when the dust has settled,' I say.

'How did it happen?' asks Zoe.

'I left a cloth on top of the gas hob.'

'But honey, how can you not have noticed?'

'Let me guess,' says Matt. 'You were too busy on Twitter?'

I say nothing. Matt looks at me. 'You can't stay here. The air is full of fumes,' he says. 'Get your stuff and Biff's bed, while I open the upstairs windows, so that the house gets a proper airing. Zoe, close the downstairs shutters but leave the windows ajar.'

Reluctantly, I do as I'm told, throwing the bare essentials – my phone and toothbrush and Biff's water bowl – into my bag. Matt picks up Biff's bed, Zoe takes his lead and, together, we cross the square towards their house. Odd and inappropriate though the situation feels, I am quite curious to finally see the inside of their rental cottage.

'After you,' says Matt, pushing open the oak door and indicating for me to turn left into an open-plan kitchen and cosy sitting room.'

'What, no brown wallpaper?' I say, looking at the tasteful deep-blue walls, and thinking back to the rodent-hued wallpaper that once blighted Maison Coquelicot.

'Oh we had it,' says Matt, throwing a log into the wood burner. 'Brown deckchair stripes. But we insisted on permission to strip it out, as a condition of the rental contract.'

'For a temporary home, it's gorgeous,' I say, taking in the distressed leather club chairs and the colourful Afghan rugs. It is far from the minimal style that I expected of them, but it is elegant in an unforced way. Even their clutter is stylish, with interiors magazines stacked up on the floor and on wooden shelves, either side of the fireplace.

'Take a seat,' says Matt, pointing towards the long refectory dining table in the kitchen.

'Would you like some tea?' Zoe asks. 'Or coffee?' She unfurls a cashmere scarf from her neck, releasing a cloud of candy-like perfume into the warm room.

'In the circumstances, I think something stronger is called for,' says Matt, producing a bottle of wine. 'How about a glass of Sauvignon?'

'Actually, the fumes have given me a bit of a headache. What I'd really love is some water,' I say.

'Sure,' says Zoe. 'Matt will sort it. I'll just run upstairs and get the guest room ready.'

'I'll help,' I say, standing up.

'No need,' says Zoe. 'Just chill.'

'Sure I can't tempt you?' says Matt, holding up the bottle of Sauvignon. I shake my head. I feel horribly awkward here. The house doesn't feel big enough for the three of us.

'So,' says Matt, handing me a glass of water and sitting down at the table, opposite me. 'What, or who, distracted you so much that you didn't notice the house was on fire?'

'OK,' I say. 'You were right. I was on Twitter.'

'Well, "On fire" is definitely worth a tweet.'

'Very droll,' I say, looking at the design magazine on the table. It includes a feature on futurist skyscrapers, thrusting confidently and phallically into the sky.

'Is this the sort of thing you do?' I ask.

'I wish,' he says. 'My buildings are a little more... down-to-earth. By the way, you've got a black smudge on your chin.'

'Probably soot,' I say, trying to rub it off.

'And there was I thinking it was the latest makeup look,' he says. 'You've missed a bit.' He leans across the table. 'Here, let me...'

'It's fine,' I say, pulling away.

'Room's ready,' shouts Zoe, coming down the stairs. 'I imagine, after all the excitement, you want to get some sleep.'

'Yup,' I say, though weirdly, I've never felt more awake. There is nothing like an unexpected encounter with the emergency services, for increasing your level of alertness.

'I guess it will be an early start tomorrow to file an insurance claim,' says Zoe.

'I probably won't bother,' I say. 'Too much hassle.'

'You must,' says Matt, 'because, at the very least, they'll have specialist cleaners to remove the toxic dust.'

'Um, I guess.'

'Let me know if you need any help with anything.'

'Yes, Matthew's good at that kind of stuff,' says Zoe, looping her arms around her husband's neck. 'He'd be only too happy to help.' She puts her chin playfully on Matt's shoulder. 'Darling, isn't it time we went to bed?'

Suddenly, I have a vision of them on the other side of the guest room wall 'going at it like monkeys', as Zoe once put it.

'You know, the fumes have probably dispersed by now. I think I'll get going,' I say.

'Don't be mad,' says Matt. 'It's no problem at all for you to stay here. Zoe's made the bed up.'

'It's really kind of you,' I say, standing up. 'But I've made up my mind. I'm going home.'

'Well, if you're absolutely determined, we'll walk you back with your stuff,' says Zoe.

'Honestly, I'm fine.'

'If you change your mind, do *frappe* on the door,' says Zoe, giving me a hug. 'Matthew, why don't you make yourself useful and carry Biff's bed back...'

'No,' I almost shout, grabbing Biff and his doughnut and edging out of the front door. 'Thanks, all the same. See you very soon.'

I walk across the square, grateful to be breathing in the cold, clean air. Back home, I lie awake with the window open, looking at the moon and reflecting on the evening's events. Oh the irony, that after so many weeks of visualising a flame in my head, when I stop – because recently I haven't been so diligent about doing the morning meditation – I end up with real-life flames. There's a lesson there, I think, as I resolve to roll out the yoga mat and start practising mindfulness again in the morning.

The next day, I survey the damage in the courtyard. The beautiful pale grey ladder that Zoe gave me is now a blackened scar against the courtyard wall, while the mirror is also scorched. I visit Pierre-Antoine, to tell him what happened. 'Ah it was you?' he says, sounding unsurprised. 'I saw the fire engine arriving.'

Later that evening he drops by to survey the aftermath and loan me an electric cooking ring, as my oven is no longer working. He also brings a USB stick on which he has downloaded 500 photos of his recent safari. It seems that he had some drama of his own, having left his passport at the airport in South Africa, on arrival.

He tells me that he only realised it was missing when the tour guide asked for passports, as their coach was about to cross the border into north Africa. 'Fortunately, our bus had an on-board WC,' he says. 'I had to hide in there for over an hour, while the border police checked everyone's passports.'

Suddenly, I forget my charred walls and the potentially carcinogenic toaster dust, and I'm doubled up with laughter at the thought of Pierre-Antoine hiding in the loo. 'Do you mind if we look at the photos another evening?' I say, when I've stopped laughing. 'I still have quite a bit of clearing up to do.'

'I'll leave the USB stick with you, so you can look at them in your own time,' he says, as if it were a huge treat to look through a friend's holiday snaps. 'There are zebras, giraffes and lions, everything.'

'Can't wait,' I reply.

'I'll take the damaged stuff to the tip for you, if you want,' he says, nodding towards Zoe's ruined gifts in the courtyard.

'Thanks, I'd appreciate that.'

'And you must make an insurance claim,' says Pierre-Antoine, before he leaves.

'It's not worth the trouble,' I reply. Over the past eight years, I've gone to great lengths to avoid any encounters with that legendary beast: French bureaucracy. I imagine the dossiers, the forms, the photocopies, the proofs of identity – indeed, the proof that I've had a fire at all – that would be required to file an insurance claim.

But the following day, after discovering how much it will cost to replace the oven, I decide to give it a go. What have I got to lose, apart from an afternoon – and possibly, my temper – if the stories of French bureaucracy are anything to go by?

And so, armed with a few iPad pictures of the molten toaster and my blackened walls, I brace myself for a meeting with my insurers, who fortunately have an office in the village. I sit down opposite the clerk. He pulls out a form – I imagine the first of many – and asks how it happened.

'A cloth left on the gas hob,' I tell him, sheepishly.

'It happens,' he says, with a cheerful shrug. I show him the pictures and settle in for an afternoon of interrogation. But less than ten minutes later, he has filled in the form on my behalf and is on the phone to a company that specialises in cleaning up fire damage. And just like that, the insurance claim is filed.

A few weeks later, after I've submitted quotes for repairing the oven, one of his colleagues comes to my house. I am staggered by what follows. He sits down with a tiny laptop, does a calculation and writes me a generous cheque. I feel almost shortchanged that I've been denied a run-in with bureaucracy.

*

Driving Zoe to Poitiers airport one afternoon in late November I notice that she is looking particularly fabulous. In a tailored, navy coat, sheer black tights and blush-coloured spindle heels, with her blonde hair pulled back into a chignon, she appears to have swapped her usual hippy-chic look for the glacial elegance of a Hitchcock heroine.

'Is it an important meeting that you are going back for?' I ask, intrigued by her sudden makeover.

'Yes. It is.' Unusually, she doesn't offer any more information and I don't ask.

The following morning, I am sitting on my yoga mat, successfully thinking about nothing, when the doorbell rings. I glide downstairs, full of love for the world and thinking benign thoughts, only to find Matt on the doorstep.

Usually, when I see him around the village he is dressed in variations of the dusty T-shirt or hoodie and jeans combination that suggests he has been engaged in hard, manual labour. But this morning he is wearing a dark jacket over his hoodie, and looks quite smart.

'I thought I'd come and see you,' he says. 'Zoe's in London.'

'I know. I ran her to the airport yesterday because you were busy with bi-folds, remember?'

'I was wondering if you'd like to have a drink?' he asks. 'Maybe this evening?'

'The thing is, I don't think Zoe would like it if we were meeting up behind her back,' I say.

'I'd just like to talk to you, that's all,' he says, eyes simultaneously smiling and boring into me. 'Actually, that's a lie. I want to do more than talk to you.'

What the hell? 'I really don't think so,' I say, trying not to be flattered by his doorstep blandishments. 'Especially, since Zoe is trying to get preg—'

'What?'

'Zoe told me that you were trying for a child,' I say.

'This is news to me,' he says. 'I've told her that I don't want any more children.'

'I'm sorry. I have to go.'

'Wait…'

But I have already closed the door. I return to my yoga mat but it's not easy freeing my mind of thoughts, as whenever I try to visualise a flame in my head, it is Matt and Zoe that keep popping up.

As Christmas approaches, I start to feel restless and, actually, a little envious of Zoe, who is perpetually in motion. Her trips to London have become more frequent. And whereas she used to go for just a few days at a time, now she is often away for over a week. She says she is busy with work – that there are a lot of office politics to deal with, and that it's important to put in 'face-time' – but I suspect the truth is that she finds the French winter a little hard going.

'What are you doing for Christmas?' she asks, over herbal tea in my kitchen, one morning.

'I'm having lunch with friends and then I'm taking Pierre-Antoine to the UK for a week's holiday, to thank him for helping me to clear up after the fire. What about you?'

'Matthew has arranged for us to go to Corsica.'

'How lovely. I've heard that it's amazing there,' I say, but Zoe doesn't look that thrilled.

A few days before Christmas, I visit Gabriella. It's dark and knee-knockingly cold outside, but Gabriella's windows are wide open. She keeps the house chilled deliberately, 'because it keeps the flesh fresh'. She answers the door wearing a Barbour jacket over a thick grey sweater over a navy and white striped shirt-dress, with sheepskin boots. Even at ninety-five, she has a recognisable sense of style.

'Aren't you cold?' I ask, shivering in the kitchen.

'I haven't had the heating on all year,' she tells me, 'but I've lit the fire in the library for you.' We go through to the book-lined room, where a fire is blazing in the stone fireplace.

'One of my friends, an opera singer, has just died,' she says.

'Oh dear, that's bad news,' I say.

'On the contrary, it's fantastic,' she declares.

I looked at her aghast. Surely she can't mean it?

'He died on stage singing, doing something that he loved,' she continues. 'He had a massive heart attack and just keeled over – terrible for his poor wife and friends, but fantastic for him. What a wonderful way to go.'

Gabriella is the only person I know who can make death sound like a fabulous event.

'My address book is a cemetery. They're all dead,' she continues. 'That's what happens when you get to ninety-five.'

I laugh. 'But I'm very happy to see you,' she says. 'Would you be so kind as to read me a letter from a friend?'

I fetch the wicker basket in which Dolores puts Gabriella's post. Speaking slowly and in as low a tone as possible so that Gabriella can hear me, I begin to read the letter, which is twenty pages long. It is written by the sister of a woman whose sister died in a plane crash in 1980 – thought to have been caused by a terrorist bomb – along with her lover, the then prime minister of Portugal, Francisco de Sá Carneiro.

'So many of your friends seem to have led extraordinary lives,' I say, when I've finished reading it.

'Well, you only have one life. You have to live it running,' she says. 'And never stop to worry about what people think of you.' To demonstrate the point, she tells me how she left her first husband after sixty days of marriage, having realised that she was attracted to another man.

'In the 1940s, that must have been a brave thing to do,' I say.
She shrugs. 'As I say, so much of life is fate.'

'What did he do, your first husband?' I ask.

'Something in rubber,' she replies. 'He was a biochemist. But enough about me; what have you been up to?'

'I'm in a slightly weird situation,' I say, 'in that I'm being pursued by a friend's husband.' I figure she will find it amusing, in a French-farce kind of way.

'Is he charming?'

'Yes.'

'Are you attracted to him?'

'Um, I suppose he is attractive, yes.'

'Then what's the problem?'

'He's married.'

'Moron! What's that got to do with anything?' she cries.

'The thing is, I was brought up a Catholic and I still have a Catholic conscience.'

'Listen to me, you moron. You sleep with him, then come and see me and I will absolve you of your sins.'

'It's not as simple as that,' I say, once I've stopped laughing. 'His wife is my friend.'

'Ah well, that's different. But life is too short to worry about religion or what people might think about you. Forget all that.'

It's nearly midnight when I leave. Gabriella has become strangely animated by the Matt story and looks as if she could stay up chatting for hours. It's funny how I met Gabriella at ten minutes to midnight on the timeline of her life, so I'm a fairly insignificant part of it. Yet in the few years that I've known her, she has had quite an impact on mine. As I walk home under the smooth navy sky, I smile at her latest nugget of advice. I have to admit that I love the idea of behaving badly and then visiting Gabriella for absolution.

Chapter 17

A Typically English Experience (Pratt's Bottom to Topsham)

THE DAY AFTER Christmas, I drive back to London with Biff, having booked a flight for Pierre-Antoine to join us the following day. He prefers to fly, he says, 'because it will be quicker and much less hassle', which turns out to be an erroneous assumption. I've instructed him to text me when he's on the train to London, so that I can meet him at Liverpool Street station. But two hours after his flight landed, I haven't heard anything. Surely he didn't get lost on the five-minute walk from passport control to the Stansted Express?

I call his mobile. To my surprise, I get a French ringtone. To my even greater surprise, he answers.

'Allo?'

'You're still in France?'

'Yes,' he says, sounding surprised that I am surprised.

'You missed your flight?'

'It's tomorrow.'

'It was today,' I say, wondering how he made the mistake.

There is silence on the end of the phone, followed by some shuffling of papers and then a loud, '*Merde*!'

An hour later, he phones back to say that he is now booked on a Eurostar and will arrive tomorrow. And so, the following evening, I drive to St Pancras station and wait among the remains of the festive tinsel, for my friend to arrive. He eventually appears, in jeans and a leather jacket, a rucksack slung casually over his shoulder. He looks nowhere near as sheepish as the circumstances might merit.

'*Salut*!' he says, kissing my cheek.

'How was your journey?'

'*Impeccable*,' he replies with a grin.

As we walk towards the less-than-salubrious side street where I parked my car, Pierre-Antoine finds much to admire – the facade of St Pancras, the red London buses, even the number of people on the streets. 'It's certainly very lively here,' he observes, as we pass a woman yelling at a man in a doorway and calling him 'a lying b*****d'.

'Oh la, la, London is much bigger than I thought,' says Pierre-Antoine, as we drive over the Westway, to Kensington. 'I imagine one could get very lost here.'

'Don't worry,' I say, with unwarranted optimism. 'You're with me, so you won't get lost.'

We are staying in a flat belonging to an old friend, who is away for Christmas.

'*C'est Versailles*,' says Pierre-Antoine, looking around the guest room and en suite bathroom. He drops his backpack on his bed, hands me a carrier bag containing two bottles of champagne, then patrols around the apartment, scoping out the possibilities for improving the insulation, and looking for draughts, two of his favourite obsessions. It's good to see his holiday getting off to such an enjoyable start.

'I thought we could go to the local pub for dinner,' I say, as Pierre-Antoine examines the gaps around the sash windows in the sitting room.

'*Nickel*!' (Perfect!) he replies, though I'm certain that he has no idea what a pub is. 'If I'd known about these gaps, I could have brought something with me to fill them.'

'Well, don't worry about that now. You're on holiday.'

In the pub, I go to the bar to order our drinks – a glass of Fleurie for me, a pint of lager for my guest, who is determined to adopt our English ways.

When I return to our table, he is studying a French phrase book, called *Je Parle Anglais*. This contains over forty different scenarios that a French person might encounter in the UK, many of them involving illness or a visit to the doctor. It's enough to put anyone off a trip to the land of boiled potatoes and *rosbif*.

A section beginning with the phrase, 'I heard her cough', for example, rapidly escalates to, 'She has no pulse'. Another chapter, dealing with food, places particular emphasis on portion size. Key phrases include, 'Look at that sirloin! It's so big!' and 'I think I won't be able to finish my chops,' as well as, 'I've had enough boiled potatoes, thank you.' As I flick through the 'Accommodation' section, meanwhile, I find myself fervently hoping that no French visitor will need the phrase, 'The smell was so bad that we had to leave the room.'

'Shall I translate the menu, for you?' I ask.

Pierre-Antoine shakes his head. 'Just order me something typically English,' he says, with touching faith. I scan the blackboard menu, which includes a goat's cheese salad, pan-seared foie gras, and confit of duck. The only 'typically English' dish on the menu is bangers and mash – and even then, the sausages are from Toulouse.

Knowing that the French take a dim view of mashed potato, I order Pierre-Antoine a prawn curry. 'Why not?' he beams, when I warn him that it might be spicy. 'It is very interesting for me to eat like the English and see them in their natural habitat.'

I don't have the heart to tell him that many of the people around us are speaking Polish or French.

As we walk home – he pronounces the curry 'excellent', by the way – Pierre-Antoine expresses surprise at the lack of garages. 'So many beautiful houses,' he exclaims, 'but nowhere to put your car. Where are the garages?'

'There aren't any. They've all been turned into luxury apartments,' I explain.

When I ask him what he is most looking forward to doing in London, he replies that he wants to visit Big Ben and 'a typical English café'. Just a small problem: in London, the independent café has gone the way of the garage. A 'typical English café' now means Starbucks or Café Nero.

The next day, I take my guest on a tour of London's key sights: Trafalgar Square, the Houses of Parliament, Big Ben, and the London Eye. Outside the Houses of Parliament, I hold his rucksack and his jacket while he zips into action with his zoom lens, jumping on walls and lying on the ground, to get the best possible angles. I notice the police watching us, but nothing can curb Pierre-Antoine's enthusiasm for all things *anglais*.

Over dinner (another local pub; this one serving Thai food) my guest asks if we could visit a 'typically English' village, tomorrow. Quietly panicking, I try to think of somewhere suitable. My guest has no idea how difficult it is to deliver a 'typically English' itinerary. I find the answer in the *Evening Standard* property supplement, which has a feature on Horsham, 'an old, historic market town', less than a two-hour drive from London. Admittedly, it's a town not a village, but Pierre-Antoine seems excited by the plan. Me, I'm hoping that Horsham will be picturesque enough to impress my guest, who comes from a region of France that is not exactly lacking in picturesque places. *Horsham, please don't let me down*, I pray, as we follow signs for the 'historic market town', the next day.

As we drive into the centre, we see no evidence of anything historic or old. Instead, we arrive in a multi-storey car park and a modern shopping precinct of the kind that exists all over the UK. The effect on Pierre-Antoine, however, is instantaneous. 'Frankly, this is magnificent,' he cries, as he claps eyes on Poundland and Phones 4 U.

At first I think he is being sarcastic but, no, he is genuinely blown away by Horsham's town centre. 'We don't have anything like this in France,' he declares, admiring the water feature, the flats above the shops and the 'excellent' layout of the precinct. Everything is '*super-beau*' or '*sympa*' or '*nickel*'. Keen to leave no centimetre of Horsham unexplored, at one point he sticks his head around a narrow alley where the Biffa bins are kept.

'I think you'll find that's it's just where the rubbish...' I say, but he has already gone, emerging a few minutes later to say that it led to a car park, but was '*jolie quand même* (pretty all the same).' People of Horsham: you will never know what pleasure your town gave to my French friend, one grey afternoon in winter.

We have lunch in Pret-a-Manger, having failed again in the quest to find a 'typically English' café, and then drive on to Eastbourne, where I've booked two rooms for the night in a seafront B&B. The signs are good for a typically English experience. In the window there is a synthetic white Christmas tree, probably dating back to the seventies; inside there is pine panelling and a red and gold swirly carpet, most likely of similar vintage. 'Frankly, you're spoiling me,' cries Pierre-Antoine. Once again, I think he is being sarcastic, but he isn't. Everywhere we go, he sees only charm.

That evening, I take Pierre-Antoine for fish and chips in a seafront restaurant. I can't have him thinking that we live on boiled potatoes, as *Je Parle Anglais* implies. Sometimes we have them fried too. He insists on paying but when he hands over his debit card, it is declined, which is odd as the one thing that Pierre-Antoine isn't short of, is money. (Most likely, he forgot to tell his bank that he was travelling abroad, and as a result, they've blocked his account.)

'Don't worry, I can pay cash,' he says, producing a wodge of notes from his wallet.

'Perhaps you should phone your bank later?' I suggest. 'And find out why they have blocked your card.'

'It's not worth the trouble,' he shrugs, as if there is no point in trying to reason with a French bank.

The following morning, sitting in a basement room surrounded by pensioners, Pierre-Antoine enjoys a traditional English breakfast. He tackles it all with enthusiasm – including the stewed prunes from the buffet – and even manages to put a positive spin on the instant coffee. 'It's... different,' he says, gamely dipping his buttered toast into the bitter water, before declaring that 'I certainly won't need to eat lunch after this.'

On the way back to London, faced with a sudden choice between three motorways, I take the wrong one and we find ourselves heading towards Dover.

'I'm not ready to go back yet,' says Pierre-Antoine, looking panicked, when I tell him we are heading back to France. When an exit appears, some thirty kilometres later, it takes us onto another motorway, where the traffic is stationary.

'*Merde*,' I say, since the only thing worse than a traffic jam, is being stuck in one that is going in the wrong direction.

'Oh la, la, English roads are very complicated,' says Pierre-Antoine, shaking his head.

Eventually, we manage to escape the motorway and stop at a petrol station to ask directions. Here, fate deals me a lucky break, in the form of a policeman who has stopped to buy a pasty. 'Excuse me, could you possibly tell me where I am?' I ask.

'Pratt's Bottom,' he replies.

'Sorry?'

'You're in Pratt's Bottom, in Kent.'

'Is it far from London?'

'It depends what part of London,' he says, before explaining how to get back to the city.

As usual, Pierre-Antoine puts a positive spin on the situation. 'I'm certainly seeing a lot of London,' he says, as we crawl back through Croydon and Streatham.

'Yes, you're seeing the parts that most tourists don't go to,' I reply, pressing the automatic door lock.

To make up for the impromptu tour of south London, I decide, on impulse, to take Pierre-Antoine to Devon, which will also circumvent the problem of what to do on New Year's Eve. And so, the following morning, we throw our bags, Biff's bed and the two bottles of champagne into the car, and drive down the M4 towards the West Country.

In less than four hours, we are pulling up in front of the dog-friendly holiday cottage that I managed to secure via a last-minute cancellation. Our cottage, or wooden chalet, is one of twelve in an alpine-inspired holiday park. It's warm and cosy, with two bedrooms, a well-equipped kitchen and an open-plan kitchen and sitting room.

'*Impeccable*,' says Pierre-Antoine, opening a bottle of champagne and looking out at the late afternoon drizzle. 'Now I am about to see the English on holiday.'

A few minutes later, a transit van draws up outside a neighbouring chalet and four people dressed as clowns jump out. I later discover that they are part of a travelling theatre group, though I briefly toy with the idea of telling Pierre-Antoine that dressing up as a clown on New Year's Eve is a 'typically English' tradition.

At midnight, we watch as fireworks are set off on the green lawn in front of the cottages, while the clowns next door, high on local cider, perform cartwheels.

In the days that follow, I take my friend on a lightning tour of East Devon. We visit Agatha Christie's house in Torquay, eat fresh crab sandwiches while shivering on the slipway in Salcombe, and marvel at the number of shops selling lumps of rose quartz and citrine in Totnes, where I struggle to translate into French the concept of the affluent hippy. Pierre-Antoine loves it all. 'Frankly, I could live here,' he declares, time and again.

The delights of Horsham, meanwhile, pale to insignificance when he claps eyes on the thatched cottages in the small East Devon village of Otterton. For me, peak excitement is reached in Topsham, an upmarket estuary town, where I spot a sign for the 'Farm Shop of the Year'. I love a farm shop at the best of times, but Dart's Farm turns out to be a farm shop with knobs on. Forget gnarled carrots and think luxury, rustic department store, selling everything from artisanal spelt breads and celery chutney to mint green Agas.

While I drool over a beast of a stove in a shade of grey called 'Pearl Ashes', Pierre-Antoine gets very excited by some mugs, featuring quirky illustrations of dogs. He heads to the counter with four of them, but his debit card is again declined.

'So you didn't call your bank?' I say.

He shrugs. 'I can pay cash,' he says, unconcerned. He checks in his wallet. 'I've still got £80 left.'

Some would consider it unwise to blow your last remaining cash on porcelain – the mugs are not cheap – when you still have several days of holiday to fund, but not Pierre-Antoine. Instead, he picks out two more mugs. 'A present for you,' he says.

'Really, Pierre-Antoine, this is not a good idea...' I say, my anger rising, as he waves me away.

'For me it is not a problem. I don't mind not having any money,' he declares.

I mind that he no longer has any money. And while it might not be a problem for him, it is now a problem for me, as I will have to pay for everything.

'I cannot believe you did that,' I say, 'and that you haven't phoned your bank to find out why they blocked your card.'

'Oh, but they are very nice mugs. I adore the expressions on the dogs' faces,' he says, not noticing the thunderous expression on mine.

'I'm sorry,' I persist, my anger ratcheting up a notch. 'That was a crazy thing to do.'

He looks at me, suddenly sheepish. 'Maybe it was not the best idea,' he says.

And then, just as I am about to further expand on the gross stupidity of blowing your last £80 on porcelain, while in a foreign country, I pull back. Pierre-Antoine is my guest and a good friend. I think of all the hours that he spent plugging the gaps around my windows with insulating foam, and force myself to take a deep breath.

'Well,' I say. 'You're right. The mugs are charming. But don't forget to phone your bank.'

Devon offers one more delight before we leave. In the seaside town of Budleigh Salterton, we finally find a typical English café – albeit one that is not quite of our era. It has granny-style lace tablecloths and gramophone music, and the waitress is wearing a full-length, frilly pink apron. In normal circumstances, I'd run for the door, but, today, I can't believe my luck.

'Magnificent!' declares Pierre-Antoine.

Job done, I think, as the waitress serves warm scones with clotted cream, and Earl Grey in a sturdy brown teapot. 'That,' he declares, as we leave, 'was top. Frankly, there is nothing more to say.'

Afterwards, we walk up the cliff path to watch silvery waves crashing onto the lavender-grey and rose-coloured pebbles of the shoreline below. East Devon has got it all: soaring coastline, Enid Blyton-esque countryside, hundreds of kilometres of cliff-top walks – and a Waitrose in nearby Sidmouth.

'Frankly, I could live here,' says Pierre-Antoine, as we gaze into an estate agent's window before leaving Devon. And so, I think, could I.

We arrive back in France to find a sign in the window of the Café du Commerce, announcing its 'Indefinite Closure'. This comes as a surprise to no one. The gossip that follows the closure, however, *is* surprising. Zoe provides the lowdown, as we are driving into Poitiers one day to visit Le Pois Tout Vert, the organic supermarket.

Basile's wife was bankrolling the restaurant – she had a 'mattress of cash' Zoe explains, using the French expression for someone who is well-off. But it turned out that she pulled the mattress from under her husband, after discovering that he had been up to various *conneries*, or affairs.

'I think it was obvious that Basile was running the café as an extension of his social life,' says Pierre-Antoine when I mention it to him over drinks one evening. But like everyone else in the village, he maintains a discreet silence as to the nature of the affairs. Whatever the story, white screens once again cover the windows, and Basile has disappeared from the village. His waiter is now working in the local butcher's.

February arrives and, with it, snow. In a few hours, the upturned terracotta pots in my courtyard are turned into snowy domes and the village is cloaked in a chilly white mantle. Biff is super-excited, kicking powder into the air as he runs in circles in front of the chateau, while I feel a similar thrill as my boots crunch across the crisp, untrampled snow.

But within days, the roads around Villiers have become dangerously slippery, because the local mayors – with the exception of Delphine, who planned ahead and ordered salt back in August – do not bother to grit the roads. The snow turns to sludge and refreezes into treacherous compacted ice, so that even the village square becomes a no-go zone.

It's great for getting work done, but after three weeks under icy siege, only venturing out to give Biff the briefest of walks or to check if Gabriella needs any groceries, I have cabin fever. So, when Delphine phones to ask if I'd like to go to my favourite restaurant, in Usson, for dinner and offers to pick me up, I jump at the chance.

'Are you sure you'll be OK to drive? The roads are still really bad,' I say, gazing through the window, as the late afternoon light fades to a crystalline blue.

'Yes, it's no problem. I'm used to driving in bad weather. I'll pick you up at seven,' she says.

My friend arrives, cheerful as ever, in red lipstick and a purple coat. We drive sedately through the cold, dark country-side in a cloud of Chanel No 5 until we see the warm, orange glow from the windows of the Auberge de l'Écurie. Inside, the fire is roaring and a surprising number of people have braved the weather to come out for dinner, including, I notice, Matt and Zoe. They wave at us from a corner table.

'Oh, you're wearing a skirt. You look… different,' Zoe says. It's true that, after weeks of wearing a knitted hat and multiple layers of clothing, I've made a bit of an effort in a short A-line skirt and makeup, but surely this can't be the reason why she appears noticeably less friendly than usual?

'How's it going with the house?' I ask.

'Why don't you pop over and have a look?' says Matt.

'I'm sure she's got much better things to do, darling. Like write her books,' says Zoe.

I'm a little taken aback by the glacial edge to her voice and the use of the word 'she'. Perhaps I've been in France too long, but it seems unspeakably rude. I wouldn't dream of referring to a friend standing in front of me, by anything other than their name.

When I mention this to Delphine, over dinner, she agrees. 'I think this woman is a little unhappy with you, for some reason. She seems very wary.'

I think of how Matt has flirted with me and wonder if Zoe has found out about it. Given that I spend most of my life in wellies and a bobble hat, I'm hardly husband-bait, so it's odd. We are seated quite far away from them, at a table near the fire, but when I glance over, they seem to be having an intense, not entirely happy, conversation.

'I have some news about the wind farm,' says Delphine. 'The mayor and the four councillors in Bonillet who voted in favour of the farm, have been forbidden to have a turbine on their land. And that's not all. They've each been given a fine of €1000.'

'Well. That's good news for the monkeys…' I say.

'FOR GOD'S SAKE…'

I look over as Matt's angry voice travels across the restaurant and see Zoe trying to shush him. Shortly afterwards, they get up to leave. Matt hovers by the door, looking uncomfortable, as his wife comes over to say good-bye.

'We're off,' she says, with a smile that is noticeably brittle, bordering on fake. 'Let's have coffee soon.'

I know from my fashion editor days that when someone says 'Let's have coffee/lunch/drinks soon,' with no specific time frame, it means, 'Let's *not* have coffee/lunch/drinks soon.' So I smile back and say, 'You know where I am.'

The snow and ice eventually clear, and as March arrives, so do the first signs of spring. Hopeful tufts of green, which will eventually become lush stalks of wheat, appear on the flat brown fields, and, as I pull out my yoga mat each morning to meditate, I do so to a soundtrack of birds singing. I see no sign of Zoe or Matt in the weeks that follow and assume that they have both gone back to London for work.

Then, one afternoon, as I'm driving to a farm track in a nearby hamlet to walk Biff, a car comes flying around a blind bend, forcing me to swerve into the grass verge. The driver is young, in his early twenties. Immediately, I feel the anger start to rise at his idiotic driving and the narrow escape from a head-on collision. I pull up the handbrake and wind down the window. He shrugs as if to apologise.

'Listen,' I say. 'You are going far too fast for this road. You had no idea what was coming round the corner and you could have caused a serious accident.' He looks at me nervously. 'I am telling you this,' I say, 'because a friend of mine died as a result of a car accident caused by reckless driving.'

I can see that I have his attention. 'But that wasn't the worst of it,' I continue. 'He wasn't killed immediately. He was in a coma and spent the last nine months of his life in a hospital bed, paralysed from the neck down.'

'I'm sorry...' he says looking genuinely remorseful.

'And I don't want this to happen to you...'

In certain parts of the UK, this little homily would be enough to get you murdered. But the young French guy nods meekly, holding up his hand in a *mea culpa* gesture. He drives away, probably cursing me, but I don't care because I feel incredibly calm and in control. I am not raging. Could it be that the meditation is working?

Suddenly, I notice the driver behind getting out of his car and coming towards me. It's Matt, dressed in a black jacket layered over a thin grey sweater and jeans. (Architects, I've noticed, seem to have a recognisable uniform, though fortunately he hasn't succumbed to the thick-framed 'character' glasses that seem to be synonymous with the profession.)

'What's going on?' he asks, leaning towards my window, one arm placed proprietorially on the roof. 'Are you OK?'

'Yes, all good, thanks.'

'Then why have you stopped in the middle of the road?'

'I just had a near-miss with a French driver.'

'Ah,' he says. 'I hear you're a bit of a demon behind the wheel. Zoe told me about your run-in with the gendarmes.'

'Yes, well I wasn't the one that was speeding.'

'I was joking,' he says. 'Where are you off to?'

'I'm walking the dog.'

'In the car?'

'I'm going to a farm track.'

'Anywhere near Puy-Felix?'

'Why?'

'Because you're on the road to Puy Felix, which is where my barn is,' he says, putting his hand through the window to stroke Biff, who is watching him from the passenger seat. 'I'd love to show it to you, if you're interested? The barn that is.'

I stifle the urge to laugh. 'I don't think so. I have to walk the dog before it gets dark.'

He looks at his watch. 'We've got two hours,' he says. 'Before it gets dark. And by the way, Zoe is at a fabric fair in Florence.'

'Right. And I'm sure she'd be thrilled to know that you were showing me your bi-folds.'

'Listen,' he says. 'The barn is on the left once you've gone over the bridge into Puy-Felix. I'll meet you there in five minutes.'

I am staggered by his self-confidence. Suddenly, another driver sounds his horn behind us. 'Oh, fuck off,' says Matt, turning to address the impatient driver.

'Yes,' I say, turning the key in the ignition. 'I'd better. Biff will be miffed if I don't walk him soon. Thanks for the invitation, all the same.'

As I drive off, I glance in my rear mirror, at the wiry figure left standing in the road, and I make a mental note to avoid any walks near Puy-Felix for the foreseeable future.

Chapter 18

Frond Life

AS SPRING APPROACHES and the scent of cut grass replaces the smell of wood smoke and damp earth, I decide to escape the village for a while. Sarah and Steve agree to look after Biff for a couple of weeks, so that I can go back to Portugal, this time to Lisbon. When I mention this to Pierre-Antoine, he hints that he would like to come too.

'I could do with some days in a spa,' he says, when I tell him, in the hope of putting him off, that my final destination is a detox retreat in Madeira. I'm momentarily tempted to invite him along. He's an easy-going chap, pleased by almost everything, but I also know that he is a travelling disaster. I imagine lost passports, blocked credit cards and missed departures, and the various travel agent duties that I would have to perform as a result. My plan is to do some thinking and writing, while gazing at the sea. I want to go alone, so I don't mention Portugal again. Pierre-Antoine gets the hint, as he doesn't either.

Lord Byron, who visited Portugal in the eighteenth century – by chance, since he'd missed his boat to Malta – was not very complimentary about the city. 'Except the view from the Tagus which is beautiful, and some fine churches and convents, it contains little but filthy streets and more filthy inhabitants,' he complained. Still, he wrote, 'I am very happy here because I loves [sic] oranges.'

I arrive at Lisbon's gleamingly clean airport, with its fresh, minty-green tiles, at close to midnight. As my taxi speeds towards the city, it is too dark to be able to comment on the cleanliness of its streets or its inhabitants, but my hotel is shiningly clean, and the night porter greets me with a big smile and the offer of a glass of port.

On my first morning in the city, I'm struck by how uncrowded, bordering on empty, it is, as I walk to Figueira Square to take one of Lisbon's famous yellow trams to the Belém district. It was from here that Vasco da Gama and many of Portugal's other explorers set off on their extended travels. The key attraction is the church of Jerónimos Monastery, where Vasco da Gama is buried. There's a long queue to get in, so I keep walking and visit the adjoining Maritime Museum instead, which, inexplicably – given that Belém is all about nautical achievements – has no line outside.

In the entrance hall, there are colossal statues of Portugal's A-list explorers. In pole position is Henry the Navigator, the prince who inspired the Portuguese voyages of discovery in the fifteenth century. It seems that he wasn't that keen on sailing himself. And who can blame him? Sailors and navigators of that era were reluctant to sail towards Africa and what was termed the 'Sea of Darkness', fearing sea monsters and boiling water near the equator. Factor in the claustrophobic and squalid living conditions and a frankly rubbish diet for months on end, and you can understand why 'explorer' would not have been the first career choice of many.

I speed past the nautical instruments, and linger over the portraits of famous explorers. You'd think they would look a little ravaged thanks to the rigours of the nautical life: scurvy; the lack of fresh fruit and vegetables; and the stress of stepping ashore, not knowing if you'd be barbecued by the natives. But, as young men at least, many of them were strikingly handsome. A 'portrait while young' of Bartholomew Diaz (the first European to get to the southern tip of Africa) shows a man with long blondish hair, an aquiline nose and penetrating eyes. If my niece were here, I'm pretty sure she would be instant messaging her friends, 'This navigator dude was HOT.' Cristóvão Colombo, on the other hand, is grey-haired and rather pasty of face, and I can't see her getting excited about him.

In addition to the big names, there are the lesser known stars of the sea: Nuno Tristão, who explored from Senegal to the Gambia; Diego Cão who bagged Namibia; and João Gonçalves Zarco, who 'discovered' Madeira in 1420. I wonder if they were the Premier League footballers and rock stars of their day, scoring countries rather than goals. This they did by erecting padrões, limestone crosses inscribed with the Portuguese coat of arms, which explorers carried on their ships to claim new lands for Portugal. Basically, it was a more official way of stating, 'Vasco woz here'.

At the end of my museum tour, a single item puts their expeditions into context. Displayed in a small black room with a soundtrack of a menacing drumbeat, is a tribal headdress trimmed with twigs and bunches of straw and topped with bronze horns. Brave was the sailor who set foot on new land with the possibility of meeting that. Many of the ships, it seems, carried convicts for precisely that purpose: they'd be forced to row ashore first, to test the warmth of the welcome.

When I emerge from the Maritime Museum, the queue for the church of the Jerónimos Monastery has disappeared. Inside the church, however, it's as if all the tourists that you don't see in Lisbon have congregated here. 'Where the f*** is Vasco da Gama?' asks someone in the melee behind me. I imagine that Mrs da Gama and many of the explorer's contemporaries asked themselves the same question when he disappeared off to sea, for months on end. And it's a fair bet that the man himself often stood on the bow of his ship, staring out at the blue and wondering 'Where the f*** am I?'

In fact, in his final repose, Vasco is lying to the left of the entrance in an ornately carved tomb.

Belém's other historic attraction is Fábrica de Pastéis de Belém, the famous pastry shop that is said to produce the best custard tarts in the world. They've had some practice, as they've been making them since 1837, so I join the long line, stretched out along the pavement, and wait until it is my turn to choose from the various trays of baked goods.

I then head across the road to the Jardim de Belém, to eat my little cache of warm custard tarts and mini empanadas (savoury Portuguese pastries). It's not the healthiest lunch I've eaten, but the custard tarts are definitely 'dope', as my niece might say. The filling is perfection: a not-too-sweet blend of sugar, egg and vanilla, balanced by a hint of salt in the pastry. The Portuguese rarely hold back on the salt, but, in this instance, it really adds something – other than an increased risk of heart attack.

I spend a few hours checking out the Warhols and Picassos in the nearby Berardo Museum of modern art, then take the tram back to the centre of Lisbon, arriving at the Praça do Commerce, just in time for cocktail hour. With its elegant architecture, cluster of outdoor cafés, and the River Tagus lapping one side, Praça do Comércio is one of the most congenial city squares in Europe, yet few people, I imagine, will even have heard of it. It reminds me of St Mark's Square, in Venice, but unlike St Mark's Square, the cafés here are not charging €15 a pop for a cappuccino – or anything close to it – the shops aren't full of sinister-looking Venetian masks and other tourist tat; and the clientele also includes Lisboetas, or locals, enjoying after-work drinks.

The square looks so inviting that I decide to stop for a glass of sparkling water (well, I am checking into a detox spa in a few days' time). As the smiling waiter shows me to a table, I notice another of those exquisite details at which the Portuguese excel: a fine mist of water is sprayed into the air at regular intervals, to cool the terrace. The subliminal message, as with sun canopies in supermarket car parks, is that every aspect of the customer's comfort has been considered.

For the lone traveller, this is supposedly the most challenging hour of the day, but Lisbon is an easy city in which to be alone. The waiters are pleasant – they don't seem at all surprised to see an unaccompanied tourist – and the atmosphere is relaxed. A Portuguese Water Dog, its black coat glistening after a dip in the river, arrives with his owner and shakes himself down majestically, adding to the laid-back ambience.

Glancing around the restaurant, I notice one couple, almost certainly British – I've lived abroad long enough to be able to recognise my fellow nationals *en vacances* – sitting in glum silence. Physically they're both at the same table, but emotionally they might as well be sitting alone.

I'm actually quite pleased to be here with only William Beckford for company. You could never be bored with him. His memoirs of his various stays in Portugal between 1787 and 1799 are full of humour and exquisite descriptions – if you're a writer, gallingly so – of his surroundings. Thanks to him, I'm especially looking forward to visiting Sintra, aka 'the garden of Lisbon', where he rented a house for six years.

Beckford, according to one of his biographers, 'evoked love, wearied of it, slipped from its fetters and began again elsewhere.' As a lifestyle choice it probably has much to commend it, though my guess is that it gets exhausting after a while. I glance at Mr and Mrs Glum, and sense that at least one of them would like to slip from their fetters and begin again elsewhere. Suddenly, I find myself thinking of Zoe and Matt.

When the waitress arrives to take my order, I force myself, in the spirit of investigation, to forgo the sparkling water in favour of a sparkling wine called 'Mateus Rosé Brut'. For many people, myself included, the words 'Mateus Rosé' mean a sugary pink wine, bottled in what looks like a giant perfume flask. With the exception of Cliff Richard (allegedly) and Saddam Hussein, who apparently kept stockpiles of it in his palace, I don't know of anyone who drinks the stuff. Not even the photograph of Jimi Hendrix swigging it straight from the bottle – what was he thinking? – could make Mateus Rosé cool. But this, according to the menu, is a dry, sparkling – and by implication, less naff – version. I'm not entirely convinced but, at €5 a glass, I'm prepared to give it a go.

The waitress returns with a flute of sparkly pink wine. It's crisp and chilled and, although obviously not as much of a buzz as discovering India or Africa, one of the best things that I've discovered in a while. Sadly, I have not seen it anywhere in the UK or France, which leads me to believe that the Portuguese, who apparently don't drink the syrupy original, are keeping all stocks of it to themselves.

Sitting under a sugar-pink sky, as vintage Massive Attack flows seductively from the sound system, I decide that Lisbon is my favourite city in Europe. It is sophisticated without being up itself, or trying too hard. And although it might have fallen upon its uppers, it is still cultured and gracious, with many clues to its illustrious past.

I imagine the excitement, five centuries ago, when a vessel sailed up the Tagus, stuffed to the gunwales with exotic treasures from the Orient, like a latter day Liberty department store gliding into port. And I can imagine, too, the euphoria of the merchants, looking out at the Tagus to see their ship literally coming in.

My phone pings with a message, sent through a social media site, from Matt. 'Gone away?' he has written. 'Saw your shutters were closed.' It seems that I can't escape him, even here, but it's a weird coincidence that he has contacted me, just when I was thinking of him and Zoe. A waiter appears to ask if I would like to order any food. I wasn't planning to, but the tuna with lemon butter rice sounds tempting, and this has to be one of the best city settings in Europe for evening victuals, so why not?

Glancing at the river shimmering calmly on my left, and the yellow trams gliding by on my right, it's hard to believe that the square has seen some horrible events, including the assassination of Portugal's second-to-last king in 1908. Even more difficult to believe is that this was the scene of a devastating tsunami. Shortly after 9.40 am, on a Saturday morning in 1755, Lisbon was hit by an earthquake, followed by a fire. Then, some twenty minutes after the quake, a six-metre wave roared up the Tagus, killing people who'd fled to the seafront to escape the flames. With horrible irony, the people that conquered the sea, suffered terrible devastation when the sea came to them. In less than an hour, poor old Lisbon was reduced from a sophisticated, prosperous city to a pile of waterlogged rubble.

As the sun starts to drop over the Tagus, I walk through the triumphal arch that leads out of the square, planning an early night. When I get back to my hotel, I find another text from Matt. 'When I'm in bed with Zoe, I think of you,' he has written. *What the hell?*

It could be the daily dose of custard pies and caffeine, but as I walk towards Baixo metro station, the next morning, I am boiling over with love for Lisbon. There is something to admire at every turn, even the dazzling modernity of the metro, which makes the London and Paris underground systems seem quite shabby. Everything is pleasing to the eye: the opalescent white tiling, the futuristic blue lights along the platforms – you could just as easily be waiting for a gin and tonic as a train – and the fact that the station smells of caramel and vanilla, thanks to the cart selling custard tarts on the concourse.

I am on my way to the Gulbenkian Museum, taking advantage of the fact that on Sunday mornings, many of Lisbon's museums are free. There are a lot of them to choose from, specialising in everything from fado and tiles, to er... electricity and water, but if you visit only one museum in Lisbon, I urge you to make it the Gulbenkian, which has to be the most under-recognised private art collection in the world. It just about blew my silver-hooped Marni sandals off.

Behind the grey concrete walls of the rather squat building, lie stunning works by some of the most famous names ever to have picked up a paintbrush. There are Renoirs, Gainsboroughs, Turners and Monets, along with paintings by Rubens, Degas, Van Dyck and Fragonard, and richly hued carpets, vases and embroidered tapestries, cherry-picked from all eras and empires.

What makes this museum so eye boggling is that Calouste Gulbenkian, the Turkish oil magnate who amassed this incredible collection, had impeccable taste, and a motto of 'only the best will do'. It is difficult to conceive that he could, and did, have many of these masterpieces in his home. His four-storey house in Paris was packed to the chimney pots with pricey pieces of art. Various thoughts run through my head: how high must his insurance premiums have been? Who did they trust to do the dusting? And Mrs Gulbenkian: did she ever demand a declutter, or think to herself, as her husband came home from yet another shopping spree, '*Dear God, not another Gainsborough?*'

Gulbenkian's life-long splurge, multi-buying Manets and Ming up until his death in 1955, certainly puts the occasional handbag purchase into perspective. But the Gulbenkian sums up how beautifully understated Lisbon is. Here is one of the best private art collections in the world, yet it barely registers on the international radar.

I have whipped myself up into a frenzy of excitement over Sintra, or Cintra, as it is also known. The so-called 'garden of Lisbon' – a half-hour train journey from the city – has inspired a lot of gushing praise down the centuries, particularly from those of a poetic sensibility. 'The village of Cintra about fifteen miles from the capitol is perhaps in every respect the most delightful in Europe,' wrote Lord Byron, while the poet Robert Southey described it as 'the most blessed spot in the habitable globe'. My old friend William Beckford was also a fan: 'I must go to Sintra or I shall expire,' he wrote.

And so on Sunday afternoon I head to Rossio station, which is as empty and calm as the rest of Lisbon – where is everyone? – to take the train to this ferny paradise. Trains to Sintra run every twenty minutes and in no time at all, I'm speeding out of the city, past flotillas of pink and vanilla-coloured tenements and buildings defaced with tumultuous graffiti, with flags of white washing fluttering from their balconies. Eventually, the high-rise kingdoms give way to pastel houses and green flat-lands. Soon we are pulling into a charming station, with pink hydrangeas spilling over a stone wall onto the platform, and beautiful panels of tile work on the ticket office walls.

In keeping with the descriptions that I've read, Sintra is lavishly green, a place of trees and turrets and pastel buildings. And tourists. The place is alive with them, coming downhill in a straggly line, after a day of sightseeing. I realise now why Lisbon was deserted: everyone is here.

It's too late for me to check out any of Sintra's castles, *quintas* (estates) or palaces today, so, after dropping my bag at the guesthouse, I stroll around the streets, up and down narrow alleys, getting the measure of the place and looking for somewhere for dinner. I pass several cafés and snack bars boasting something called *bifana* on the menu, which is unnerving as it conjures up visions of a small, female version of Biff, served, almost certainly, with boiled potatoes. (An internet search later reveals *bifana* to be a piece of grilled meat in a bun, or a hamburger.)

Proper restaurants appear to be thin on the ground, but eventually I find one in a side street. The waiters seem excessively delighted to see me. 'Come on in, sit wherever you want,' says one of them, waving his arm expansively at the rustic, and mostly empty, interior. It is early, so presumably my fellow tourists are back at their hotels, stretching out their hamstrings after a rigorous day on Sintra's hilly terrain.

On previous trips to Portugal, I've successfully avoided such national dishes as rooster-in-its-own-blood stew, and sparrow casserole, but this evening I'm determined to travel beyond my culinary comfort zone. To start, I order coriander soup served with a 'poched' [sic] egg, not because of a burning desire to eat it, but because I'm intrigued. How do you make a soup from coriander, without it tasting like shower gel? The answer: with chunks of fried bread and a lot of salt and oil. It's not terrible but it's not terrific.

My main course, the rooster-in-its-own-blood stew, turns out to be less sinister than it sounds. It's basically a Portuguese version of coq-au-vin, with rice thrown in. My waiter helpfully points out – fortunately after I've eaten it – that the rice has been soaked in blood for several hours, which is the kind of detail that no diner wants, or needs, to know.

But the big question, with regards to the national cuisine, is this: 'how do the Portuguese manage to eat so much salt without suffering cardiac arrest?'

I suspect that their passion for salt is something to do with their seafaring past and the need to preserve food for months on end. But not for the first time, I find myself wanting to say, 'Guys, calm down with the salt. We're not going to sea for a year.' After my gastronomic adventure, I return to my hotel to plan tomorrow's sightseeing. There are an awful lot of palaces, villas and grand estates to see in Sintra, built by wealthy aristocrats and merchants who were no doubt attracted to its verdant hills by the possibility of some climbing of the social kind, Sintra being the summer retreat of the royal family.

The next morning, I join an eager scene in the tourist office, which is the place to buy tickets for almost everything. After standing around in a crowd of people, shoving and shouting in all languages, I eventually emerge triumphant, with a combined ticket and all-important day pass for the buses that shuttle around Sintra's hills and palaces.

I join another excitable crowd at the bus stop. The tourists in Sintra certainly haven't come to Portugal to toast their buttocks on the beach. Instead, they're determined to load up on culture and it's a case of survival of the fittest. People fight to board each bus with the same outta-my-way enthusiasm as Biff attacking a bowl of chicken and basmati rice.

After I've trodden on an elderly tourist or two to claim my place on the bus, I'm transported up into a pleasant green landscape. Every now and then I glimpse an impressive villa, most likely owned by a wealthy Lisbonian or maybe a British expat, much, I imagine, as it was in Beckford's day.

First stop is the Moorish castle. The views from its ruins are stupendous, but you have to earn them. Up and down, down and up, I go, climbing steep paths, steps and parapets, to admire vistas that stretch as far as Lisbon and the sea. (The castle would have provided one of the first sightings of Vasco da Gama returning from India.)

There is, I notice, a thrilling disregard for health and safety. Several walkways have potentially fatal drops, with not even a rope to prevent the clumsy from making a faster-than-planned return to the old town. I decide to walk the 650 metres back to town from the castle gardens. It's a steep descent but strangely enjoyable in a schadenfreude kind of way, since a surprising number of people are hauling themselves uphill, presumably because they lost the battle, or the will, to get on the tourist bus. 'Am I nearly there yet,' several ask, as they pant their way up the winding paths. The truth is too cruel, so I smile encouragingly while thinking, *Not even close*.

Pena National Palace is my next stop. Here, another steep climb is required to reach the entrance of the palace, which was built in the 1840s as a summer residence for Portuguese royalty. Inside, assuming you haven't collapsed and been carted off by paramedics as you haul yourself uphill, you are rewarded with the kind of claustrophobic crush that you can enjoy on London Underground for half the price. And, unlike the London Underground, you cannot get off at the next stop.

Within a few minutes, I deeply regret entering this hellish place without a bottle of water. The only route through the palace is a single-file line, which comes to an abrupt halt shortly after I've joined it. I am at the mercy of the people in front, armed with their smart phones and cameras. If one person stops, we all stop. And we do. Often. The tourists in front of me are the most diligent kind, determined to admire every last tile and piece of decorative cornicing, oblivious to the back-up behind them. I am trapped, roped in on both sides, with no chance of doing a U-turn thanks to the people pressed up behind my shoulder blades. To misquote Beckford, I have to leave Pena, or I will expire.

I cannot say how long I am held hostage in Pena, but after an age of shuffling through its fancy rooms like convicts, we are eventually released onto an open terrace. Gasping for water and air, I am tempted to rush across it like Maria, running open-armed across an Austrian mountain in *The Sound of Music*.

The most fascinating thing about the palace, which is designated one of the Seven Wonders of Portugal by the Portuguese Ministry of Culture, is that the interior is just as it was on the night that the Portuguese royal family fled for their lives in 1910. The last queen of Portugal, Queen Amélia, is said to have been Portugal's equivalent of Marie Antoinette, but despite studying modern history at university, I had never heard of her, although she is exactly the kind of historical figure I'd be interested in. Did she, I wonder, ever say, 'Let them eat custard tarts?'

Regardless of her extravagant tastes, one has to have some sympathy: her husband, King Carlos I, and son, were killed by terrorists, as they rode through Lisbon in an open-carriage. Queen Amélia, fortunately, made it out of Portugal with her head intact and spent most of her remaining years in France, her country of birth.

I'm flagging a little by the time I leave Pena, but after glug-ging back a bottle of water, I'm back on the bus – my combined ticket is good for one day only – and heading for the Quinta da Regaleira. The palace and its gardens provide another excel-lent cardiovascular workout. I start in the palace, which was built in the early twentieth century for a Portuguese million-aire. I'm much taken by his cheerful colour schemes – lovely corals and yellows – the lavish cake-icing-style stucco on the ceiling and the eye-catching mosaic of birds-of-paradise on the dining room floor. By Sintra's standards, this palace is cosy in its proportions and has the advantage that you can wander around at liberty, rather than travelling through in a hot tourist sandwich.

But the real pull-factor at Quinta da Regaleira is the gardens. Difficult though it is to believe, in the bright sunshine, the summer playground of the Portuguese nobility was once also a place of cult worship, with links to the Freemasons and the Knights Templar. Guidebooks hint at funny goings-on in Sintra's caves and forests, with vague mentions of Celtic worship, madness, eccentricity, and, according to the locals... light bulbs popping frequently, though that could just be the eco bulbs that they are using, as I have the same problem at home. But I can easily imagine strange, if unspecified, "goings-on" at the Quinta da Regaleira. As well as being a fiesta of chloro-phyll, ferns and deepest green fronds, its gardens are filled with Masonic symbolism and strange quirks, chief of which are two wells, leading to a series of underground passages.

No one knows what the wells were used for – certainly not collecting water – or what went on there, but the gardens' unusual features seem to have been carefully planned. As I go up and down the steep paths, there is a surprise around every corner: statues, grottos, towers, and lookout points, secret foun-tains, terraces and hidden pools of water. The wells, however, are annoyingly elusive. Onwards and upwards I go, along avenues of palms and exotic fronds, past moss-covered stones, only to be led into a series of fern-lined cul-de-sacs, so that I have to go down again. It's encouraging to see that many other people appear to be playing the same game of garden Snakes and Ladders.

Just as I'm about to give up on the wells, I hear strange echoing voices and suddenly I am standing with a cluster of fellow tourists peering into a mossy void. It looks like a reverse tower, built underground with a stone staircase spiralling around its sides. I climb down into the darkness of its damp, echoing interior. At the bottom there is a tiled floor, featuring some weird but obviously meaningful pattern, which I later discover is the compass and the cross of the Knights Templar. It is thought that the wells may have been used for ceremonial purposes and possibly Masonic or tarot initiation rights, but no one knows for sure. It's creepy even in daylight. And it gets weirder.

Pausing on the way back up, I notice people disappearing into a dark tunnel off one of the landings. I follow the person in front of me, who is using the torch app on their phone to light the way, into a dark, narrow passage. After a while, we emerge into daylight, by a hidden lake and grotto. Apparently, the well and dark tunnels symbolise death (descending into darkness), leading to rebirth (light) and the Garden of Eden (the lake and grotto). Who knows? But I can imagine the Facebook update that my niece would have posted: 'Man, some seriously weird shit must have gone down here.'

Madness is also said to have flourished on Sintra's posh estates. A kind of madness – or that common expat affliction known as *too-much-time-itis* – would certainly have been necessary to design those gardens. But whatever weirdness went on underground, an equal amount of fun would have been enjoyed, above it. The hidden benches, secluded terraces and summerhouses would, no doubt, have hosted many illicit trysts.

Exhausted from climbing up wells and steep paths, and suffering from fern-fatigue, I shoehorn myself back onto the shuttle bus to return to my hotel. I've saved the best, Monserrate, until last. This is the estate that William Beckford rented from 1793 to 1799, spending some of his own vast wealth on land-scaping its grounds. He even imported a flock of sheep from England, putting into perspective the Marmite and other home comforts that modern expats ship in from the motherland. I cannot wait to see it.

The following morning, when I leave my hotel to take the bus up to Monserrate, I am surprised to find Sintra deserted. I also seem to have the palace gardens to myself, wandering alone among the fountains and the ferns, appreciating the sharp green freshness of the place at this early hour.

Although I've enjoyed many stunning views since arriving in Sintra, those from inside Monserrate are stupendous. It is a beautiful palace, built in the best possible taste. The entrance hall features astonishingly intricate stone carving from floor to ceiling, so that the walls look as if they are made of lace. And oh, the views… I experience a euphoric rush every time I look through a window or step onto a terrace and see the canopy of green forest below. How could anyone live here and not feel insanely happy all the time?

Yet Francis Cook, the wealthy Englishman who bought the villa half a century after Beckford had moved on, does not look at all happy in a photo with his extended family. Their glum expressions suggest that money, a beautiful house and all the ferns and exotic shrubs you can buy, do not necessarily make you happy. But I bet Beckford had fun here.

Chapter 19

Be Like a Bee

I KNOW THAT I'm going to love Madeira from the moment that I step into the arrivals hall and see the ocean shimmering on the other side of the floor-to-ceiling windows. Madeira is a mini-Portugal, with impressive slices of cliff, topped with a whipping of green forest and spirit-lifting views of the Atlantic. Like Portugal, it has an abundance of EU-funded highways and tunnels – more, possibly, than is appropriate for a small volcanic island.

Until recently, I had no idea where Madeira was, mainly because it's not on many maps. Once a poverty-stricken outpost of Europe, it now appears, on the surface at least, to be a relatively affluent outpost of Portugal, thanks to lavish (some would say ill-advised) spending on marinas, helicopter ports and industrial parks. But the truth is that it is laden with debt. Madeira is a highly leveraged garden, floating to the south west of Portugal.

The cab driver takes the motorway rather than the scenic inland route to my spa hotel, so there are disappointingly few glimpses of the island's inner, evergreen beauty. But we eventually arrive in a residential neighbourhood, dominated by gated villas and frills of bougainvillea, where he deposits me in front of a single-storey pink building.

I have booked a room with 'superior sea view' and cannot wait to be in it. My plan is to sleep for a few hours – I had to get up in the middle of the night for the flight to Lisbon – book some spa treatments, and then sit on the terrace with my laptop and work until sunset. Right now I can't think of anything more delightful than four days in a room overlooking the sea. The only thing that stands between that sea view and me is the stern-faced boy behind reception, currently holding a lengthy phone conversation in German.

My first thought is that he is on work-experience, but he exudes an authority beyond his years. Unusually for a spa, where members of staff tend to drift around in tunics and pyjamas, on a cloud of peace and love, he is wearing a tailored suit. Where is the whale music, the burning incense and the obligatory statue of Buddha, I wonder?

When he finally gives me his attention, it is with all the warmth of a winter dip in the Atlantic. He hands me a programme in German, which includes activities such as *Wassergymnastik*, a workout called 'Thump' and something called *Body Combat Am Strand*, which turns out to be 'combat on the beach'. I'm supposed to be checking in for a peaceful break, not World War III. At least the *Poncha Abend*, or 'Punch Evening' as I'm able to deduce from my limited German, sounds as though it has potential, assuming it refers to the alcoholic beverage rather than physical assault.

As the stern receptionist escorts me around the spa, introducing me as *Frau* Wheeler, I realise that everyone is speaking German. I have landed in a German-speaking colony of Portugal. He shows me the yoga room, the computer room – 'You will only use wifi here, *ja*?' – and the dining room, where breakfast is being served on a terrace overlooking the sea. 'Here you will be told what you can eat,' he says. Finally, he takes me back to reception and opens a door opposite his desk: 'Here, *Frau* Wheeler is your room.'

The view from the room stops me in my tracks, mainly because it is not what I booked. Instead of an unspoilt view of blue Atlantic, what I see from my terrace is... a large shrub. There is a small patch of sea visible in the distance, but a land-scaped cliff encroaches from the right, blocking most of the view, as if it were nature's very own photobomb.

'Um. This isn't what I was expecting.'

'It's a sea view, *ja*? You can see the sea, *Frau* Wheeler,' he says, as if anticipating a complaint.

'But it's not the view on your website,' I say. 'It is a sea view obscured by a large shrub.'

'There is nothing I can do, *Frau* Wheeler. All of the rooms have superior sea views. There is no difference.' He marches back to his desk before I have time to argue.

The view is not the only disappointing thing about my room. It is next to the reception (lots of shouting in German) and above the kitchen (lots of shouting in Portuguese, accompanied by clanging pots). I've been in airports that were more peaceful. I march back out, wearing the same 'don't mess with me' expression as the receptionist.

'Excuse me,' I say. 'I would like to be moved to another room.'

'Not possible, *Frau* Wheeler. All the rooms with superior sea views are booked.'

'Then please move me to a room with an inferior sea view that is at least quiet. I am not staying in that one.'

Perhaps sensing a kindred spirit in my steely eyes, he picks up a key and says, 'Follow me, *Frau* Wheeler'.

And so I find myself in a room that is, at least, quiet. I throw my bag down and head to the terrace for breakfast. Those who have booked the Ayurvedic programme are seated at a long table eating seeds and sipping herbal tea, their self-discipline rigorously tested by the aroma of coffee and bacon drifting over from the non-Ayurvedic buffet (not everyone is here for the detox). I help myself to a coffee and sit at a table overlooking the sea, pretending that I am nothing to do with the detox programme, which I will start tomorrow.

I've been to an Ayurvedic spa before (Ayurveda being the Hindu medical system for the prevention and cure of disease) so I know the drill. Panchakarma, the detox programme, can include vomiting and purging – yup, people pay good money for something that happens in many UK cities on a Friday night – but for western tastes, a less traumatic version has evolved, a kind of 'Ayurveda-lite'.

It is important to ease yourself in gently, starting with a treatment called padabhyanga (a foot and leg massage), leading up to abhyanga (full-body oil massage) and, finally, the most powerful treatment of all, shirodara, whereby a continuous stream of warm oil is poured onto your forehead. This is said to stimulate the so-called third-eye chakra, which is connected to intuition and mental clarity. It's fashionable to scoff at the mention of 'chakras', but I'm fully on board with the concept of the body's different energy points.

At midday, I take my place with the detoxers on the terrace, having noticed that, unlike breakfast, the Ayurvedic lunch looks surprisingly good. The women at the table radiate good health and the self-righteous glow that comes from several days of lentil dhal and downward dogs. Seated in the middle of them is a slightly built Indian man, dressed in jeans and a checked shirt. Dr Jafri, or Dr J as everyone calls him, looks young, earnest and somewhat ill at ease. I slide in at the end of the table, next to Angelika and Elspeth, who seem to be generating the most laughter.

Most of those present have been doing the programme for over a week and have clearly bonded over the chia seeds. Very generously, they switch to English for my benefit and, even more generously, they share a key piece of insider knowledge: Antonio is the name of the therapist that everyone wants on their spa card. A session of abhyanga with him, according to Angelika, 'is better than bad sex'.

'*Come on,*' says Elspeth, pushing her Chanel sunglasses back on her blonde bob. 'It is better than any sex.'

For a bunch of people who've been deprived of toxins and stimulants for over a week, my fellow conscripts are excellent company. After lunch, we all file into the dining room for a talk by Dr J, entitled 'Ayurveda in Everyday Life'. A couple of people are making notes, so I get out my notebook too, although I'm pretty sure I can predict most of what Dr J is going to say: eat more vegetables, avoid coffee, wine and sugar, and so on. Whatever the type of spa, with the notable exception of the French thalassotherapy kind, the advice always boils down to avoiding life's most pleasurable comestibles.

The doctor speaks very softly and with a heavy accent, so I find myself dipping in and out of his talk. 'The first thing in Ayurveda is time-management... eight hours to work, eight hours to sleep... eight hours for friends, cooking and exercising,' he says.

To pass the time, I decide to play a private game of spa bingo, ticking off the most predictable phrases in my head. Dr J is talking about the importance of hydration (tick!), warm liquids, especially ginger tea (tick!), and avoiding coffee, sugar and alcohol (tick, tick, tick on my imaginary bingo card). He then moves on to less well-charted territory, beginning with the benefits of a 'daily application of oil'.

'If you do this before yoga or sports activity, it gives mobility and softness to the muscles and joints,' he says. He also recommends applying warm oil to the head and heels – that's coconut or sesame oil, not engine, if you're planning to do this at home – while applying warm oils to you heels before going to bed, is good for insomnia.

You could, it seems, fill a large part of your day with oil-based activities, filling your ears with warm sesame oil, swilling out your mouth with a tablespoon of sesame oil for twenty minutes every morning – 'good for gums and general health as it pulls out toxins' – and dipping your fingers in sesame oil and putting them up your nose. Presumably, this regime is easier to follow if you're living alone. And if you don't, you soon will be.

As the doctor expounds on the benefits of massaging the inside of your nostrils – 'the entry point to your head' – I find myself switching off. There is a limit to what I'm prepared to do to be toxin-free. But suddenly I'm yanked back into the present by the words 'introducing a bag of oil to your anus'. *What the hell?* I glance around the room, thinking I've misheard, but my German friends look equally startled. This manoeuvre, Dr J is explaining, is 'good for lubricating your intestines'.

My game of bingo in ruins, as 'bag of oil to your anus' is not a phrase that I've encountered in a spa before, the doctor moves on to the detoxifying power of yellow lentils and the benefits of drinking warm milk. (Sadly, cappuccinos and hot chocolate don't count.) If you're not partial to warm milk or lentil soup, and if all this oiling of one's orifices sounds exhausting, there is some good news: 'Reading, loving and hugging' are also 'cleansing' activities, according to Dr Jafri.

He finishes with a piece of advice that sounds almost poetic. We should all close our eyes more often, he says, as 'the inner world is more beautiful than the outer world'. It's a lovely thought that you can block out the stress or the ugliness of everyday life, simply by slipping inside your own head.

'It all seems very good advice, *ja*,' says Elspeth afterwards. 'But where is the fun? Warm milk and sticking your fingers up your nose before bed? This is not so sexy. I think your husband or boyfriend would leave you.' Angelika is quiet. It seems that her treatment card includes forty-five minutes of intestinal lubrication.

I'm rather dreading my one-on-one consultation with Dr Jafri. Prior to our meeting, I fill in a twenty-page medical questionnaire, unlike any other I've ever encountered. The questions range from, 'Do you have small, medium or large eye sockets?' to some frankly embarrassing enquiries about the workings of one's digestive system.

Dr Jafri sits with his back to the ocean in his small, luminous office. He looks thoughtful. I am not sure if he has read my questionnaire, but, fortunately, his questions focus more on personality than bodily elimination. We establish that I am not the most patient person in the world and that I can sometimes get very angry, very quickly. He nods knowingly, before diagnosing me as a 'Pitta' personality, with a predominance of fire. (A central belief of Ayurvedic medicine is that we are each made up of a combination of mind and body characteristics relating to the elements of air, water, fire and earth.)

As I gaze out at the Atlantic shimmering in the floor-to-ceiling windows behind him, he tells me that attachment – be it to a person, a situation or a place – is bad for me. I need to continually make changes in my life. Pitta types it seems, like their freedom. I should also avoid any kind of exercise that makes me hot, which rules out just about everything apart from yoga and swimming, and effectively gives me the green light to hang up my running shoes for good. It gets better. 'Between 10 am and 2 pm is when you should do your intellectual activity,' he tells me. Only four hours of work a day? To be an angry, fired-up Pitta is to win the Ayurvedic lottery it seems.

His advice is surprisingly specific, though it does not extend to how to quell your Pitta rage when being tailgated down an Iberian motorway. As a fiery personality, my best colours are greens (for creativity) and blues (for relaxation). Yellow, red and orange on the other hand, spell aggravation. I look down at my yellow dress and think, *Oh, dear*!

It seems that I should spend more time in forests and that gardening would be good for me, although not, if previous experience is anything to go by, for the plants. The bad news, given that Pittas are over-prone to temper, is that alcohol, coffee, spices and red meat will stoke up a Pitta-person's ego and hot headedness.

'In Ayurveda, it is important to keep your head cool and your body warm,' says Dr J. To quell the Pitta fire, he advises eating green-coloured foods – particularly broccoli, cauliflower and cabbage – and drinking mint tea.

His final piece of advice suggests that he has been chatting with the stern receptionist. 'Don't always be competitive,' he says. 'Be relaxed with what you have.'

Afterwards, I have a head and foot massage with Antonio, which is everything Angelika and Elspeth said it would be. Forget the private chef, chauffeur or housekeeper; if ever I find myself on *The Sunday Times Rich List*, Antonio will be the first person I call.

Later, I join my new German friends and Dr J, on the terrace for a lentil burger, which tastes better than it looks.

The company is so convivial that I feel I am at a particularly dynamic dinner party. There is just one thing missing: wine.

Angelika tells me that a carnival is taking place in a nearby village and asks if I'd like to go along. And so, after dinner, six of us pile into a yellow taxi van, driven by a tiny red-haired woman called Rosa, who talks loudly and euphorically of the procession, the 'carpets of flowers' and the singing that we are about to experience.

She drops us in the central square, where people are milling around outside a church. The main procession and singing is due to start at 8 pm. We stand around for an hour waiting for something to happen but nothing does. (I should have realised that 8 pm in Portuguese time probably means midnight.) My new German friends are unimpressed and unwilling to wait – I wonder if they are Pitta types too – so we decide to walk back to our hotel, without having seen any singing, processions or carpets of flowers.

Our leader, Erika, seems to have inbuilt GPS, so accurately does she guide us down the mountain and back to base. The route we take is pretty much as the crow flies, down a steep incline and across four lanes of fast moving motorway, the dangers of which I hardly notice, as I'm too busy chatting to Elspeth. I learn that she owns a cosmetic dentistry practice in Berlin, and that her husband of twenty years recently left her and her three children for a 'Polish prostitute' that he met on *sugardaddy.com*. That's the thing about spas. Over the dry crackers and nuts, almost everyone has a juicy story to tell.

The following morning, I walk up the hill to the spa's sister hotel, where I've arranged to meet Angelika and Elspeth for the 7 am levada walk, the levadas being the trails of irrigation channels or mini-canals that crisscross Madeira's mountains.

The foyer is empty when I arrive, which unnerves me. If I'm the first to arrive for something, it usually means that I'm in the wrong place, or I'm so late that everyone has left without me.

Suddenly I spot a familiar face behind the front desk: the stern receptionist. *Gott im Himmel*, I wasn't expecting him to pop up here.

'*Guten Morgen*,' I say, braced for psychological warfare. 'Is this where we meet for the forest walk?'

'Yes, *Frau* Wheeler, but you will need to be on the list if you want to do the walk,' he says. 'Are you on the list?'

I sense that he is willing me not to be. He has the same look of vindictive satisfaction about him as the people who carry out the security searches at Stansted airport. 'I think you will find I am on the list,' I say, as I know that Angelika added my name the night before. He takes his time, staring at the form and looks crestfallen when he confirms that I am on it. I wonder if he will also be checking our identity cards before we get on the bus, or assessing if we are suitably dressed for a forest walk.

Angelika and Elspeth arrive, clutching water bottles and looking jauntily sporty in baseball caps, trainers and leggings. I too, am wearing trainers, but with a sarong and a cardigan, the least inappropriate items for a hike that I have brought to the spa with me, as I hadn't planned on doing any jogging.

Carlos, the hotel's fitness instructor, who is everything you might expect of a Portuguese fitness instructor – tanned of skin, dark of hair and dressed in a tight black T-shirt – drives us to the start of the walk in a mini van. He tells us to set our own pace and that we can walk or run, but we must turn around and come back after twenty minutes. He makes it clear that he won't be joining us, which is a relief. No pressure to keep up, then.

Accompanied by my two fit friends, I jog along the track at a respectable pace – though it is not easy jogging in a sarong – and then as soon as I've rounded the corner, out of Carlos's sight, I slow down to a stroll, waving Angelika and Elspeth on. There is no point in spoiling the scenery by running through it.

I'm surrounded by glossy evergreens, with palm trees and soft ferns sprouting at every turn. Occasional pops of blue hydrangeas break up the greenness, while the air is scented with eucalyptus and rosemary. I stroll along, occasionally over-taken by a jogger or fast-paced hiker, to a gentle soundtrack of running water. It's possible to hike Madeira's levadas for days, as there are 2500 kilometres of them. Dipping into the cool green landscape for twenty minutes is barely breaking the surface, but this enchanting forest is everything Dr J prescribed for a fiery Pitta like myself.

The sight of Angelika and Elspeth jogging back towards me is the cue to turn around, and, just as I do, my phone pings with a message. It is from Zoe in France, and all I can say is that it is a good job that I'm in a calming green forest when I read it, as otherwise my Pitta fires would be blazing.

Dear Karen, I am dismayed to discover that you have been having an affair with my husband. I know that Matthew can be flirtatious – I'm sorry to disappoint you but he is like that with everyone – and I realise that you are especially vulnerable, but to find that you have been running after him behind my back has come as quite a shock. I considered you a friend. It's unfortunate that we live in the same village but I would appre-ciate it if you could stay away from my husband. Yours, Zoe.

I struggle to control my anger during the bus ride back. *Running after my husband.* I can't believe the injustice of this accusation, especially since I have been running *from* him. And what does she mean by *especially vulnerable*? It makes me sound like the village idiot.

'Are you alright, *ja*?' asks Elspeth. 'You have gone very quiet. Didn't Dr J tell you not to do any running?' Back at the hotel, I meditate on my terrace for ten minutes, in order to calm down. Then I go to the computer room with my laptop to reply:

Dear Zoe, would you mind telling me who or what gave you this idea? I am not 'running after your husband' thank you very much. You are targeting the wrong person. Yours, K.

I am not going to let this ruin my stay in Madeira, but over breakfast – boiled apples and nuts – I start to crave caffeine. As my fellow detoxers melt away for their respective treatments, it looks as if I might be left alone to indulge in my favourite toxin, even if it does stoke up the Pitta fires. Frankly, they've already been thoroughly stoked by Zoe's email.

But, just as I'm reaching for a coffee cup, Dr Jafri appears with his own breakfast of puree and powders, scuppering my plan. Behind him is the stern receptionist, who fixes me with steely eyes and then looks pointedly at his watch. '*Frau* Wheeler, you are wanted in the spa. You are late for your abhyanga appointment, *ja*.'

Obediently, I get up to go. The abhyanga treatment, if I'm honest, is a little disappointing, mainly because it is not administered by Antonio. In a health spa, it's not the best sun loungers that people compete for, but the best therapists and masseurs. And unfortunately, they cannot be bagged by the strategic deployment of a beach towel.

At least the after-dinner entertainment sounds promising. Over sweet potato curry and rice, Dr Jafri tells us that he will be doing an evening meditation 'with some singing, clapping and dancing' and anyone who is interested should join him in the yoga room. The immediate uptake is not overwhelming. But given the absence of alcohol and internet in my room, it's not as if I have alternative plans for the evening. And I'm already a believer in quietening the mind, thanks to my meeting with the guru in Gabriella's garden.

But singing and dancing in daylight? Without alcohol or other social lubricants? No chance. Elspeth and Angelika are prepared to give it a go, but Angelika says that she will leave immediately if it involves chanting any *Oms*. Having done a fair bit of yoga over the years, a few *Oms* do not bother me. Dancing in daylight does.

Dr J is waiting for us in the yoga room, sitting cross-legged on the floor. Behind him, through the floor-to-ceiling windows, the sky is turning syringa-pink over the sea. How delightful it would be, to be able to summon up a Madeiran sunset in your head, replicating, at will, the same sense of stillness and beauty.

A few other people shuffle into the room in their yoga kit, making half a dozen of us in total. What follows is extraordinary. Dr J begins with some breathing exercises of the kind that would be familiar to anyone who has done a yoga class. He then announces that we are to close our eyes and, 'Be like a bee'. He demonstrates by making a buzzing noise from deep within his throat. A couple of people exchange nervous glances, but then we join in, and, gradually, the communal humming rises to a crescendo, as if the room were inhabited by a swarm of bees.

So realistic is the noise that we are making that I fear someone will come along with a can of insecticide and try to exterminate us. It doesn't help that I'm wearing a yellow dress and black footless tights – yes, another entirely inappropriate outfit – and actually look like a giant bee. The noise seems to vibrate upwards from the solar plexus, resonating through the body and creating a bond with everyone in the room – one big, communal buzz, if you like. The buzzing turns into *Oms* – the noise is said to be the sound of life, of the universe vibrating – and I open my eyes expecting to see Angelika creeping out, but she is *Om*-ing with the rest of us, her eyes closed. I have no idea how long the *Oms* go on, but I will say this: by focusing your energy on keeping the *Ommm* going, you forget about problems with your neighbours and accusations of infidelity.

Dr J then announces that it is time for singing and gives each of us a small piece of paper containing the lyrics. Obviously, we are not talking Coldplay or Beyoncé here. Instead, the lyrics consist of just four words. Despite having aligned my energy with the universe via the *Oms*, I am sceptical. But Dr J presses a button on an old-fashioned CD player and the room is filled with a sonorous voice.

'*Hey Ram Ram Ram, Sita Ram,*' sings the voice, and we all follow.

'*Ram Ram Ram Ram Sita Ram,*' it chants, and we repeat the refrain.

'*Sita Ram Sita Ram Ram Ram Sita Ram.*'

And so it goes on. I have no idea what we are singing, but the voice is so compelling, so macho and sure in what it is singing, that I am mesmerised. It seems to resonate with an energy as primal as the forest that we walked in this morning. As the sound of our charismatic but invisible choirmaster fills the room, I wonder if it is possible to fall in love with someone without actually seeing them?

The *Rams* and the *Sitas* (pronounced 'zeeta') and the *Sita Rams* eventually speed up, building to a crescendo. Then suddenly we are clapping along. (Later I google '*Sita Ram*' and discover that the mantra is believed to balance both sides of the brain and create a state of mental harmony.) The energy in the room is unlike anything I have ever experienced. Such is the state of collective euphoria that when the good doctor says, 'Let's dance', instead of cringing, I find myself thinking, *At last!*

I open my eyes to see if anyone is looking embarrassed or making for the door – no one is – and suppress a momentary urge to giggle at the sight of the doctor moving backwards and forwards, his loose white trousers flapping around his ankles as he kicks his feet. I'm sorry to say that he does not look good on the dance floor. But that is not the point.

Suddenly, we are all up and twirling around, arms above the head, in a blur of *Sitas* and *Rams*, as sea and sky merge in swirling pink outside. It's as if Mother Nature has given us all an ecstasy pill – or at least a double gin and tonic. Who knew you could feel this happy without alcohol and for no particular reason? The music, the light, the colour, the singing and the celebration of being alive, well, I can honestly see how people join cults or end up in saffron robes, dancing around town with a tambourine.

Afterwards, as I head up the hill with Elspeth and Angelika to watch a fado performance in a nearby hotel, Elspeth echoes my thoughts. 'My God,' she says. 'In that room just now, I think I would have done anything that Dr Jafri asked me to.'

We march into the bar on the hotel terrace, where the fado performance is about to begin. A woman in black and a morose-looking man with a mandolin, proceed to entertain (if that is the word) the assembled crowd, with a series of sad, emotion-charged songs. But I'm not feeling the misery; I'm still buzzing like a bee.

Chapter 20

A Ronaldo in Madeira

SOME PEOPLE HAVE great flashes of insight or spiritual awakenings after shirodhara, the most powerful of the Ayurvedic treatments. Me, I decide to go to the Cristiano Ronaldo museum. As a steady stream of warm oil pours onto my scalp from the copper bowl swinging gently above my head, my thoughts jump about like Biff on a beach. Is it possible to get a bus to the museum in Funchal? Where can I buy some Ginja before I return to France? (The Portuguese cherry liqueur is brilliant for making cakes and trifles, though obviously I'm committing a thought-crime by even thinking about such things in a detox spa.) And what to do about the Matt and Zoe situation when I get home?

After a while, my mind starts to slow. The warm oil seems to melt away my thoughts. Shirodhara, considered the cherry on the cake of Ayurvedic treatments, is said to take you to a deep state of inner silence – much deeper than standard meditation. It is also said – forgive me for slipping into spa-speak here – to awaken your intuition and inner wisdom, improve your mental clarity, release negative emotions, help deal with anger, and enable you to fly like Superman.

I'm joking about the flying, obviously, but having had this treatment once before in India – all hail the beauty press trip! – I know that you do see the world differently afterwards. It makes you feel like the mistress of your own universe, but in a quiet rather than an over-caffeinated way. And as with meditation, I've noticed that the first thoughts that come into your mind after silencing it, tend to be the most important.

As the oil continues to trickle over my forehead or so-called 'third eye', I realise how restless I have been feeling of late. I need to make some changes – and not just jettisoning every-thing that is red or yellow from my wardrobe. And suddenly, right there, with my third-eye fully open, I can see what needs to be done when I get back to France.

'How was the shirodhara?' asks Angelika, over lunch. I tell her that I slept like a stone for two hours afterwards and now feel as if I have a hangover. 'Ah, but you shouldn't have slept,' she says. 'Amazing insights are supposed to happen after shirodhara. You are supposed to note down any impulses and then act on them.'

My immediate impulse is to go to the Ronaldo museum. Elspeth was planning to come with me, but at the last minute, she calls my mobile to say that Antonio has just covered her entire body in a sticky rice paste and instructed her to lie down in a dark room for an hour, presumably until her pulse rate returns to normal.

When my cab arrives, it is Rosa, the driver who took us to the religious festival. When I tell her that I'm going to the Ronaldo museum, it's as though a starting pistol has been fired. 'Is easy for people to be nasty about 'im... but he has dan a good thang for Madeira...Ronaldo 'e works very 'ard... all the time workin'... since he was a boy... very poor family... when he was twelve they see he iz different... they send 'im to Portugal...'

(People in Madeira talk about Portugal as if it were a separate country; though to be fair, it does have its own president.)

As Rosa whizzes along Madeira's highways and through its tunnels, she seems to have inbuilt oxygen tanks which allow her to talk without refilling her lungs: '...some people they are jealous and say all kinda nasty things about him. Me, I am proud of 'im, you know...'

'Does he come home to Funchal very often?' I ask, seizing a nanosecond gap between words.

'Yeh, he come back here. He has built an entire apartment block... not a big one, y'now, a small one... for 'im and 'is family.'

Really? You've got to love him for that alone. Many people would pay good money *not* to live in an apartment block with their family.

I've come out of curiosity – what kind of man opens a museum in his own honour? – but I might have to revise my view of Cristiano Ronaldo. Slightly.

'And what about Irina, his former girlfriend, the beautiful model?' I ask. 'Did she come to Funchal very often?'

'Yes, she az been here too,' says Rosa, a little more reticent on the subject of Ronaldo's love life. 'You know... very nice parks in Funchal... afterwards you gonna walk through the park of the casino into the town...'

CR7, as the Ronaldo museum is called – for those who don't follow football, that's his initials plus the number of his former Man United shirt – is in a side street near the harbour. As we pull up in front of a modern building, a man with black hair and aviator shades emerges. 'I think tha's his brother,' says Rosa, winding down the window and summoning him over in rapid-fire Portuguese. One imagines that the Ronaldos are the closest thing that Madeira has to royalty, so I have to admire the casual way that she does this.

'*O cliento*,' she says several times, nodding to me in the back. I feel a little foolish – I make an unconvincing football fan – but he is surprisingly charming. Speaking in perfect English, he confirms that he is indeed Cristiano's brother and his name is Hugo.

There isn't much of a family resemblance, though maybe if he wore diamond car studs and highlights in his hair, the link to footballing greatness would be more obvious. Instead, in jeans and a white polo shirt, he looks more like the bouncer to his brother's rock star.

'Are you younger or older?' I ask.

'Older. I'm thirty-nine and Cristiano is twenty-nine,' is the polite reply. Then, really hitting my journalistic stride, I ask, 'And how many brothers does Cristiano have?' I'm expecting the reply to be in double figures – after all he's from a good Catholic family – and if he's one of say, twelve, it will considerably reduce the cachet of having met 'Cristiano Ronaldo's brother'.

'Just one. And two sisters.'

Ronaldo has only *one* brother and this is him? *Result.*

'I hope you enjoy the museum,' he says, with a polite nod. 'It was nice to meet you.' And before I can continue with my probing questions, he is gone.

'See. Wadda I tell yer?' says Rosa, nodding with satisfaction at a job well done. The fare is €25, even though I was told at the hotel that it would be €16, but it is worth the surcharge to be able to say that I met a Ronaldo. All the same, I'm a little disappointed that he was so charming, as it makes it more difficult to poke fun at his kid brother.

In fairness, when you've got as many trophies as Ronaldo, you can't just put them on the mantelpiece. And maybe this museum is not just an exercise in ego, but an attempt to give something back – to create a reason for people to visit Madeira.

Unfortunately, my impression of Cristiano was forged by a memorable fashion shoot and interview in American *Vogue* some years ago, in which he pouted, looked petulant and referred to himself in the third person. And I have never forgiven him for expediting Wayne Rooney's exit – swiftly followed by England's – from the quarter-finals of the 2006 World Cup. (For non-football fans, Rooney is Ronaldo's former teammate at Manchester United – the one who looks like Shrek.)

True, Rooney had stamped on one of Portugal's players, so probably would have been given his marching orders anyway, with or without Ronaldo pleading with the referee to issue a red card. But as he trudged off the pitch, a smug Ronaldo gave a sneaky victory wink, for which he will remain forever unpopular among England fans.

In the lobby of the museum, I'm faced with a floor-to-ceiling image of Ronaldo's head and chest. Once I've paid the €6 entry, the enormous, puffed-up chest splits down the middle to let me in. Inside, a TV screen plays a video of the footballer arriving to open the museum with his former girlfriend, Irina Shayk, who looks as if she'd rather be modelling for the Ryanair charity calendar than spending time with her boyfriend in Madeira.

I watch the footage of him patting small children on the head, flashing his blinging white teeth in a thoroughly professional manner and posing next to the waxwork statue of himself – which anyone can see, is not a patch on the real thing – and conclude that CR7 has mostly been dating himself for the past decade.

There are lots of pictures of Ronaldo kissing things, mostly trophies and football pitches, and, bless him, his mum. Fortunately, there are no pictures of him kissing Alex Ferguson. But by far the most interesting exhibits in the museum are the letters from fans. Enterprising youngsters from around the world have written to the footballer requesting his autograph, his footballs, his shirt or his boots. Resisting the temptation – admittedly, not huge – to stand in front of an interactive screen and have my picture taken with a virtual Ronaldo smiling cockily over my shoulder, I leave and walk through the casino gardens to the centre of Funchal.

Madeira's capital is small and perfectly groomed, with a harbour, gleaming white pavements and an abundance of palm trees, fountains and outdoor cafés. It exudes money, taste and good civic maintenance, reminding me a little of Monte Carlo. But I don't hang around as, by now, I have a penalty shoot-out happening in my head. Ayurveda is supposed to put the body back into balance, but I suspect that the caffeine and alcohol levels in my body *were* perfectly balanced and I shouldn't have messed with them.

The bus back to the hotel takes the scenic route, corkscrewing up the narrow roads through the centre of the island and providing some bracing views. Back at the hotel, I take a couple of painkillers before heading to the terrace for dinner, where I find everyone leaning over the balcony, pointing out to sea. The cause of the excitement is a pod of wild dolphins performing back flips on the horizon. Once the dolphins have departed, I inspire similar levels of interest by describing my visit to the Ronaldo museum, though I suspect that my German pals are more fascinated by the fact that I went there, than its contents.

The following morning, Elspeth and Angelika wait with me in the lobby until my taxi arrives and we swap contact details, although we all know that we won't use them. It's the unspoken spa rule: no matter how closely you've bonded with someone, you should never, ever initiate contact once you're back in the real, toxin-riven world. Which is a shame, as Elspeth and Angelika were great fun, and I liked them enormously.

I arrive back in Lisbon in the late afternoon and take a taxi to the Hotel Memmo Alfama, my treat to myself on my last night in Portugal. And what a treat it turns out to be. Normally, I avoid any place that describes itself as a 'design' hotel, since there is usually an inverse relationship between contemporary furnishings and good old-fashioned service. But this hotel, discreetly tucked away in a side street, is a real find.

I slip into the dimly lit reception to be met not by a uniformed receptionist, but a chap in a T-shirt and tattoos. He shows me to my room, which is cool and calm with an expanse of snowy-white bed linen. Then he leads me up to the bar on the open rooftop and a view over the orange and pink rooftops towards the River Tagus.

There are comfortable-looking sofas, while candles in glass jars flicker at strategic points around the bar. But the standout feature is the open-air laptop counter with power points, where the solo traveller can enjoy the view and a glass of something glacial, while checking their emails and maybe even doing a bit of work. The marble counter is such a simple and perfect idea that every hotel should have one. Sitting there with my laptop, a glass of sparkling Mateus Rosé and a front-row seat on the unfolding sunset, I couldn't ask for more from life, apart from maybe Biff curled up at my feet.

There is only one thing spoiling my enjoyment: the thought of seeing Zoe and Matt on my return to France. Zoe has not replied to my email, so I have no idea why she thinks I have been enjoying a dalliance with her husband.

I wake at dawn, the following morning, and log on to my laptop to book a train from Lisbon to Porto, departing shortly after 9 am. The tattooed chap on the front desk – he's still there – prints my ticket and my Ryanair boarding pass and calls me a taxi. I think back to northern Spain, where everything was too much trouble, and imagine the effort one would have to expend there, in order to achieve such results. Here in Lisbon, everything is marvellously glitch-fee. Gliding past the cruise ships on the Tagus towards Santa Apolónia, Lisbon's oldest railway terminus, it's all so lovely that I am loath to leave.

I hope that no one ever tries to modernise Santa Apolónia, as it is quite the most charming mainline train station I have ever encountered. It looks more like a private mansion than a railway terminus, with an old-fashioned façade painted in bird egg blue. My train is already waiting on the white-tiled platform. The three-hour journey from Lisbon to Porto – where I will catch my flight back to France – costs just €23.

At Porto Campanhã station, I catch another train for the short journey to the airport. This boasts a most unusual feature in this security-conscious age: a car park situated directly under the departures hall. Now, I'm the first to complain about overzealous security arrangements, but it strikes me that this set-up offers a remarkable opportunity for anyone seeking a fast track to notoriety. Armed with four wheels and some explosives, someone could cause considerable inconvenience in the departure hall.

But in all other respects, the security arrangements at Portugal's airports are a model of sense and restraint. At Lisbon, Porto and Madeira, the airport stewards operate under the somewhat shocking assumption that you really are going on holiday, rather than plotting aviation disaster. In the unfortunate event that you set off the alarm, they do not assume the sour-faced, 'guilty until we've had a good grope' approach, so familiar to users of UK airports. Instead, they use a wand detector and are almost apologetic.

Portugal holds one last delight: the airport shopping. I must say that the offerings at Porto really are tempting. There is port, obviously, if you're a fan of the wine that gives a hangover like no other; but there is also the sparkling Mateus Rosé that I so enjoyed in Lisbon (for less than €6 a bottle) and Ginja (possibly Portugal's best-kept secret). *So long, Portugal*, I think, as my plane powers into the sky. It's been wonderful, and I'll be back.

Chapter 21

See You Later, Alligator

THE END OF the summer marks the eighth anniversary of my move to France. It is also the moment that I decide to sell Maison Coquelicot. Buying the house on impulse was one of the best decisions I ever made, leading me to some lovable, quirky people and memorable times. It proved to be a quiet haven – I wrote four books there – but also a place of loud laughter and many boisterous gatherings.

I don't make the decision lightly. Instead, I write lists of reasons 'for' and 'against' selling. Topping the list of 'against' is that it is Biff's home and he might not want to move. I picture him stretched out along the back of the sofa, watching me work with his big black eyes, his paws parked in front of him. But I am restless and it is time for a change. And Biff's home is wherever I am. In truth, I made my decision several months ago as warm oil dripped over my head in Madeira. In the moment of clarity that followed the shirodhara treatment, I realised that the time had come to move on. The fact that I have recently registered on the radar of the gendarmes (thanks to the white line incident) and the *sapeurs-pompiers*, also feels like a sign, that life is waving me forward.

When I tell Gabriella what I'm planning to do, she says, 'Do you feel it in your tripe?'

'Yes,' I say, laughing. 'My gut instinct is that it is time for a change. So yes, I feel it in my tripe.'

'Well that's fantastic,' she says. 'Look at what you have. You are free. Free to buy and sell houses [well, one house] and move around. You have wonderful friends, a dog that loves you and a portable talent. You are blessed.'

And so, early in November, I contact Jérome, the dynamic local estate agent, and ask him to sell my house. Sitting in the courtyard in the honey-coloured light of an Indian summer, he tells me that it is a buyer's market at the moment and important to set a realistic price. The financial crisis and fear of President Hollande's surprise taxes, such as the 'social charges' levied on the sale of second homes (subsequently declared illegal by the European Union) have resulted is a glut of properties for sale and few people buying.

As I sign Jérome's contract, I reassure myself that Maison Coquelicot will take at least a year to sell. This will give me time to pack up my books and Le Creuset casserole dishes in a leisurely fashion, and decide where I want to go next. So it is a shock when my house sells in less than two weeks, to the first and only couple that comes through the door.

On their first visit, the potential buyers – a small, intense Frenchwoman and her smiling husband – stay for over forty minutes, while I walk Biff up and down rue St Benoit. They seem particularly interested in the garage. On the second visit, they arrive with a tape measure and an architect and stay for over an hour, again mostly in the garage.

They make an offer, which I accept, and a few days later I go to the estate agent to sign the *compromis de vente*, the legally binding document of sale. Jérome greets me with a big smile and invites me to sit down at his desk to go through the contract. Biff hesitates for a moment – he has seen the plate of croissants on Jérome's desk – before draping himself casually over the estate agent's feet.

Jérome proceeds to run through the key points of the contract. After reassuring him that I won't remove the electric sockets before I leave – apparently some people do – and that I am sound of mind (all things are relative), he pushes the pile of forms towards me for signing. And at that moment, the strangest thing happens: a loud and sorrowful wailing starts up from under the desk. Biff is crying.

I put the pen down. This is obviously a sign. My furry soul-mate will never forgive me for selling our home. I'm about to back out of the deal when I spot the reason for the plaintive wailing: someone has just removed the croissants from Jérome's desk. Biff is staring at the spot where they had been, his face a portrait of disappointment.

I sign the final page and hand it back to Jérome. 'Are you happy?' he asks.

'Yes, thank you,' I reply. The truth is that I'm also a little sad when I think of the hours that I spent sanding floors and painting walls, and of all the people who have sat around the kitchen table or in my the courtyard, a magical den of colour and scent and candlelight. But there is no going back now. The speed and ease with which the house has sold, makes me think that this is meant to be.

Jérome tells me that Monsieur and Madame Jolie who have bought my house, already have their mortgage in place, so he does not foresee any problems. As he stands up to shake my hand, he tells me that the signing of the *acte de vente*, or final contract, should take place in January and that he will contact me as soon as he has a date.

'Don't worry, you're going to have a garden to dig up very soon,' I tell Biff, as we walk back across the square. I notice the council workers in their high-vis jackets, preparing to hang the Christmas lights around the *mairie*. Even the timing feels right. I will have one more Christmas in Maison Coquelicot before packing up and leaving in the New Year. As luck would have it, a friend has offered me his house in a nearby village, Château-Vallois, as a stopgap. It is in the middle of the countryside, the real *France profonde*.

Pierre-Antoine, who is busy unpacking a consignment of embroidered boleros when I drop by his shop to tell him the news, finds this hilarious.

'Oh la la, Château-Vallois? It's not the metropolis, that's for sure,' he says. He's especially amused that I will have to drive fourteen kilometres and back to buy milk. I don't have the heart to tell him that I'd be reluctant to drive even two kilometres for a carton of milk, but a bottle of Sauvignon Blanc? That's a different matter.

On the way home, I bump into Zoe, dressed in a navy pea coat and jeans tucked into knee-boots. It's the first time that I've seen her since I got back from Portugal. She looks pale under her knitted hat and, to her credit, a little embarrassed. 'How are you?' she asks.

'I'm good thanks.'

'Look, about that email…'

'Don't even think about it,' I say. 'I've already forgotten.'

'Do you fancy a coffee? I've got lots to tell you.'

'Sorry, I'm in a bit of a hurry.'

'I'm going back to London tomorrow and I probably won't be back,' she says.

'Perhaps another time.'

'I mean that I won't be back, ever,' she says.

'Well, good luck with everything,' I say, walking away. I can't deny that I'm intrigued, but I'm about to declutter my life and Zoe is top of the list of things to go.

'Gee whiz, that was quick,' says Gabriella when I tell her the news, but she doesn't question my decision. In the weeks that follow, word spreads among my neighbours that I have sold my house. People start asking if I've finished packing up yet, but as a last minute operator I am not even going to start until after Christmas. In the meantime, I throw my energies into buying the largest Christmas tree I can find.

Pierre-Antoine helps me to get it home, the two of us carrying it across the square at dusk. There is the usual flurry of late afternoon activity in the square – cars speeding up to the *boulangerie* or the *tabac*, in the daily last-minute rush for those French essentials, bread and nicotine. Blue and white lights now twinkle around the village, thanks to the mayor's investment in new Christmas decorations.

'It's all part of the push to get re-elected,' Delphine explains. 'All the mayors are doing it.'

Early on Christmas morning, I visit Gabriella. We sit in her kitchen, chatting over Italian coffee and panettone, which she orders every year from the same baker in Italy. Before I leave, I read her the messages inside the many Christmas cards she has received from all over the world and in several different languages.

I feel guilty when I leave to go to friends for lunch, but Gabriella is perfectly happy on her own. She has three sons, one of whom is arriving tomorrow with two of her grandchildren, so she has a lot of cooking to do.

'You've made my day. Thank you,' she says, as I kiss her goodbye. 'See you later, alligator.'

'In a while, crocodile,' I reply, thinking how lovely it is to be able to make someone's day. I head down to the lake to give Biff a walk before we go out to lunch. Just as I'm admiring how beautiful the grass looks, flecked with frost – like green and white tweed – a man in his twenties approaches with a rather ferocious looking dog.

'Ah, it's the lady with the nice car,' he says, in French.

I look at him blankly.

'I want to thank you,' he says.

'For what?' I say, thinking this is a case of mistaken identity.

'You don't remember? The day I nearly had an accident because I was driving too fast?'

'Ah,' I say, remembering how I called him out for his dangerous driving. I assume that he is being sarcastic and suddenly feel a little scared. His dog looks as if it could have Biff as an hors d'oeuvre.

'I mean it. I drive much more calmly now, as a result of what you said to me that day,' he says. 'So I'd really like to thank you for being so frank.'

By the time I realise that he means it, he has walked on. I am stunned by the unexpected manifestation of gratitude. I made Gabriella's day and now this stranger has made mine.

The following week, Pierre-Antoine drives around to my house, his trailer laden with cardboard boxes that he has been saving for me from his various deliveries of blousons. Finally, I begin to pack up. It's always a bittersweet experience, moving home. As you edit your possessions, selecting what to take forward to the next chapter, you find yourself carrying out an audit of your life.

But as I pile my books into plastic carrier bags – a much easier way of transporting them than boxes, Gabriella tells me – I find that I am enjoying myself. As I realised on my Iberian road trip, I am never happier than when I'm packing up to leave. Soon the *petit salon* is piled high with boxes and bags of books, which I start to move over to Château-Vallois at weekends, helped by Pierre-Antoine.

By mid-January, I still don't have a date for the final signing. Having committed to the sale of Maison Coquelicot, I'm keen for it to conclude. At least once a week, I call into the estate agent's to see if there is any progress or visit my *notaire* for an update. Monsieur Guillon is a charming man, known throughout the region for his integrity – a surprising number of French *notaires* are corrupt – his fluent grasp of English and movie star looks.

Perhaps for this reason, his receptionist, a fierce lady with grey hair, guards his office as if it were the strong room of the Louvre. She becomes less friendly – and let me tell you that we started from a low base point – each time I visit, fixing me with an unfriendly stare and saying, sotto-voiced, 'We will call you when there is news.'

When the news comes, it isn't good. It seems that no one noticed that that part of the property next door, is built above my garage, making it a shared freehold. One of Jérome's colleagues calls to tell me that they have arranged for a *géomètre*, or surveyor, to come and measure the garage. I'm surprised as this information should already be in the deeds, but the *géomètre* shows up the following day, spends five minutes in the garage and then asks how I'd like to pay.

'Pay?' I repeat, astonished, not least because I didn't book him.

'Yes, that will be €90,' he replies.

Annoyed, I march over to the estate agents. The basic principle when selling a house in France is that all fees – other than the initial condition report and energy certificate – are paid by the buyer. The estate agents are earning over €8000 commission for the one and a half hours that Jérome spent showing my house. Admittedly, estate agents in France also do some of the preliminary form filling, but, even so, the fee is lavish given the amount of work. And since they failed to notice the shared freehold over the garage, I feel that they should cover the additional cost of the *géomètre*.

Jérome is out, but the suggestion does not go down well with his colleague. She replies with a curt, 'Go and see the *notaire*. It is the *notaire* who organised the *géomètre*.'

And so I do, arriving in the peach-coloured bleakness of the solicitor's offices to be met with the usual glare. Today, the receptionist does not bother to reply to my *bonjour*. Instead, she picks up the phone, says something along the lines of 'Bloody hell, it's her again' – at least that's what I imagine she says, as she speaks very quietly – and a young female colleague descends from the offices above.

I ask why the issue of the garage has only come to light now. She shrugs. 'It is you who pays the *géomètre*,' she insists, before advising, 'Go and see the estate agent.'

I give a Gallic shrug and give in. I will pay the *géomètre*. The alternative is to shuttle backwards and forwards between the two offices, forever. Later, I discover that the question of 'Who pays the *géomètre*?' is often a bone of contention in France.

I move my remaining furniture over to Château-Vallois, helped by Pierre-Antoine and one of his friends and, lured by the prospect of hot water and heating, I finally move in. (The Beast, as I call the oil boiler at Maison Coquelicot, has run dry and it seems pointless pouring €500 of oil into it – the minimum cost of an oil delivery – when I'm moving out.)

At the end of January, I go once more to the *notaire's* office. This time I use a different tactic. I don't bother with a cheery *bonjour*. Instead, I employ the journalistic technique of silence, which usually puts the onus on the other person to speak.

But the receptionist merely picks up the phone and says, 'My colleague is coming.'

'It's Monsieur Guillon that I want to see.'

'It is not possible,' she says, just as the door opens and Monsieur Guillon appears.

'Madame Wheeler,' he says, with a warm smile. 'Come in.'

Finally, he has a date for me. The signing will take place next week in Douhé, at the office of the buyers' solicitor. Madame Jolie, I discover, is a psychiatrist and Maison Coquelicot will be her new practice. The reason she and her husband spent so much time in the garage is that they are planning to convert it into a waiting room.

The night before the sale, I clean the house from top to bottom with the help of Carmen, my cleaner. She has news of Magda, who is apparently now living in the UK with her children and a new boyfriend. 'She has a job in Brighton [she pronounces it *Bright*-on] in a café, and is very happy,' says Carmen. 'That is why you could not find her in Coimbra.'

'Ah,' I say, thinking that Magda is living her life in a way that Gabriella would approve of: if not running, at least jogging, and never stopping to worry what people might think.

'The other man, the one that she went to Portugal to be with, was no good,' says Carmen flicking her duster. 'So Magda, she don't hang around.'

'Good for her,' I say.

When we are done cleaning, I walk around the bare rooms one last time, admiring the antique iron radiators and glass-panelled interior doors. I hope that the new owners will love the small but charming details, such as the hand turned wooden knobs and glass fingerplates on the cupboards, as much as I did. I hope, too, that they will appreciate the wood burner, the built-in bookshelves and the watery-green mosaic tiles in the bathroom, which are the legacy of my tenure, along with the oak kitchen floor. It feels as if part of me will forever be embedded within these walls.

Downstairs, the doorbell rings. I'm surprised to see that it is Matt. 'I was wondering if you needed a hand?' he asks. 'I heard in the Liberty Bookshop that you were moving out today.'

'Thanks, but it's all under control,' I reply.

'I'm sorry to hear that you're leaving the village. I hope it wasn't because of me.'

'It had nothing to do with you,' I say, which is the truth.

'I suppose you heard about Zoe?'

'That she thinks you were enjoying an extra-marital liaison with me?'

'No, not that.'

'She's going back to the UK.'

'So? That's what she's always done, for work.'

'No, she's going back permanently. We've "consciously-uncoupled" or whatever the phrase is.'

'Ah.'

'It seems that Zoe has been enjoying a cross-Channel relationship with her boss for the past few months.'

I think of all the times that I drove Zoe to the airport for her 'work trips'. Now that I think about it, she always seemed exceptionally cheerful when going back to the UK.

'And you didn't notice?'

'I was too busy building a house.'

'So, what made her think that I was having an affair with you?' I ask.

'She probably realised that I would like to,' he says.

'There must have been more to it than that.'

'I think someone, another expat or a neighbour perhaps, saw us together at the café opening and possibly mentioned it to her. You know how people gossip out here.'

'Everyone here has drinks with everyone, usually without any rumours of an affair.'

'I don't know. Maybe she found some of the messages that I sent you. Anyway, she has gone and won't be coming back.'

'Well, I'm sorry to hear that,' I say.

'I'm not. It's over. It was a mistake to marry her,' he continues. 'We had nothing to talk about. France was actually a last ditch attempt to make things work.'

A last ditch attempt to make things work? It never looked that way. Zoe and Matt seemed like a happy couple. If he is telling the truth, it's a reminder that appearances are never quite what they seem.

'So, will you sell your French house?'

'We haven't finalised the details of the divorce yet, but I'm hoping to keep it.'

'Well, better luck with the next wife,' I say. 'Third time lucky and all that.'

'Very droll,' he says. 'Anyway, where are you going?'

'Not far.'

He laughs. 'Don't worry, I'm not going to stalk you.'

'I'm almost disappointed,' I say, as I see Pierre-Antoine coming down rue St-Benoit.

'Well, hope to see you around,' he says. 'I'm having a party soon to celebrate finishing the barn. I hope you'll come along.'

'Will I have to dress up in rhinestones?'

'No. Themed parties aren't my style. You can come along as you are.'

'I'll think about it.'

After saying goodbye to Carmen, who has agreed to continue working for me in Château-Vallois, I run back upstairs and place a pair of decorative iron firedogs in front of the fireplace in the main bedroom.

'You're not leaving those, are you?' says Pierre-Antoine, looking at me as if I'm mad. 'They're very old and almost certainly valuable.'

I shrug. I have decided that everything that was in the house when I arrived – I found the firedogs in the attic – must remain here, as they are part of its history. The pale pink climbing rose and the hollyhocks that I planted are also now part of that history and should hopefully burst into life every spring, for many years after I've moved on.

I lock the door for the final time and we walk up rue St Benoit, Biff's tail bobbing with excitement, towards Pierre-Antoine's shop. In his apartment above it, he opens a bottle of champagne, which seems like a suitable ending.

Early the next day, I take Biff for a walk on one of the new tracks that we've discovered near Château-Vallois. It's crisp but bright, and the sky is a smooth wash of blue. I can hear birds singing and the ground feels firmer, the air fresher. Everything is starting over. I look at my watch. I've got time to drive to Villiers for a coffee in the Liberty Bookshop, before setting off to Douhé for the signing.

'I've heard that you're leaving us?' says an elderly expat at a nearby table, as I surf a property website on my laptop.

'Only temporarily,' I say. 'My plan is to find a little bolt-hole in the UK – a place to escape to in the winter months, before returning to France for the summer.'

Almost as I'm saying this, a 'property alert' pings into my inbox, from an estate agent that I have registered with in Devon. I click on the link and find a powder-blue cottage, with a window box sprouting French lavender, and baskets of white geraniums hanging above the door. It has lots of original features, including architraves and wide wooden floorboards.

Best of all, there is a walled garden at the rear, with wisteria, climbing roses and a palm tree. A palm tree!

Scrolling through the photos, I suddenly have the same feeling that I had when I saw Maison Coquelicot for the first time. I feel it in my tripe: this house is going to be mine. It even reminds me of my French house, but instead of croissants and countryside, there will be Devon cream teas and coast, because – oh joy – it is minutes away from the sea, with a magnificent view of the estuary from the top floor guest room.

Heart thumping with excitement, I phone the estate agent in Exeter and arrange a viewing for the following week. I then drive to Douhé for the signing. My *notaire* is waiting, along with Jérome and the Jolies. We all squeeze into their *notaire*'s office to sign the final documents. I then hand Monsieur Jolie the keys to Maison Coquelicot, which are still attached to my silver key fob inscribed with the word *château*. He takes them with a smile, and we shake hands and wish each other '*Bon courage*'.

And just like that, on a cold but sunny day in March, my French adventure – or this particular part of it – comes to an end. As I drive to L'Auberge de l'Écurie in Usson du Poitou to meet Delphine for lunch, I feel lucky to have had this experience, but excited by the new chapter that is about to begin.

Delphine is waiting at a corner table, wearing a necklace of electric yellow sunflowers. I tell her that the new buyers are lovely and seem happy with their purchase. There is only one thing that bothers me: Maison Coquelicot is going to be a psychiatry practice.

'Imagine! All those unhappy people offloading their problems and sadness within its walls,' I say. 'My poor little house.'

'Ah *non*,' replies Delphine, demonstrating once again the importance of perspective. 'It means that your house was a place of great healing and this lady picked up on that. It has worked its magic for you. Now you don't need it anymore.'

The truth of this suddenly hits me. Maison Coquelicot was a haven. It gave me physical and emotional shelter when I limped out to France with a broken heart eight years ago. But the time had come to hand it on to someone else.

I imagine Madame Jolie's troubled clients in the cosy salon in winter, baring their souls by the log fire, or sitting in the private courtyard in summer, the edge taken off their anguish by the scent of the jasmine and the beauty of the pink roses and hollyhocks.

So much has happened in the past eight years. I've made many dear friends, including Delphine, who is like a sister to me, and Gabriella, my self-appointed mother-in-law. I've also met the love of my life – the one with big paws and a wet nose – written four books, and learned the difference between a Madiron and a Malbec.

I love France and I love belonging to a small village community, but I love nothing more than a new beginning and the possibility of a new set of old floorboards to sand. (Although this time, I've decided, I won't be doing the sanding myself.)

'You have new glasses,' I say to Delphine, as Fred, the restaurant proprietor, brings our aperitifs.

'Yes,' she replies. 'The optician said I could have something inscribed inside, like a personal motto.' She takes them off and hands them to me to look at. Written in French is the phrase, 'The best is yet to come.'

I laugh and click her glass. 'Here's hoping.'

Underneath the table there is a loud woof, and Biff-dude, when I look down, is smiling.

Afterword

May 2016, East Devon

WHEN I VISITED the pale blue cottage for the first time, I knew immediately that it was going to be mine. As with my French house, I didn't hang around. Immediately after the viewing, I made an offer, which was accepted a few hours later, proving my theory that houses – like people – present themselves at the right time.

Since then, life has been a lengthy to-do list of floor levelling, rewiring, and plumbing works before, finally, the fun bits of choosing paint colours and kitchen cabinets. The builders are now gone, my books are unpacked, and I am no longer washing dishes in the bathtub and using my desk as a dining table when friends come to stay.

To begin with, my social life arrived on the 7.05 pm train from Paddington on a Friday, but in the two winters that Biff and I have spent here, we've acquired some fabulous new friends, met an intoxicating mix of people, including writers and artists, in a nearby coastal enclave; learned that 'dimpse' is a West Country word for dusk; and walked many kilometres of jungly Jurassic Coast. I've also discovered how polite drivers are in Devon (incidents of road rage: nil) and how fierce the competition for a beach hut.

As I write from my top floor office, I can see the fronds of the palm tree swaying in the walled garden, and a band of sea, sparkling like an eternity ring, on the horizon. Downstairs my bags are packed ready to drive to Poole this evening, where we will take the ferry back to France for the summer, to visit Gabriella, Delphine, Pierre-Antoine and all the other friends that my readers have come to know and love.

The plan is to rent out the house in Devon as a holiday cottage during the summer months, and I will live there in the winter, swapping the French countryside for Jurassic Coast. But life has a funny way of sabotaging a plan, so as Delphine likes to say, 'Let's wait and see.'

Several readers have written to say how sad they were to discover that I'd sold my house in France. Well, cheer up dudes, because I've found another one, close to my old village, with several barns attached and an orangey-pink roof. It's a charming, single-storey building, which a friend has already nicknamed 'The Magic House'.

Like the cottage in Devon, it too, has wisteria and roses, and is positively crying out for an enthusiastic *anglaise*, armed with a paint chart and a plan of renovation.

As for Arianna, she has raised her game on the academic front since our road trip, which she describes as 'the best experience of my life' – a statement, I swear, that was not made under duress or induced by the promise of Pop Tarts. When she finishes college, she is planning to come and live with me. As Gabriella says, life never stops delivering surprises.

But right now, the sun is shining, seagulls stand guard on the inky slate tiles of the nearby rooftops, and Biff is jangling his lead, demanding to be taken to the beach. To the many readers who've wished me happiness: finally, and quietly, I think I may have found it.

Acknowledgments

THANK YOU TO my niece, Arianna, for being the world's worst navigator but the sweetest company; to Gabriella Mellen for her friendship, humour and inspiring advice; to Martine Mousserion, Patti Huisse, Eileen and Wally, and Wilma Johnson; and to 'Miss Offley', my lovely, inspirational primary school teacher, for a surprise appearance at my book signing in Eymet.

Thank you to Andy Robert Davies for his wonderful cover illustrations and for striving to reproduce exactly the shade of yellow that I saw on the wall of the Quinta da Regaleira in Sintra. I'd also like to thank Wendy Driver and *The Mail on Sunday*, and *Living France* magazine. Thank you to Stephen, Stefanie and my friends in London, including 'Perfume Club'. I don't see any of you enough, but when I do, it's always fun. I'd also like to thank my friend and Alexander Technique teacher, Noel Kingsley, both for sorting out my shoulders for the past twenty years, and for suggesting that I write *Tout Sweet*, in the first place. Yes, blame him.

Finally, thank you to my readers – I'm sorry that this book took longer to produce than the Chilcot Inquiry – and to all the fun and fabulous people that I've had the good fortune to meet in France and Devon. In Devon I'd particularly like to thank Katie W and Jazz, Lesley, Dean, Matthew, Cathy and Jane, for dog care, decor advice, walks, champagne, and moments of great hilarity. May there be many more to come.